MALCOLM LOWRY'S *VOLCANO*

By the same author:

The Ballad of Dingus Magee
Going Down
Springer's Progress

MALCOLM LOWRY'S *VOLCANO*

Myth
Symbol
Meaning

DAVID MARKSON

Times
BOOKS

Library of Congress Cataloging in Publication Data

Markson, David.
  Malcolm Lowry's Volcano.

  Includes index.
  1. Lowry, Malcolm, 1909-1957. Under the volcano. I. Title
PR6023.096U58   813'.5'4   77-92329
ISBN 0-8129-0751-5

Otra vez: Elaine
—and for my mother

PREFACE

A preface, I suspect, is typically a kind of *a priori* defense. And since most readers of literary criticism are to some degree "specialists"—which I take as euphemistic for kind hearts with harsh preconceptions—I further suspect it might be salutary to announce at the outset precisely what this book is not. It is not a new biography of Malcolm Lowry, and, indeed, with the exception of a reminiscence I have attached as an appendix, very few references to the man are made within its pages. It is also not a look into the full corpus of Lowry's work; a number of stories and poems are mentioned, but only as they prove relevant to *Under the Volcano.* For those who would rebuke me for failing to do something I never intended to do, I can only recall the irascible Westerner whose own "preface" was fixed to his gate: "This is King Fisher's ranch. Go elsewhere." (His name really *was* King Fisher.)

To me at least, my premise seems beyond argument. Some twenty-five years ago, at Columbia University, I devoted a 30,000-word master's thesis to *Under the Volcano* because I believed it the finest single novel in the English language in my lifetime. Nothing written since then has reduced that estimate. But because I also find the book as suggestively intricate in mythic and literary parallelism as anything since *Finnegans Wake,* I am all the more convinced that a detailed, "Joycean" reading —in my case, an exhaustive rethinking and expansion to more than three times its length of that earlier essay—is long overdue.

But if I have restricted myself here to the one task, I scarcely mean to dismiss the remainder of Lowry's work out of hand.

Having known the man well in the last years of his life, I can
venture that he would have contemplated mayhem before allowing the posthumous *Dark as the Grave Wherein My Friend Is Laid*
or *October Ferry to Gabriola* to be published in that unrevised,
patchwork form in which we have them. Just as vehemently,
however, do I disagree with those who would condemn the
stories or novellas in *Hear Us O Lord From Heaven Thy Dwelling
Place* for no reason other than that several have to do with
"writers," surely another quixotic "preconception" of recent
criticism. Certainly "Through the Panama" and "The Forest
Path to the Spring" will last; along with the neglected "Strange
Comfort Afforded by the Profession," these strike me as perhaps the only efforts in which Lowry ever again approached that
same layered resonance which vivifies his one masterwork.

Yet neither is Lowry shamed by the earlier novels *Ultramarine*
or *Lunar Caustic,* particularly in that the former was accomplished at twenty-three. And if my feelings about the poems are
mixed—often they seem more like sketches for poems than the
finished product—several refuse to let me rest.

Be that as it may, and for all that I am hardly eccentric in my
devotion to *Under the Volcano*—though it was a fairly lonely business, once—I must admit to finding myself disheartened by the
nature of most existing Lowry commentary. A rare exception is
Malcolm Lowry (Twayne, 1972) by Richard Hauer Costa, an acute
evaluation of success and failure in the entire Lowry canon,
ratified by a remarkably creative understanding of Lowry's intent throughout. Another, also called *Malcolm Lowry,* is the biography by Douglas Day (Oxford, 1973), a volume which my own
memories of Lowry forced me to approach warily, but which I
find extraordinarily close to the mark on all levels of psychological speculation. While Day himself remarks the need for a more
comprehensive exegesis of *Under the Volcano* than his biographical format permits, his generalizations about the work (they are
more than that) remain indispensable.

Conversely, the only existing full-length effort centered upon
Under the Volcano alone is paradoxically far more narrow than my
own, meaning Perle Epstein's *The Private Labyrinth of Malcolm
Lowry* (Holt, 1969). By comparison, in her single-minded inves-

tigation of Lowry's cohabitation with the Cabbala, Dr. Epstein is practicing secret Faustian incantations where I am making house calls.

The Canadian critic Tony Kilgallin, in *Lowry* (Porcepic, Ontario, 1973), is extremely good on *Ultramarine* and on Lowry's response to film; if his explication of *Under the Volcano* is somewhat fragmented, I will in fact make use of several insights from it in an "afterword" to my text. And an eclectic selection of essays edited by George Woodcock called *Malcolm Lowry: The Man and His Work* (University of British Columbia, 1971) would be of value if only for offering a translation of Lowry's preface to the French edition of *Under the Volcano,* even if this in turn is based upon a considerably more elaborate document he had contrived for his British publisher, Jonathan Cape, available in the *Selected Letters* (Lippincott, 1965).

I have also already mentioned my thesis, placed on file little more than four years after the original publication of *Under the Volcano.* After the first reviews, nothing else had then been said about Lowry, and while the case was something less than that of Balzac proclaiming to the world the genius of M. Beyle, he seemed pleased: "As a matter of fact it is about the only thesis of its kind I have ever read which seemed to me to be organized with an actual feeling of dramatic excitement working through its architectonics." For reasons to be explained in my introduction, any such "excitement" in the present volume—an altogether new book—can occur only in its later chapters. But I can also see where my own "specialization," even with Lowry himself having found the approach apposite, might raise objections among certain types of readers—this insofar as I have essentially chosen to "retell" *Under the Volcano* in terms of those Joycean utilizations of myth and symbol that comprise its texture, dictate much of its interior form, and evince most of its meaning. If my efforts have any model, though I have not looked into it in years, it is probably Stuart Gilbert's early work on *Ulysses.* Which is to say that where Gilbert follows, sequentially, Joyce's Homeric episodes, I do much the same with Lowry's far more variegated parallels, but without the introductory overview to which Gilbert devoted the first section of his book. Gilbert's catechizing, after all, occurred only five or six years after *Ulysses* itself, and *Ulysses* was revolutionary. Mine follows the post-Joycean Lowry by three decades.

But in the same regard I might also comment on this predilection of mine toward things "Joycean," a matter for which I have already been taken to task, on the basis of a solitary essay, by Stephen Spender in his preface to recent editions of *Under the Volcano.* As I hope my introduction indicates, I mean to make of the word a generic term—though "mythic" will do equally well. For all the differences in their ultimate aesthetic orientation, there remains between Lowry and Joyce an undeniable affinity of *method,* i.e., that constitutional insistence upon reference and allusion which calls forth archetypal equations; or cf. Eliot also, with quotations from thirty-five different writers in the 400-odd lines of "The Waste Land." Lowry is not Joyce; nor Eliot. But he would have been a radically different Lowry had not both irremediably infected the contemporary literary bloodstream before him.

In fact it is a basic contention herein that no less a reader than Lowry's early mentor Conrad Aiken was always remiss—if with a deliciously studied crustiness—in insisting that Lowry simply "tucked into" the book whatever bits and pieces of esoteric knowledge he stumbled upon, "whether or not pertinent." On one plane my entire purpose is to repudiate that notion; or, less charitably, Mr. Spender's *sufferance* of Lowry's Joycean devices as having presumably derived from "a kind of inspired misunderstanding."

By its intrinsic nature, however, this stance leaves me open for still another accusation, that of turning something I know full well is first of all a novel—the best of novels—into an arcane literary puzzle, or worse, of self-indulgently displaying private erudition. ("Gentlemen, this semester we commence our study of the *Oedipus at Colonus* by Sophocles, a veritable treasurehouse of grammatical peculiarities!") As will soon enough be certified —if his own exhortative letter to Jonathan Cape has not certified it long since—the youngster making it hard for the rest of the class is Malc Lowry.

For all this, I have arbitrarily decided against any top-heavy apparatus of reference notes, most sources being self-evident in context; where they aren't, I am drawing on what can only be termed "general information." Footnotes, too, are infrequent. And any question of bibliography becomes redundant with the availability of the dozen analytical pages on the subject in Costa, or the extensive listing in Day.

I should add that the reader will not have had to set *Under the Volcano* aside less than nine minutes ago to follow me, since what I have assayed is a wholly self-contained critical narrative. As a point of reference, however, I have incorporated a brief plot outline into my table of contents (my chapter numbers correspond with Lowry's own).

Also, to avoid clutter I have cited page references for only selected Lowry quotations; those not cited generally fall in near sequence or at least in the chapter under discussion. Pagination applies to the original Reynal and Hitchcock edition, but is valid for the Lippincott hard-cover reissue and the current Plume paperback.

And one possibly touchy point. In churlish demonstration that this entire reading is my own, almost nowhere do I refer to any other Lowry commentators except Lowry himself—though it is patent that where we are all of us fetching our pitchers to the same well, some duplication is inescapable. More than once over the years, however, that "well" has become my antique thesis, grandly pillaged without acknowledgment even *after* the writer had corresponded with me about it. Since many allusive or symbolic recognitions in Lowry are no more than should be anticipated from any equipped reader, I am perhaps not quite the maiden despoiled; but in those several instances where I myself may appear to be echoing someone else, and am actually echoing *his* echo of my own work, neither will I appreciate being indicted for promiscuity.

Presumably the sheer abundance of my discoveries will readily verify their independence anyway. For that matter there are few secrets at Lowry Interpol, and the important Lowry critics —again Costa, Day, Kilgallin—are all aware that my entire manuscript was finished before their books became available. *Honi soit qui* Malc *y pense.*

Short excerpts from what follows, in different form, were once in *Prairie Schooner,* and my appendix, abridged and altered, appeared in *The Nation.* Friends like Catharine Carver, Glauco Cambon, Peter Kaldheim, Alan Koblin, Sterling Lord, and Kevin Sullivan will recall individually the gestures for which I now express thanks to each—as will even more particularly, I hope, Dick Costa and John Simon.

Sadly, on the other hand, one can no longer thank old Aiken for years of Lowry-*cum*-martini conversations—or anticipate that growl with which he would have waved aside most of what I have to say. He is missed.

Most importantly, I trust that my appendix—and especially to Margerie Lowry—will make evident the profoundest debt of all, which in small part the very existence of this book is meant to discharge. "Who the hell am I?" Lowry once asked. "What an incredible privilege! Did I really know Conrad Aiken? And did he actually once come to see *me?*" At the present writing, Lowry himself is dead twenty years; a like wonderment at his own friendship gives me pause still.

Quotations from *Under the Volcano* are used with the permission of J. B. Lippincott Company, as are brief excerpts from published Lowry letters. Everything else appears with the permission of my wife.

—D. M.
New York, 1978

CONTENTS

CONTENTS

Shaving the Consul. They and Yvonne encounter Laruelle.

MALCOLM LOWRY'S *VOLCANO*

INTRODUCTION

"It is simply a way of controlling, of ordering, of giving a shape and a significance to the immense panorama of futility and anarchy which is contemporary history."
—Eliot, *"Ulysses,* Order, and Myth"

The opening scene of *Under the Volcano* occurs in a hotel called the Casino de la Selva. Elsewhere in the first chapter a character stands "looking into the abyss," a ravine breaking precipitously across Lowry's fictional landscape, and at the end of the chapter a bell speaks: "dolente . . . dolore!"

The word "selva," in the Spanish appropriate to the Mexican setting of the book, means forest or wood. It means the same in Italian, as in the famous "selva oscura," or dark wood, where Dante finds himself at the start of the *Divine Comedy*—before he too approaches an "abyss." Of themselves, such associations are tenuous at best. They become demonstratively less so when we consider the words ascribed to the bell:

Per me si va nella città *dolente,*
Per me si va nell' etterno *dolore* . . .

Since the lines occur in the inscription Dante places above the gate of hell—

Through me is the way into the doleful city,
Through me the way into the eternal pain . . .

—their deliberate evocation must suggest a good deal about certain of Lowry's thematic implications. Yet that evocation must simultaneously raise questions about the intrinsic nature of Lowry's approach to fiction, or at least about the approach his critic must take. To protest that, in such exegesis, the wood may be obscured by the trees—or indeed, by the "wood"—is to forget that it is assuredly not the critic who has echoed Dante in that bell.

And there is something effectively more significant here than any mere penchant for literary "embellishment" (even if the pun is perhaps avoidable). Milton and Shakespeare reek of traditional classic "borrowings," as did Virgil for his contemporaries fully two thousand years ago; but what is meant to be perceived in "charged" fiction of this contemporary sort is finally a method of *juxtaposition.* A novel like *Ulysses,* concerned literally with a circumscribed temporal situation, is seen to deal with something else entirely when we become conscious of Joyce's parallels with the *Odyssey.* Time is bridged, past and present occur in effect simultaneously—and in this same removal from the ephemeral, the writer gives the lie to our contemporary sense of dissociation.

"Brave men lived before Agamemnon," ventured Horace, but Horace was only guessing. If today we can document the fact, it is the "mythic" artist, more profoundly than any archaeologist or anthropologist, who will project this timeless "shared" continuity of human experience.

By "myth" in this context is meant *any* prototypal image, of course. An inconsequential sixteenth-century necromancer called Johannes (or George) Faust, after his paradigmatic literary transformations, has come to exemplify man's darker broodings as readily as does Tiresias, though the latter is far more truly "mythic." Very little myth is "pure" anyway, in the sense of originating in primitive religious ritual; the most viable of the Greek myths are to be found in Ovid, which is to say they are literature, and not even Greek literature. What matters is the way such usage reaffirms man's unvarying estate.

That bell strikes: "dolente . . . dolore!" Once it does we are missing a point—and it is a point that is undeniably seminal—if we fail to perceive that Lowry's Mexican "selva" is also Dante's, or that his abyss is an immemorial Inferno.*

Joyce, here, is the master, *Ulysses* the watershed. But even Homer nods; and it is ironic that such few reservations we maintain about *Ulysses* may arise from the very direction its author chose to pursue in his own mythic interpolations.

Joyce more than once remarked, for example, that his identification of Leopold Bloom with Odysseus occurred because the latter is literature's "complete man." Yet Bloom is not Odysseus solely; almost as if in afterthought he is equated with the ghost of Hamlet's father, or again with Christ. And it was through these "incidental" parallels that Joyce took a clue from himself, as it were, in establishing the far more inclusive mythic scheme of *Finnegans Wake.* There we have no single predominating mythic analogy. The dreaming H. C. Earwicker is the legendary Irish figure Finn MacCool to be sure, but by deliberate extension he is an incalculable number of others from Moses to Dean Swift—"Here Comes Everybody," as his initials proclaim. The concept remains immensely provocative: Any man's myth increases me, for I am "Mankinde."

But was Earwicker's improbable dream necessary? Foregoing traditional chronology, much of contemporary writing demands to be read as we look at a mural: where individual stanzas or even lines may bear no immediate relationship to those nearest them, they hold their decisive, reflexive place in the whole when

---

*While there remain, even this long after Joyce and Eliot, certain professional readers who balk at this sort of thing, in his *Anatomy of Criticism* Northrop Frye has postulated an entire *theory* of criticism based in good part upon such awarenesses—i.e., those archetypal patterns which, whether deliberate or otherwise, essentially "link" one work of art with another "to unify and integrate our literary experience." The same basic premise can be drawn from Joseph Campbell's comparative mythic schematizations in his monumental *The Masks of God,* though it has also long since been adumbrated by writers from such diverse disciplines as Jung, Susanne Langer, Lord Raglan, Cassirer, Robert Graves (in *The White Goddess* and *The Greek Myths*), Maud Bodkin, Heinrich Zimmer, Jessie L. Weston, the Cambridge classicists, etc.—several of whom must, in fact, be mentioned subsequently here.

viewed spatially. Yet with a volume the length of *Finnegans Wake*, such perception requires a kind of intellectual peripheral vision. A perspective can certainly be achieved, nor does it cost that lifetime of dedication Joyce half-seriously asked of the ideal reader. Nonetheless Joyce's own shifting focus begs the question: if the "multimythic" richness of *Finnegans Wake* is what the novelist is after, must he cease to be novelist? Can this wealth of prototypal allusion, which after all evokes nothing if not the essence of man's creative tradition—which *is* man—be integrated into a fictional form that is itself traditional?

After Joyce, it can. The guilt of the protagonist of *Under the Volcano* is that of Adam after expulsion, his agony that of Christ at Golgotha, his frailty Don Quixote's. Through degrees of highly specific analogy Lowry's hero so to speak "becomes" Faust, Dante, Prometheus, Heracles, Buddha, Oedipus. He is Aeneas, Hamlet, Noah, Judas, Prospero, Narcissus, Trotsky, Macbeth, Shelley, Scrooge, Quetzalcoatl, Bix Beiderbecke, Candide, Moses, and Gogol's Tchitchikov—if not to add Peter Rabbit and the Fisher King, among many more. There is even a touch of Alice in his makeup, and at one juncture, as if to assert that one man's myth scarcely need become another's poison, he boldly enacts a Homeric parallel of his own. Each of these projections vastly amplifies the meanings of Lowry's narrative, but —and this remains crucial—that narrative does exist, with its own organic structure, its cohesive surface sequence. Such identities are proclaimed only through allusion or metaphor *integral* to the contextual reality of the book itself, and even when lengthy equations of "episode" are created, again Lowry's surface is not distorted. The mythic content is there, and then some; but *Under the Volcano* remains always a novel first of all, with its own profoundly dramatic *literal* impact.

In fact it is a paradoxical tribute to the richness of Lowry's achievement, because of this very indivisibility of surface and symbol, that even where he is most unstintingly praised he is often less than perceived. Inevitably, Joyce does become the basis of comparison, but only insofar as *Under the Volcano* occurs within the frame of a single day, that it makes use of interior monologue, that it is characterized by pun and verbal excess and what far too many otherwise sophisticated readers still think are "literary references." All this is true so far as it goes: *Portnoy's Complaint* and *On the Origin of Species* both deal with aspects of family life.

But where that use of myth is, then, a key Lowry strategy, to seek out such patterns at the expense of his more traditional fictional center would be equally to miss the point: obviously, an "abyss" is sometimes a hole in the ground. (Though there is also St. Augustine: "If by 'abyss' we mean a great depth, is not man's heart an abyss?") Yet even in essentially traditional terms Lowry presents difficulties. He differs from Joyce in having propounded tragedy—if maintaining a redemptive sense of the absurd throughout—and too, a tragedy in which his subjectivity serves to create a *drama* of the consciousness rather than any mere representation of its workings. But he has also written a book in which concepts from Jung, Spengler, Freud, the comparative anthropologists, Spinoza, Plato, Oriental religion, and the occult all function *operatively* to become part of the texture of events themselves; moreover he has made organic use of the philosophic idealism of George Berkeley, and in an oblique but inescapable manner the entire novel is meant to be seen as unreal.

None of which has anything to do with "myth"—but where then a way in? Ortega y Gasset says somewhere that great novels are "lavish of particulars," meaning that in Tolstoy, in Stendhal, in Laurence Sterne, we are always assaulted by more details than it is possible to remember. Normally such details are intrusions of fictional reality, to a degree inconsequential. But in a mythic novel *nothing* is inconsequential; as already indicated, even the most ostensibly trivial reference, when viewed in conjunction with its reflexive echoes and repetitions, will be understood to speak volumes. (Indeed, such is Lowry's control that even a subtle use of *clichés* will prove meaningful.) But thus too then, any larger question like that of philosophic idealism, once pinned down of itself, will subsequently demand to be seen in relationship to such analogues as Lowry's occultism and the mystic "vision," his borrowings from abstract Hindu and Buddhist metaphysics, and more.

In consequence, and since I intend to follow Lowry chapter

by chapter, it has seemed serviceable to reserve discussion on *all* such topics for appropriate points of departure fairly late in the text—once the evidence is in. This line of attack has its own pitfalls, since a number of first interpretations will undoubtedly appear conjectural until that evidence does verify Lowry's intent; yet while some few anticipations will be unavoidable, by its inherently "spatial" nature the mythic novel can define its terms only gradually, and that *process* itself seems worth exploring. Early allusions to Dante's wood afford a telling metaphor for the spiritual dislocation of Lowry's characters, for example, but elsewhere in the novel several of those characters will find themselves in an actual dark wood—quite "real" enough to cause death—and thus a basically literary symbol, once its meaning on that earlier level has been made evident, will become part and parcel of the book's dramatic substance. But the *creative* construct in that transformation, or in countless other structural subtleties like it, can be apprehended only if we have built toward it as Lowry himself does.

Said differently, what follows is an *inductive* investigation, from the inside out, "under" *Under the Volcano*. Commentary on the more conventional aspects of Lowry's effort—theme, character, even as it were the very "life" of the novel—will also then remain deliberately inconclusive until Lowry himself brings such matters into largest focus, my contention being that these, likewise, are in their way most rigorously effected by his cross-referential, mythic strategies, i.e., that gradual accretion of allusive detail. If one result of this approach is that, in addition to some unconvincing early interpretations, a certain prosaic "exposition" becomes necessary in the first few chapters, the latter accusation is one that *Under the Volcano* itself has not always escaped. But the "trivia" must be recorded before being seen whole. Well before the end, however, Lowry's multiple clusters of meaning will have become virtually *dehiscent;* there, the effort is to keep them from spilling off the page.

At risk of repetition: what is being so insistently intimated in those last two paragraphs is, simply, that this book gets better as it goes along. But it is a point the writer would ask be held in mind. In dealing on a linear basis with materials which assume meaning only when seen spatially, much of the introductory exposition in the first three full chapters may appear oversimplified and overqualified (the problem will be reflected stylistically as well); and in that same context a number of symbolic attributions may *seem* wrongheaded. From there on, as the *reflexive* configurations come into focus, there is an almost geometric progression in both authority and intensity.

CHAPTER ONE

It is something other than chance that in a novel making use of myth to order a world where order is not, a salient theme should be that very climate of *disorder*. The setting of *Under the Volcano* is a town in Mexico called Quauhnahuac, a town where "a fine American-style highway leads in from the north but is lost in its narrow streets and comes out a goat track." This from Malcolm Lowry's opening page, a directional signpost for the age: civilization one way, dissolution the other. In the shadow of Lowry's symbolic volcano, the balance is critical.

But "place" in *Under the Volcano* is more than contemporary microcosm; simultaneously, "the name of this land is hell." And as we have seen, that hell will become specifically Dante's, Faust's, Adam's after the Fall. Yet if such metaphors are projected to their logical extremes—as Lowry never fails to do—then against this same symbolic backdrop Dante will achieve a vision of the divine, Faust will glimpse salvation, Eden will be redeemed. Thus it is also no accident that the premise of eternal cyclic return—the concept of death and resurrection which has informed man's beliefs since belief began—underlies implicitly all statements in the novel.

Indeed, the events in *Under the Volcano* occur on the Mexican holiday known as the Day of the Dead, during which, in words Lowry borrows from an unnamed Strauss song, "Once a year the dead live for one day." (The song is "Allerseelen," "All Souls.") Processions of Indians are visiting the cemeteries of the apparently peaceful town: "Only if one listened intently . . . could one distinguish a remote confused sound—distinct yet somehow inseparable from the minute murmuring, the tintinnabulation of the mourners—as of singing, rising and falling, and a steady trampling—the bangs and cries of the fiesta that had been going on all day."[4]*A day of mourning, likewise a day of celebration—while typifying its paradoxical motif of continuance is an enormous Ferris wheel, to be remarked repeatedly.

But the structure of the novel itself is cyclic. Its main action takes place in a twelve-hour period in November, 1938, while the circumstances of Chapter I occur one year later to the day. Thus by preceding the story in sequence, but following it in time, the chapter must be considered both introduction and epilogue: in commenting after the fact it demands to be reread with a knowledge of those facts. And since it closes with the Ferris wheel leading "backwards" once again into the past, this circle, too, revolves ceaselessly.

As introduction, Chapter I naturally fulfills those same obligations of "exposition" necessary here, familiarizing us with the novel's central characters—through reminiscence, these being "the dead" in question—and permitting us to break into that main narrative at a moment of crisis. Lowry gives us this prefatory material through the perspective of M. Jacques Laruelle, an expatriate French film director. Laruelle is seen first in conversation with Dr. Arturo Díaz Vigil, his physician and tennis partner, like himself a spectator at the events of a year before; separating from the doctor he strolls through the darkening Quauhnahuac countryside, then at a cantina in the town itself holds a second conversation with a theater manager named Bustamente. The framework is scant; Lowry himself has said of the chapter, in his preface to the French edition of the novel, that Laruelle "establishes a kind of survey of the terrain, just as he expresses the slow, melancholy and tragic rhythm of Mexico itself."

Lowry's methods are acutely subjective, however, and in addition to such externals it is Laruelle's consciousness upon which emphasis is placed. Yet neither is it the Frenchman alone who emerges here. Throughout, Laruelle is obsessed with the memory of a man named Geoffrey Firmin, late British Consul in Quauhnahuac and protagonist of *Under the Volcano*.

*Numbers thusly placed indicate page references.

The first spoken words of the novel refer to the Consul; he is the subject of Laruelle's other talk as well. Laruelle's perspective ranges back almost a quarter of a century, to a period when he and Geoffrey had been boyhood friends before meeting again by chance in Mexico, but in the main its focus holds to the latter's existence before "that day." An alcoholic, ridden by undefined and seemingly hallucinatory guilts, the man at first glance would appear hardly tragic in stature, and the same highway that terminates so abruptly in the town can easily be read as symbolic of his own personal estate: in Quauhnahuac he had come to the end of the road. At the chapter's end, however, we read with Laruelle a long, agonized, remarkably eloquent letter of Geoffrey's—a plea to his wife Yvonne, who had left him, that she return—which more than alters that judgment:

> . . . . . . Night: and once again, the nightly grapple with death, the room shaking with daemonic orchestras, the snatches of fearful sleep, the voices outside the window, my name being continually repeated with scorn by imaginary parties arriving, the dark's spinets. As if there were not enough real noises in these nights the color of grey hair. Not like the rending tumult of American cities, the noise of the unbandaging of great giants in agony. But the howling pariah dogs, the cocks that herald the dawn all night . . . the eternal sorrow that never sleeps of great Mexico. For myself I like to take my sorrow into the shadow of old monasteries, my guilt into cloisters and under tapestries, and into the misericordes of unimaginable cantinas where sad-faced potters and legless beggars drink at dawn, whose cold jonquil beauty one rediscovers in death. So that when you left, Yvonne, I went to Oaxaca. There is no sadder word. . . . [35]

Yet Lowry is concerned not only with Geoffrey's individual humanity here. Speaking of the man, in his uncertain English Dr. Vigil suggests to Laruelle: "Sickness is not only in body, but in that part used to be call: soul. Poor your friend, he spend his money on earth in such continuous tragedies."[5] That a comment of this sort must be seen as pertinent to the age itself is made evident almost immediately by the essential tone of Laruelle's retrospection:

What had happened just a year ago to-day seemed already to belong in a different age. One would have thought the horrors of the present would have swallowed it up like a drop of water. It was not so. Though tragedy was in the process of becoming unreal and meaningless it seemed one was still permitted to remember the days when an individual life held some value and was not a mere misprint in a communiqué.[5]

On this explicit a level, Mexico itself—"place"—does emerge initially as political microcosm. To quote from Lowry's preface again: "Mexico, the meeting place of many races, the ancient battleground of social and political conflicts where . . . a colorful and talented people maintained a religion which was virtually a cult of death . . . is the ideal setting for the struggle of a human being against the powers of darkness and light." The country at the time of the novel is disturbed by characteristic internal strife —"the eternal sorrow that never sleeps of great Mexico." Beleaguered by labor unrest and pressures from foreign oil interests, the Cárdenas government is also in conflict with the pro-Nazi "Union Militar" party of Almazán. Belated newsreels of the Spanish civil war are showing in the Quauhnahuac theater, and Maximilian's decayed summer palace in the town reminds Laruelle of another era of tension: "The shattered evil-smelling chapel, overgrown with weeds, the crumbling walls, splashed with urine, on which scorpions lurked . . . this place, where love had once brooded, seemed part of a nightmare. . . . France, even in Austrian guise, should not transfer itself to Mexico."[14]

Projected even more deeply into the past, the same themes are reiterated by a calendar illustration of a meeting between Cortez and Moctezuma, conquistador and victim, and are then thrown again into contemporary focus by a sudden storm which causes a power failure and sends Laruelle hurrying to shelter— inevitably suggesting impending "blackouts" and "shelters" of another sort. Or more portentously: "It was still raining, out of season, over Mexico, the dark waters rising outside to engulf his own zacuali in the Calle Nicaragua, his useless tower against the coming of the second flood."[29]

Similar political undertones mark Laruelle's recollection of Geoffrey's half-brother Hugh, another participant in the events of the preceding year; at twenty-nine, and as a committed Loyalist, Hugh "still dreamed, even then, of changing the world (there was no other way of saying this) through his actions."[9] Conversely, we are also told the story of a ship, the S. S. *Samaritan,* upon which Geoffrey had been an officer in World War I. Ostensibly a freighter, in actuality a camouflaged gunboat, the irony in its name will typify latter-day Samaritanism as the theme is enlarged upon.

But Lowry's individual characters themselves also become, in effect, political symbols. Impersonally to be called "the Consul" throughout the novel, Geoffrey is even this early mistaken by the theater manager for an "Americano." This is a typical case in which the full extent of a symbolic "identity," even of a non-mythic sort, cannot be appreciated until understood in terms of the novel as a whole; but Lowry is laying the groundwork for an embodiment within the man of that indifference on the part of both England and America which precluded intervention in Spain, and which by extension will have to be read as the indifference of Western civilization itself to the outcome of such a conflict. And Laruelle here is cast of the same mold, seen to persist in that indifference even *after* the fascist victory. For all that it too involved fascist machinations, he has learned nothing from the personal tragedy in Quauhnahuac of a year before, and —this in late 1939—is left with "few emotions about the war, save that it was bad. One side or the other would win. And in either case life would be hard."

Most crucially, what Laruelle has failed to learn is simply that "love is the only thing which gives meaning to our poor ways on earth." "Not precisely a discovery, I am afraid," the Consul adds, the line being his in the letter; banality or otherwise, however, the statement will become central to the novel's various levels of meaning. Yet in his talk with Dr. Vigil, when Laruelle refers to another declaration of this truth actually painted across the facade of his house—"No se puede vivir sin amar," "One cannot live without love"—he insists that it has been inscribed there by an "estúpido."[6] Or again, when he and Vigil drink a Spanish toast, traditionally "Health and money and love, and time to enjoy them," Laruelle offers only "Salud y pesetas," and Vigil's response is limited to "Y tiempo para gastarlas."

As a result, the doctor is forced to speak of a church "where is the Virgin for those who have nobody with," and Laruelle after his four years in Mexico still feels "like a wanderer on another planet." Suggesting yet deeper ramifications of this isolation—the failure of communication itself—Lowry interposes several references to the Tower of Babel, and the theme is then echoed in Geoffrey's letter; separated from Yvonne and desperately in need of her return, he is nonetheless forced to write, on pages he will not, significantly, mail: "I could not, cannot ask you. I could not, cannot send a telegram." Or, estranged in another way, remarking in this instance the incommunicable depths of his suffering, Geoffrey thinks of himself "as a great explorer who has discovered some extraordinary land from which he can never return to give his knowledge to the world."

Insofar as it stems from this same bankruptcy of love, a corollary motif here is that of guilt. Showing at Sr. Bustamente's theater is *Las Manos de Orlac, The Hands of Orlac,* a Peter Lorre thriller of which, as Laruelle contemplates a poster advertising it, Lowry writes: "An artist with a murderer's hands; that was the ticket, the hieroglyphic of the times. For really it was Germany itself that . . . stood over him.—Or was it, by some uncomfortable stretch of the imagination, M. Laruelle himself?"[25]

The theme is also emphasized in the tale of the Consul's gunboat, in connection with the disappearance—and alleged incineration—of some German officers it had captured. The facts of the episode are never made quite clear, and since Lowry is rarely otherwise imprecise, the deliberate ambiguity would seem to imply that guilt is entertained only insofar as man *desires* his suffering (the concept will be reiterated later). In any event, although the Consul had been acquitted by a court-martial in the case, and indeed then awarded a medal, he persists in "imagining that a stigma would cling to him because of it throughout his whole life." Yet if the man is labeled a "more lachrymose pseudo 'Lord Jim,' " Laruelle also recalls that he had been at times "enormously funny" about it all. "People simply did not go round," the Consul has said, "putting Germans in furnaces." (Which is not to fail to remind us, if in typically oblique Lowry fashion, that Germans shortly did go round putting *people* in them.)

Spurious or otherwise, these same guilts manifest themselves additionally in the Consul's sense of persecution. Considered from Sr. Bustamente's Latin viewpoint, the very fact that Geoffrey was a "Consul" signifies irrefutably that he was some sort of spy, or "spider" in the theater manager's term; Bustamente is insistent enough about this so that Laruelle conceives of the Consul "pursued by other spiders who, without his ever being quite certain of it, a man in dark glasses he took to be a loafer here, a man lounging on the other side of the road he thought was a peon there, a bald boy with earrings swinging madly on a creaking hammock there, guarded every street and alley entrance."[30] Whether or not such presences *are* "spiders," or involved at all in the very nearly revolutionary Mexican political subterfuges of the moment, it happens that all three are to be seen during the Consul's day, remarked in each instance with distinct overtones of mystery.

Again there is no connection here with myth, yet the lines further exemplify the extent to which seemingly casual imagery demands attention—especially since this whole concept of "spiders" will become a contributory factor in the Consul's murder. But even in the limited context of Chapter I, the description adds credence to the picture we are given of the Consul as "a man living in continual terror of his life," again a metaphor for humanity's own status in 1938. Similarly, when Laruelle remembers an occasion when Geoffrey "had run into the cantina El Bosque, kept by the old woman Gregorio . . . shouting something like 'Sanctuario!' that people were after him, and the widow, more terrified than he, had hidden him in the back room for half the afternoon,"[30] the scene is thrown into far larger focus when we find it said of that "hieroglyphic of the times" the Orlac film, "what a complicated endless tale it seemed to tell, of tyranny and sanctuary."

This constant shifting from a particular image to a broader suggestiveness is also characteristic. Take Laruelle during his walk:

How continually, how startlingly, the landscape changed! . . .
you would find every sort of landscape at once . . . you could
change climates, and, if you cared to think so, in the crossing of
a highway, three civilizations; but beautiful, there was no denying its beauty, fatal or cleansing as it happened to be . . . [9]

On one level, considering the admixture of beauty and fatality
in his anguished letter to Yvonne, if not to mention the range
of his intellect—as when Laruelle recalls him speaking of "the
god of the storm, 'Huracán,' that 'testified so suggestively to
intercourse between opposite sides of the Atlantic' "—the description might apply to the landscape of the Consul's own
consciousness, to become the heart of the novel. (There is
something of the same in Lowry's picture of the Casino de la
Selva, characterized by an "air of desolate splendor.") But the
lines must certainly also make it clear that Lowry intends a
universality of meaning in things to come. Likewise the barranca, or omnipresent ravine: "Quauhnahuac was like the times
in this respect, wherever you turned the abyss was waiting for
you round the corner."[15]

But the same abyss is waiting "round the corner" in a different way entirely. The following pages will summarize the
more important mythic analogies adumbrated in Chapter I,
or at least insofar as they can be discerned within that limited context.

DANTE

As already indicated, any "abyss" in Lowry's mythic framework
will most specifically be seen to recall the *Inferno*—though it
must be reiterated that the first hints of all such equations will
prove slight. The symbolic function of a word like selva, to
choose an already familiar example, cannot be fully understood
until much later in Lowry's text when he will let two of his
characters, separately, say something about their lives by quoting the verse from which it comes:

Nel mezzo del cammin di nostra vita
Mi ritrovai per una selva oscura . . .

(In the middle of the journey of our life
I came to myself in a dark wood . . .)

But in our view of that larger context, something subtle will be perceived. Likened to "the times," as by Laruelle, Lowry's abyss naturally becomes an essentially political symbol, whereas when equated with Dante's abyss it evokes a prototypal image of human misery. Similarly, however, Lowry's selva will come to represent both political *and* spiritual dislocation—and as it happens, Dante's own dark wood was also meant to represent both. Thus where Dante writes on several levels at once, Lowry will draw parallels on several.

The same pattern emerges in an equation between *Under the Volcano* and another model altogether, the *Dead Souls* of Gogol which Lowry himself mentions in the French preface. No one in *Under the Volcano* goes about literally purchasing "dead souls"— that is, titles to deceased serfs, for fraudulent tax purposes—but Lowry's narrative is of course *about* the dead, and several key lines relevant to that mania of Tchitchikov's might readily be applied to Geoffrey, or to Laruelle in his own preoccupations of Chapter I: "Whatever you know," someone suggests to Gogol's figure, "the body depends upon the soul. . . . Think not of dead souls but of your own living soul, and in God's name take a different path." (Cf. Dr. Vigil's comment on "sickness" of soul —or more pointedly the reference to Geoffrey "spending his money" to tragic end.) But more than a satire on human obsession, Gogol's novel, like Dante's poem, was intended as contemporary political commentary.

Thus the complications can be inferred, even if, again, such connections remain inconclusive in the single chapter. Witness likewise the aforementioned cantina El Bosque. Later, in the very process of quoting Dante, the Consul's familiarity with the foreign tongue more immediately at hand will lead him to substitute this Spanish word for the original Italian: "Mi ritrovai per una bosca oscura—or selva?" And even as the name of the tavern is thereby seen as less than random, the Consul will moreover enter the Bosque, and find it very suggestively "dark" —and this during a moment of dramatic spiritual distress.

Or again: in any Dantean scheme, Dr. Vigil's name can hardly fail to suggest Virgil, the poet who leads Dante through the mists. In Chapter I Vigil himself adds substantiation to this probable identity through his expression of concern for the Consul's "soul," an interest assuredly beyond the province of ordinary medicine. Much later along, however, the identity will pass beyond any realm of speculation when the doctor invites the Consul and others to Guanajuato and mention is made of an underground tomb still to be visited by tourists in that city, famous for its mummies—this then a very real "abyss" in which Vigil-Virgil will be offering to serve as guide. Similarly, while drinking here from a bottle on whose label "a florid demon brandished a pitchfork," when Vigil is described as having conjured a "flaring lighter out of his pocket so swiftly it seemed it must have been already ignited there, that he had drawn a flame out of himself," the gesture is certainly "hellish"—but it is undeniably more so from that view of Chapter I which sees it in conjunction with the full book.

One further illustration. Recalling an adolescent adventure, Laruelle mentions a golf trap known as the "Hell Bunker" in which one night he had come upon Geoffrey secluded with a girl. Laruelle remembers "the bizarre scene," and "the awkward grotesque way the girl scrambled to her feet," but otherwise never tells us precisely what he and his own companion happened to see—though we do note that while young Geoffrey is described initially as "a virgin to put it mildly," the group then proceeds to a tavern "with some queer name, as 'The Case is Altered.' " But the joke is considerably more indirect than this. Describing the "Hell Bunker" Lowry writes that it "lay in the middle of the long sloping eighth fairway"; he also refers to it as an "abyss," and remarks further that it "yawned." Hell in quotation marks, an abyss that yawns in the middle of a field, the field numbered as the eighth of a sequence. Whereas in Dante's description of the eighth circle of his own hell: "Right in the middle of the malignant field yawns a well." Some few lines later, as Dante peers into that other "bunker," we discover what

Laruelle saw: "In the bottom," Dante writes, "the sinners were naked."

One obvious point here is that while Lowry is profoundly engaged with such analogies, like Joyce he is quite capable of toying with them irreverently. But at the same time his "buried" joke is one more indication of how much we must surely miss at first reading.

FAUST

Geoffrey's letter is found in a volume of Elizabethan plays Laruelle had borrowed some months before the time of the main flashback, when thinking "of making in France a modern film version of the Faustus story with some such character as Trotsky for its protagonist." Opening the book, Laruelle misreads a line of Marlowe's: "Then will I headlong fly into the earth . . . " (The original says "run.") A moment later he is "shaken" when he brings his finger down at random on another passage:

> Cut is the branch that might have grown full straight,
> And burnèd is Apollo's laurel bough,
> That sometime grew within this learnèd man,
> Faustus is gone: regard his hellish fall—

In view of Laruelle's preoccupations, this alone should imply an association between the Consul and Marlowe's figure, or even that our "modern version" of the tale is *Under the Volcano* itself. Later on, however, the Consul will actually be called "Trotsky," and, dying, will be flung bodily into a ravine, thus literally "flying" into earth.

But the letter adds to the identity in the section at hand. "Right through hell there is a path, as Blake well knew," the Consul has written, "and though I may not take it, sometimes lately in my dreams I have been able to see it." On one level, this sentence must be taken as the first adumbration of a complex symbology of paths themselves, later in fact to be related to the fertile metaphor of the dark wood where Dante loses "the straight way"; on another, however, it harks back specifically to

a passage from Bunyan's *Grace Abounding for the Chief of Sinners*
used by Lowry as one of three epigraphs for the novel, itself
Faustian in tone:

> Now I blessed the condition of the dog and toad, yea, gladly
> would I have been in the condition of the dog or horse, for I knew
> they had no soul to perish under the everlasting weight of Hell
> or Sin, as mine was like to do. Nay, and though I saw this, felt this,
> and was broken to pieces with it, yet that which added to my
> sorrow was, that I could not find with all my soul that I did desire
> deliverance.

Meanwhile a more subtle evocation occurs in the final moments of the chapter. The Consul's letter falls from the book of
plays, and Laruelle reads it by the light of a candle; when he
finishes we hear the aforementioned bell. Lowry does not force
the issue, but the premeditation would appear incontestable:

> How! bell, book, and candle—candle, book, and bell,
> Forward and backward to curse Faustus to hell!

Furthermore it is then actually "backwards," to the eleven flashback chapters of the Consul's revisited hell, that the revolving
Ferris wheel immediately leads us.

But the relevance of such symbolism is also made evident well
within the boundaries of the single chapter, since even on the
surface the Consul emerges as a character whose sufferings bespeak a sense of damnation or an inability to achieve grace. "I
wonder if it is because to-night my soul has really died that I feel
at the moment something like peace." Too, a decidedly "occult"
aspect of his personality is several times expressed. This also
from the letter:

> Meantime do you see me as still working on the book, still
> trying to answer such questions as: Is there any ultimate reality,
> external, conscious and ever-present etc. etc. that can be realised
> by any such means that may be acceptable to all creeds and
> religions and suitable to all climes and countries? Or do you find
> me between Mercy and Understanding, between Chesed and
> Binah (but still at Chesed)—my equilibrium, and equilibrium is

all, precarious—balancing, teetering over the awful unbridgeable
void, the all-but-unretraceable path of God's lightning back to
God? As if I ever were in Chesed! More like the Qliphoth. . . .
A frustrated poet in every man. Though it is perhaps a good idea
under the circumstances to pretend at least to be proceeding with
one's great work on "Secret Knowledge," then one can always
say when it never comes out that the title explains this defi-
ciency.[39]

But this on its own part is obviously something more than
incidental documentation of that Faustian turn of mind; particularly in light of the reference to Blake, himself a mystic, and
another to Swedenborg, the passage must stand as fair warning
of esoteric matters to come. The Hebrew words used are Cabbalistic, and the image of "teetering" over a void is an allusion
to the fact that the occult Tree of Life, an emblem of the Cabbala, is said to grow near such an abyss. In seeking the "Secret
Knowledge" of which the Consul speaks, the adept runs the risk
of a fall like Faust's own—or like man's after his cataclysmic
misstep involving that other tree in Eden. But since this Cabbalistic abyss will also again recall Dante's, there are simply too
many of Lowry's key symbolisms thrown into simultaneous juxtaposition here to be separated this early; discussion of his occult apparatus will occur elsewhere.

Yet even where such complexity is most apparent, Lowry is
generally more subtle still. Thus the declaration that equilibrium is "all," while an appropriate metaphor for a precarious
state of Cabbalistic attainment, is also a calculated *literal* allusion
to the manner of Yvonne's death; she will lose her balance,
physically, and fall beneath a horse—but too, that fall will occur
from a tree, and only after she herself has noticed several manifes-
tations of balance which strike her as "admirable" during the
day. Further, the Consul's question concerning "ultimate reality," which forms the subject of his own book, will be seen in
retrospect as a first statement of such themes in *Under the Volcano*
itself.

Similarly the Consul's drunkenness, with its already mentioned hallucinatory quality—frequently to be tied in with vi-
sionary aspects of this occultism—is also found even here to

connote more than ordinary household addiction. "You will think I am mad," he has written, "but this is how I drink too, as if I were taking an eternal sacrament." And again, while it will develop that there is a studied undercurrent of Swedenborgian "correspondence" in what superficially appears an element of coincidence in the novel, it is worth note that this very word is used in regard to one such incident herein.

Another mythic ancestor of the Consul's whose presence will enhance many of these same motifs is Prometheus, one more dealer, as it were, in secret knowledges, and another who endures unending torment, although his entrance into Chapter I is amusingly surreptitious—if characteristic of Lowry's own Faustian ability to put the most unexpected objects to work for him symbolically. While Laruelle contemplates the otherwise anonymous volume of Elizabethan plays, Lowry confronts him with a representation on its cover of "a golden faceless figurine . . . carrying a torch"—the edition then being that of the Modern Library with its familiar trademark. (Laruelle also sees vultures, but not until later will one of those creatures be specifically named an "infernal bird of Prometheus.")

According to myth, it is Prometheus who instructs mortals in the useful arts; and since the Faust legend itself suggests its certain dark artifice, also relevant here is a minor Lowry theme of the hero as artist. Reference has been made to the Consul's occult work-in-progress, we know too of Laruelle's film background; Hugh in turn has been a musician and composer, more recently a journalist, and Yvonne an actress. But more significant is that without exception such pursuits are of the past. It will develop that the Consul is not at work on his book, and indeed, has even resigned his consulship; when he appears, Hugh will only recently have cabled his own resignation to his newspaper. An anticipation of this motif of withdrawal—possibly an additional corollary to the all-pervasive failure of love, a failure anyway of "contribution"—occurs in Chapter I when Laruelle looks back on his four years in Mexico: "He had acquired a Mexican mistress with whom he quarrelled, and numerous beautiful Mayan idols he would be unable to take out of the country, and he had—"[10] The summation ends that abruptly because, in fact, there is nothing more to add; that the art objects themselves have been "acquired" heightens the note of passivity.

A final Faustian point. Since he is profoundly concerned with questions of redemption, Lowry will now and then make use of Goethe's version of the legend, in which salvation is achieved; but the version by Marlowe, with its inexorableness of doom, will echo more vividly. Lowry is writing tragedy. Above and beyond what they contribute thematically then, such parallels must underscore that same inevitability in the narrative to follow.

LOST EDEN

Much of this is noted literally. Viewing the countryside from the Casino de la Selva, Laruelle remarks "the purple hills of a Doré Paradise," later attributes to that landscape "the beauty of Earthly Paradise itself." When his walk brings him to the summer palace of Maximilian and Carlotta, Mexico is described as "their Eden," and then by association becomes Geoffrey and Yvonne's as well: "Ghosts, as at the Casino, certainly lived here. And it was a ghost who still said: 'It is our destiny to come here, Carlotta.' . . . But it was the Consul's voice, not Maximilian's, M. Laruelle could almost have heard in the Palace."[14]

But as has been indicated, Eden in *Under the Volcano* is untenanted—expulsion has come to pass. Thus even while contemplating that paradisiacal landscape Laruelle spies an "abandoned plough," and in his walk deliberately avoids the Consul's old house, "where there would be a light in the window M. Laruelle didn't want to see—for long after Adam had left the garden the light in Adam's house burned on."[22]

In much the same vein Laruelle recalls the Consul once suggesting he make a film about Atlantis—i.e., another "lost" paradise—and then a plaint in the letter reiterates the notion poignantly: "Oh, Yvonne, we cannot allow what we created to sink down to oblivion in this dingy fashion."

Evocative of the Fall, such projections will naturally enrich the themes of guilt, godlessness, etc., which pervade Lowry's surface characterizations. Indeed, a Miltonic allusion lifts the concept to a level of cosmic "fall" when Laruelle remarks a cloud described as "an immense archangel, black as thunder," and moments later thinks of the barranca as "city Moloch." And conversely, since the Fall results from partaking of the Tree of Knowledge of Good and Evil, a cursory line of Dr. Vigil's is perhaps meant to invoke the possibility of a return to innocence: "Come, amigo," the doctor tells Laruelle, "throw away your mind."

Later, Lowry builds a step-by-step analogy with the Biblical events following the "first disobedience."

CHRIST

Specific detail is limited in Chapter I; what we find more often, unlike the Consul's label for drink as "sacrament," is a generally Christian "tone" which anticipates the enlargements to come. Laruelle, for example, considering the cantina by candlelight after the storm, and in spite of the room being filled with "refugees from it," senses "a sort of piety about this scene." And when Sr. Bustamente returns the long lost book of plays and mentions the Consul, referring to his beard and describing him as "the one with the blue eyes," there is much of the same inflection in the passage: Bustamente feels the Consul to have been *"simpático,"* and recalls having seen him once "in this very bar give all his money to a beggar taken by the police."

The Consul's letter does become distinctly Biblical at one point: "Lift up your eyes unto the hills, I seem to hear a voice saying." (Cf. Psalm 121: "I will lift up mine eyes unto the hills.") But almost as if to intimate something about the elusive nature of his own methods, confronting Laruelle with the ravine once again Lowry writes: "When Christ was being crucified, so ran the sea-borne, hieratic legend, the earth had opened all through this country, though the coincidence could hardly have impressed anyone then!"[15]

Conversely, two oblique allusions do demand attention. First, recalling a boyhood adventure, Laruelle mentions an island in an estuary "which you could ride out to at low tide on a donkey." It is probably still necessary to take it on faith that Lowry is never *merely* anecdotal; but because a similar act will be specifically described in New Testament terms elsewhere, the lack of other meaning in the reminiscence would indicate that a first *visual* hint of such imagery is intended, at least.

Second, already quoted from the Consul's letter, has been mention of "the cocks that herald the dawn all night." As it happens, the line occurs shortly before a reference to Christmas, sudden enough to demand an exclamation point at its implications in the Consul's loneliness. Whereas in *Hamlet:*

> Some say that ever 'gainst that season comes
> Wherein our Saviour's birth is celebrated,
> The bird of dawning singeth all night long . . .

Whether intended in this particular regard or not, however, the connection between a cock and the Christ story will become unimpeachable later, relevant to the pronouncement: "Verily, I say unto thee, 'The cock shall not crow, till thou hast denied me thrice.'" Midway through one of the most extended parallels in the book, which includes the three denials, a cock will crow in prelude to the Consul's own "crucifixion."

Naturally Lowry's Christ analogies will reassert the theme of "rebirth," likewise implicit in his uses of Dante. In his letter, the Consul goes on at length about the possibility of a new life for himself and Yvonne ("I seem to see us living in some northern country, of mountains and hills and blue water . . . "), and this vision, localized subsequently as a vision of Canada, becomes the most personal expression of the concept as the novel progresses. But the motif will also be reiterated in patterns of historical repetition—*vide* references to Cortez and Maximilian as a first illustration—and by repetitions in personal history as well, such as the renewed friendship of the Consul and Laruelle. Similarly the Orlac film, playing in 1939, will be seen to have been at the same cinema a year before. And in a line which might appear irrelevant were it not to have a curious echo at an important moment later on, Laruelle notes that because of the peculiar route he has followed, "at this rate he could go on travelling in an eccentric orbit round his house forever."

DON QUIXOTE

Strolling through the fields bordering the town, Laruelle is described as "a knight of old, with tennis racquet for shield and pocket torch for scrip"—on one plane a commentary on the decline of heroic stature in modern man, on another a first evocation of Cervantes' Ingenious Gentleman. There is mention of a Cervantes in the flesh, but rather than the novelist a restaurant owner is meant (in parallel with that same melancholy decline, where the original Cervantes fought at Lepanto, the one named here is a "cockfighter"). Geoffrey's letter refers once to "the Knight of the Sorry Aspect"—which may also be an early intimation of a Grail scheme eventually to unfold—and Laruelle considers the notion that his late friend's life had become "a quixotic oral fiction." And finally, on that estuarial island to which the two had ridden years before, a windmill is mentioned.

Yet once more: obviously, not every windmill implies a Don Quixote tilting at it. But since, like *all* such details, windmills will reappear, and once in a context involving just such an improbable combat, this one is again then less than "incidental."

Logically enough, such symbols will augment Lowry's concern with common delusion and folly, while certain of the Consul's less grotesque alcoholic hallucinations will be very like Don Quixote's own. But insofar as the parallel at least mildly suggests insanity—for which a distinct potential will be remarked in the Consul, and by extension in modern political existence—that motif might also be considered here. Already quoted has been the Consul's comment that Yvonne might think him "mad"; a second reference to the subject occurs when Laruelle is reminded of "that other palace in Trieste . . . where Carlotta went insane," and a third, if less direct, when Lowry names Cervantes' tavern the "Salón Ofélia." More obscurely, in speaking of his writing the Consul sees himself "like Clare, weaving fearful vision," an inversion from a Clare poem ("Summer Images") in which a snail "fearful vision weaves," but phrased to remind us that Clare himself spent over twenty years in a mental asylum. And not merely for reasons already cited has the Consul thought of Blake; as the narrator in Lowry's story "Through the

Panama" puts it, "he had really been drawn to William Blake in childhood because he'd read in his father's London *Times* that Blake was cuckoo." Gogol does not escape here either; and since one more reference involves Poe, again within the limits of the single chapter a trenchant illustration is to be perceived of Lowry's use of allusion for deeper purpose than literal aptness alone. (Thus also, of the two artists named, Blake and Doré, both "happened" to do illustrations for the *Divine Comedy.*)

And no rest for the weary—since Blake and Clare, like Swedenborg, must furthermore suggest mystic "visions" akin to the Consul's, while Poe's alcoholism will relate to Geoffrey's, as will his suicidal inclinations, another Consular proclivity to be discussed later. But as a matter of fact the Poe analogy is more fecund than this. "Darkness had fallen like the House of Usher," Lowry informs us, and unless Poe holds some proprietorship over the word "tintinnabulation," this would seem to be the only reference to him in the chapter. Yet the parallels between the two works are uncanny. Roderick Usher and Poe's narrator, like the Consul and Laruelle, are childhood friends who have come together after long separation; there is a "haunted" palace in the Poe not unlike Maximilian's with its "ghosts" in Lowry; a guitar (Hugh's has not yet been mentioned) is used as a comparable symbol in both narratives; there is a painting intended to represent hell in each; the occult books named in Poe are virtually interchangeable with those later to be catalogued on the Consul's shelves; Poe's Roderick, in giving up his "soul," echoes themes in Lowry already remarked; the "fissure" on the house in Poe corresponds symbolically with the barranca in Quauhnahuac; and even the ultimate tragedies in the two stories are hauntingly similar.

OEDIPUS

As already pointed out, many of Lowry's originally verbal or "poetic" symbols are subsequently transformed into fictional reality: Dante's wood becomes an actual wood, Lowry's Cabbalistic tree becomes a very real tree from which Yvonne falls, etc.

On one occasion during the Consul's coming forth by day,

Oedipus will be called into play through reference to Cocteau's dramatic version of the myth, *The Infernal Machine,* likewise to undergo such a transformation when the Consul later boards a carnival loop-the-loop called "La Máquina Infernal." As Cocteau's title is meant to imply that Oedipus is enmeshed in the diabolical machinery of the gods, so too will the Consul be briefly caught up in a literal sort of demoniacal "machine." When he is, he will find himself "hung for a moment upside down."

In Chapter I, gazing into the theater during the failure of electric power, Laruelle sees an apology for the delay "hung, magically projected upside down." There is no point in insisting again that Lowry does not repeat images without purpose; but some moments later, when Laruelle studies the Consul's letter and finds the handwriting composed in part of "Greek e's," the *rereader* of *Under the Volcano* will accept the fact that, like Prometheus disguised as a colophon, Oedipus has made his unobtrusive entry onto Lowry's subterranean stage.

Nor, for the moment, is the Theban alone in this furtiveness:

> . . . the Greek e's, flying buttresses of d's, the t's like lonely wayside crosses save where they crucified an entire word, the words themselves slanting sharply downhill, though the individual characters seemed as if resisting the descent, braced, climbing the other way.[35]

Calligraphy with a difference. Christ is here, as is Faust, whose resistance to his own "descent" has been noted previously. And since Laruelle finds himself "walking gradually downhill since leaving the Casino de la Selva," Dante is similarly present, descending as he does after leaving his own selva. Moreover the most crucial scene in the novel, from which point onward its tragic progression becomes irreversible, occurs at the site of a "lonely wayside cross."

But as a matter of fact Lowry also manages to introduce an entirely new theme in this same brief passage, that of "climb" to be expanded as the volcano Popocatepetl becomes a counterpart to Dante's Mountain of Purgatory, at the top of which Eden is situated. Thus man himself, in his striving to return to the lost garden, peers out from this same "wholly drunken" handwriting.

But to revert to Oedipus: closely allied with the parallel in the body of the novel—where it becomes considerably more explicit than these first allusions suggest—will be a more generalized theme of the "lost father." In Chapter I we are told that the Consul's actual father "had walked up into the Himalayas and vanished," a bit of information which Lowry will work to Freudian purpose on occasion; but as the subject is enlarged upon it will also connect with the quest for God, removal from His garden, etc. On a level of the Oedipus myth itself, however, any reminder of such a quest must obviously heighten our sense of impending tragedy exactly as does Lowry's Faust parallel.

The foregoing, then, are the essential mythic elements introduced in Chapter I. There remain other aspects of the chapter to be mentioned, however, many of them surface details merely, but again of larger consequence when seen reflexively. The description in the Consul's letter, for example, of "unimaginable cantinas where sad-faced potters and legless beggars drink at dawn," is no haphazard bit of coloring but an allusion to two very particular cantinas, and the Consul's attraction to one of them, situated in the town of Parián and called the Farolito, will mount with a fatality more inescapable than any implied by mythic undercurrent alone. Moreover the letter itself has been written at that cantina, where indeed, when the Consul finally does newly arrive, both a potter and a legless beggar will be in evidence.

But again wheels within wheels, or within potter's wheels; for that same image, with its connotations of age-old craft, is another which will be repeated as Indians in general come to represent an abiding human simplicity or good. In Chapter I a first nod in the direction of such symbolism occurs when Laruelle passes two ragged peons seen to be arguing, "but with the profound concentration of university professors wandering in summer twilight through the Sorbonne," and again when their carriage suggests "the majesty of Aztec princes" and their faces "obscure sculpturings on Yucatecan ruins."[11] Lest he be carried

away by his own romanticism, however—or by D. H. Lawrence's
—Lowry then proceeds to satirize himself by having Laruelle
overhear a fragment of their conversation—about nothing more
immemorial than someone's "completamente fantástico" state
of drunkenness. (Sentimentally, the inveterate Lowry reader
would like to believe they have recognized Laruelle and are
perhaps recalling the late Consul themselves—though there is
no textual evidence for the notion.) But if the potter is also then
another of those poetic symbols eventually transformed into
reality, Lowry's meaning will be all the more fully realized in that
transformation—since, when the Indian does appear, it is to
offer the Consul charity at his most desperate moment of need.

But the same single line meanwhile anticipates yet another
theme altogether, insofar as references to drinking at dawn, in
later scenes, will call to the Consul's mind a sense of peace he
has known in such cantinas at such moments, this in turn to be
closely associated with the dawn in Oriental myth—the hour of
Buddha's transcendent "peace" or enlightenment beneath the
Bo Tree. (Whereupon in Lowry even trees, already Biblical and
Cabbalistic, will be seen to proliferate symbolically.) The reference to the Vedic storm god Huracán, whose name the Consul
has said testifies to "intercourse between opposite sides of the
Atlantic," is the novel's first specific announcement of the motif
—though that "intercourse" becomes an important subject in its
own right.

But to return to the Farolito, as will the Consul's thoughts so
often. Throughout the novel the man will be troubled by the
loss of letters he had received from Yvonne. In the final chapter,
at that cantina, the letters will be returned to him, and his name
on their envelopes will be one of several factors contributing to
his death. By that time their reappearance will have its own
intrinsic inevitability; but in writing his own letter to Yvonne *at
the Farolito* six months before, and speaking of hers, the Consul
makes a casual remark certain to be forgotten by the reader: "I
think I have some of them on me."

Again in the letter, the Consul refers somewhat hyperboli-
cally to "shadows of fate at our meeting in Spain." Since mention of that Spanish meeting will be misconstrued by the fascists and lead him one step closer to death, "shadows of fate"

will have become less than exaggeration after all.

Or yet again: the central events of the novel occur on the day of Yvonne's return to Quauhnahuac, and halfway through that day a remorseful postcard she had written immediately after her departure, but had incorrectly addressed, is finally delivered to the Consul. The "coincidence" in its arrival at that time is effective enough dramatically; there is considerably more irony at hand, however, when we note here that the Consul himself has remarked: "And if you'd only written me *right away* also, it might have been different—sent me a postcard even. . . ." The italics are Lowry's; the element of contrivance in the later scene is further minimized when we find the Consul also here questioning a misaddressing of the letters themselves.

But to list several other items equally certain to be overlooked until the chapter is reread as epilogue:

—In the novel's opening paragraph, Quauhnahuac is placed geographically in approximately the same latitude, in one direction, as "the southernmost tip of Hawaii," and in the other as "the town of Juggernaut, in India, on the Bay of Bengal." In Chapter I we learn that the Consul spent much of his boyhood in India. Only later does it develop that Yvonne was born in Hawaii, but in a stroke Lowry has encompassed those extremes from which the two have been drawn into the maelstrom.

—Fairly late in the chapter, Laruelle notes that it is "already seven o'clock," a realization that reminds him of nothing more urgent than dinner. Seven o'clock will be seen as the exact hour of the dual tragedy with which, ironically, the film director has been so totally preoccupied.

—Seemingly exaggerated reference is made, in the discussion of spies and "spiders," to the fact that "one could not cross the border in a cattle truck, say, without 'their' knowing about it." Later it will be revealed that Hugh has entered Mexico in precisely this way—and in the company of a fascist who will be present at the time of the Consul's death. Moreover it will be Hugh's name signed to a political cablegram which will give "them" one further reason for accusing the Consul of being a "spider" before taking his life.

—Laruelle notices horses or uses them in simile several times; then after watching one ridden precariously by a drunken Indian, he decides that "this too . . . this maniacal vision of sense-less frenzy, but controlled, not quite uncontrolled, somehow almost admirable, this too, obscurely, was the Consul."[23] La-ruelle also once sees "dark shapes of pariah dogs" in the theater, and as omnipresent symbols of guilt the latter will follow the Consul throughout Lowry's Doomsday; but the idea of the horse "being" the Consul is something else again, and more than metaphor. In primitive mythology a dying god, or ritual priest-king, is often conceived of as being destroyed by an animal and then as being reborn into the form of that animal. And since it is a horse that directly causes Yvonne's death, and indirectly the Consul's, by the end of the novel, and with assistance from Jung and Sir James Frazer, Lowry will have managed to perform just this transformation with the Consul. Again, patently, the subtle-ties here are such that elaboration must await a fuller context; suffice it that Lowry will subsequently make use of, and literally speak about, such matters as the "eating" of the god, anthropo-morphism, ritual sacrifice, etc.—which is to say that he is writing a "modern" novel in perhaps the most sophisticated sense of the word.

On which incomplete note Chapter I may be left, if hardly dis-missed. As its wealth of detail will have already suggested, the Consul's letter alone must come to be seen as a kind of Rosetta Stone for the interpretation of much that follows, and will de-mand to be looked back at frequently. What such elements add up to as they stand, meanwhile, is a question Laruelle himself in effect asks at one point, when he finds he has not succeeded in "explaining the Consul" to Sr. Bustamente: "What, after all, was a Consul that one was mindful of him?" The answer, of course, lies in the question itself, or rather in the recurrent Old Testament line which Lowry has characteristically adapted for his own ends. No italics seem necessary:

What is man, that thou art mindful of him?

CHAPTER TWO

"For Christ Jesus sake Yvonne come back to me, hear me, it is a cry, come back to me, Yvonne, if only for a day . . . . . . "[41]

Yvonne leaves in December, 1937. The letter, read by Laruelle in November, 1939, is composed in the spring of 1938, and it is six months after that writing that the main action of *Under the Volcano* takes place. Yvonne does return, and her reunion with the Consul lasts indeed "only for a day." In her first sight of the man, and our own, he is shown holding a "Mexican National Railways timetable," stark indication that the events to follow have their inflexible schedule. Twelve hours later both Yvonne and the Consul will be dead, with, in words from Chapter I descriptive of Maximilian and Carlotta, "their only majesty at last that of tragedy."

Chapter II, like all of those written from Yvonne's point of view, is among the shortest in the novel. The letter has prepared the reader for the confrontation with which it begins: "Still holding the timetable the Consul built himself to his feet as she came forward. *'Good* God.' " (The emphasis is worth note.) But the first hesitant exchanges between the pair are interspersed by exclamations from a temporarily unidentified third party across a partition—"They shoot first and ask questions later"—and there are gaps in Yvonne's perceptions as well as in conversation. The disjunctiveness seems unquestionably "true," though the scene is perhaps difficult to follow initially.

Typically, however, the complications are deeper than those demanded by verisimilitude alone; the interjected lines themselves are being spoken by Hugh's fascist acquaintance who will be present in the final pages of the novel, where the already familiar "they" will "shoot first" in precisely the manner described. Yet the very mode of the passage reiterates an even more familiar theme, that of communication. As the tension does subside, the Consul asks if Yvonne will have a drink. Yvonne can answer only: "—"

Stressing the point, Lowry shortly forces Yvonne into difficulty in communicating with *herself,* so to speak, when she passes Laruelle's house with "its inscription on the wall she didn't want to see"—this the statement that "one cannot live without love" which underlies all such failures in the novel. Thus it is not surprising that we will find Dante at hand also; for if the *Divine Comedy* can be reduced to any sort of summary (though it cannot), the same line might express its own central premise.

Some Dantean items, again perhaps not yet wholly convincing, but to be noted as the weight of such symbolism continues to accumulate:

—In the *Comedy,* as Dante approaches the Mountain of Purgatory, Venus is rising as the morning star. Since divine love in Dante is represented by the sun, in recording that the planet appears first he is pronouncing a logical spiritual progression: man must become sensible of mundane or earthly love before aspiring to the heavenly. And thus while Yvonne arrives in Quauhnahuac at seven o'clock, she remembers leaving Acapulco earlier the same morning "when the horn of Venus burned so fiercely she could imagine her dim shadow cast from its light."

—Venus is already a recurring symbol, since the Consul envisages it "burning hard in daylight" in his letter, in fact in those paragraphs where he is speaking of a possible "new life." But this notion of Yvonne's shadow being cast by a single star, if perhaps beyond ordinary credulity, signifies that we are "in" Dante in another way: in Purgatory, where the dead cast no shadows, Dante's is equally wondrous.

—During Dante's ascent through Paradise itself, the guide Virgil is replaced by Beatrice, Dante's sublime love on earth, in his poem a personification of the spiritual love which must ultimately replace reason in man's pursuits. Seeing Beatrice closely for the first time, at the end of the *Purgatorio,* Dante feels as if "just smitten by the sun," and is forced to "remain a while without vision." Whereas when Yvonne appears before the Consul: "Then he looked up abruptly and saw her, peering shortsightedly about him before recognizing her, standing there, a little blurred probably because the sunlight was behind her."[46]

—In Dante there can be no progression toward the divine so long as darkness persists—sin, doubt, despair, etc. But after having attended an all-night Red Cross ball the Consul is now in a hotel bar, and while the town square is "brilliant in the seven o'clock morning sunlight," Yvonne enters "blinking, myopic in the swift leathery perfumed alcoholic dusk." (When they emerge together some moments later, the Consul at once puts on his dark glasses.)

In essence then, where Yvonne represents that salvation the Consul might achieve through love—both in fictional reality and on this figurative level—he himself remains in the dark wood. Yvonne herself certifies the fact, and perhaps much of the foregoing, when she considers the name Quauhnahuac (in actuality the pre-conquest Nahuatl name for Cuernavaca): "Where the eagle stops! Or did it really mean . . . near the wood?" Since the Indian word does in fact mean "place of the eagle," the alternate Dantean translation is a symbolic interpolation only.

Nonetheless, this early in the day the possibility of that return toward the light still hangs in the balance. Borrowing a fortuitously available symbol as quickly as he will improvise, Lowry may have had good reason for translating the name as it stands: it is after he dreams of being carried by a heavenly eagle—i.e., where the eagle stops—that Dante reaches the gate of Purgatory. Similarly, where Yvonne remembers "sailing into Acapulco harbor yesterday evening through a hurricane of immense and gorgeous butterflies swooping seaward," Dante speaks of man himself as an "angelic butterfly that flies to judgment without defense."

On the other hand such analogies are not particularly typical of the chapter. While a street is named "Calle Tierra del Fuego," "Street of the Land of Fire," and a bemused shopkeeper calls the Consul a "diablo," for all the groundwork laid by Laruelle much of what remains is still introductory. (Though again, Tierra del Fuego might suggest the islands themselves, an "end of the world" to correlate with the Consul's end of the road.) The same Dantean imagery of light and dark, also to become germane to Lowry's occult symbolism, most often occurs here mainly as surface coloring—essentially a first adumbration of motif. Thus when the Consul at one point is seen to be "shaking so badly" that he can barely hold a bottle, Yvonne thinks: "This is like an ultimate denial—oh Geoffrey, why can't you turn back? Must you go on and on forever into this stupid darkness, seeking it, even now, where I cannot reach you, ever on into the darkness . . . !"[50]

In much the same way, when Yvonne pauses to conceive of the Consul's own attitude toward such matters, it is with relative superficiality (italics added):

> "But look here, hang it all, it is not altogether darkness," the Consul *seemed* to be saying in reply . . . "what beauty can compare to that of a cantina in the early morning? Your volcanoes outside? Your stars . . . Antares raging south southeast? Forgive me, no. Not so much the beauty of this one necessarily . . . but think of all the other terrible ones where people go mad that will soon be taking down their shutters, for not even the gates of heaven, opening wide to receive me, could fill me with such celestial complicated and hopeless joy as the iron screen that rolls up with a crash, as the unpadlocked jostling jalousies which admit those whose souls tremble with the drinks they carry unsteadily to their lips. All mystery, all hope, all disappointment, yes, all disaster, is here, beyond those swinging doors . . . "[50]

There are depths here, of course. The new reference to insanity should be noted, as must the new intimation of drink's religious dimension, a hint again of the "eternal sacrament." Since it is not simply "raging," but burning itself out, Antares in its way becomes a celestial symbol for the Consul's own self-destructiveness, and too, the additional echo of Dante rings sharply: "Abandon all hope, ye that enter here." Yet the passage is actually much *lighter* in texture than those in which Lowry will be able to pursue similar topics later on. (Each of Lowry's first four chapters, in fact, written from four different points of view, is to a degree "introductory.")

At all events—and her partial insights to the contrary—

Yvonne's hopes persist. In another of her thoughts of Acapulco
at dawn she remembers having heard, "from the small boats
tossing in the Spanish Main, the boys, like young Tritons, already beginning to blow their mournful conch shells"—i.e., to
calm the turbulence of the seas. Yet in Quauhnahuac itself every
sign repudiates those hopes. The first words she hears the Consul utter, apropos of a regulation in the timetable, concern the
transportation of a corpse "by express"—again a note of prophecy insofar as their own corpses will perhaps soon be "transported." (Laruelle says nothing about the manner or place of
burial, however.) When they walk home together a child's funeral passes them in the street, and Yvonne thinks of the Acapulco plane as "a minute red demon, winged emissary of Lucifer." While in the hotel bar itself:

> Yvonne's eyes came to rest on the old woman, who was sitting
> in the shadow at the bar's one table. On the edge of the table her
> stick, made of steel and with some animal's claw for a handle,
> hung like something alive. She had a little chicken on a cord
> which she kept under her dress over her heart. . . . She set the
> little chicken on a table near her where it pecked among the
> dominoes, uttering tiny cries.[51]

Yvonne's heart is "chilled" by the "evil omen"—and naturally
none of this eases the difficulty of communication in the scene.
This after she makes no answer to the Consul's offer of a drink:
"Or should she? She should . . . it was what she had made up
her mind to do if necessary, not to have one drink alone but a
great many drinks with the Consul. . . . 'You have one and I'll
cheer,' she found herself saying."[47]
    The situation is rendered more poignant—echoing what has
been labeled in the letter "the common anguish of our separation"—when the Consul remarks that he had left Quauhnahuac
only once in Yvonne's absence. After which: "Did she remember
Oaxaca! The roses and the great tree . . . Or at night their cries
of love, rising into the ancient fragrant Mayan air, heard only by
ghosts? In Oaxaca they had found each other once."[48] In this
context of fulfillment, the recollection of roses would again suggest Dante—the poet's highest vision occurs in the form of a

rose—while the "great tree" in that same context must newly
imply Eden. Actually, however, the latter reference is to a tree
in Santa María del Tule, some few miles from Oaxaca proper,
claimed the oldest in the hemisphere and said to antedate Christ
—a veritible Tree of Life in reality then, if not of Knowledge.

But that Oaxacan fulfillment, like Eden, remains only memory. "—Divorce. What did the word really mean? She'd looked
it up in the dictionary, on the ship: to sunder, to sever." Whereupon this concept finds its physical counterpart also as, walking,
she and the Consul are arrested by a photograph in a shop
window "purporting to show the disintegration of a glacial de-
posit in the Sierra Madre, of a great rock split by forest fires."
The photograph is labeled "La Despedida," "The Farewell."
"After the damp and the detritus had done their work both
severed halves of that blasted rock would crumble to earth. It
was inevitable, so it said on the picture."[54]

Yvonne longs "to heal the cleft rock," but she is also fully
aware of certain difficulties in the process. Not unlike Bunyan's
sinner who does not "desire" deliverance, "the other rock," she
imagines, "stood unmoved. 'That's all very well,' it said, 'but it
happens to be your fault, and as for myself, I propose to disin-
tegrate as I please!' "[55]

Here then something new—though the fact that the divorce
hasn't, in truth, been wholly a result of the Consul's drinking has
actually been hinted at before this. In Chapter I, Laruelle makes
essentially innocuous mention of his "passion for Yvonne," and
the Consul's letter speaks of "the unity we once knew. . . . Knew
even in Paris—before Hugh came." Earlier in Chapter II, however, Yvonne has described the last leg of her journey, "—From
Acapulco, Hornos," at which the Consul has replied: "Ah, Hornos.—But why come via Cape Horn? It has a bad habit of wag-
ging its tail, sailors tell me. Or does it mean ovens?"[47] Lowry has
deliberately confused the Consul here, since Yvonne has sailed
originally from Los Angeles only; the Hornos she mentions is
not Cape Horn—again the end of the world—but an area in
Acapulco. The Spanish word does also mean ovens—this time
perhaps a "furnace" into which *Dante* puts people—but the
point, finally, is the play on the Consul's own "horns." Rather
less subtly, in fact, one of the first things Yvonne notices in the

bar is a calendar showing a woman in a "scarlet" brassiere—while she herself carries a scarlet bag.

When Laruelle's continued presence in the town is subsequently remarked, almost immediately the Consul makes a still more obvious reference to the subject by speaking of "Cuckolds-haven, that town cursed by the lost love of Maximilian and Carlotta." Shortly after this Yvonne learns that Hugh, also, is in Mexico, but her guilt—in regard to infidelities with both men—will have taken hold before she is aware of the proximity of either. As they approach Laruelle's house it strikes her "that recently in her picture of Quauhnahuac this house hadn't been here at all! . . . it was as if the house had never existed, just as in the mind of a murderer, it may happen, some prominent landmark in the vicinity of his crime becomes obliterated."[57] Or more to the archetypal point: "The grass, she thought, wasn't as green as it should be at the end of the rains."

In the guise of the first of the "hideous" pariah dogs, these guilts follow Yvonne and the Consul to the house at the close of the chapter, but an altogether different aspect of this symbolism of being "followed"—a word itself to become a motif in later Yvonne chapters—has already emerged. Leaving the bar a moment before the Consul, Yvonne finds that she has "almost taken the arm of another man wearing dark glasses, a ragged young Mexican leaning against the hotel wall," whom the Consul in turn greets "with something enigmatic in his voice." After some moments, viewing the Cortez palace from below, Yvonne then speculates that "a man standing gazing over the valley . . . looked less like Cortez than the poor young man in the dark glasses who'd been leaning against the wall of the Bella Vista."[56] The episode is hardly ominous, but since this same man will appear so to Yvonne elsewhere—"following" through the day's events as will the old woman of the dominoes—on one plane it must be read as an elaboration of the chapter's general pattern of "omen," whether recognized by Yvonne or not. But at the same time the man in question is of course the first of those several "spiders" described as if in metaphor alone by Laruelle—possibly, as their portentousness does become evident, to be read collectively as a sort of slowly "objectifying" correlative for such guilt and/or paranoia as Lowry portrays.

In spite of all this, Yvonne is able to feel a "sense of a shared, a mountain peace," as they approach the house; "it was false, it was a lie, but for a moment it was almost as though they were returning home from marketing in days past."[64] The contradiction here, or rather the paradox of simultaneously conflicting emotions, is a characteristic Lowry construction which has occurred before; as quickly as Oaxaca reminds Yvonne of fulfillment, it reminds her that love is now "dying." Nor are such contrasts always subjective: even as she studies the shop-window photograph of the split rock, since the shop happens to be a printer's she also notices the "spinning flywheel of the presses" —and for that matter the same window is otherwise filled with "wedding invitations." Repeated oppositions of this sort, as in the dialectic of the Tao, will eventually be understood to form a pattern of complementary polarities, or "opposing motions" as Lowry calls them in one of his short stories, which provide the novel in good part with its surface tensions and will later be seen to have certain occult meanings as well. Elsewhere in Chapter II, in other early illustrations, it is while expressing amusement over some absurdity that the Consul is cut short by the passage of the child's funeral, and even within the brief description of the procession itself we find "the women behind, very solemn, while several paces back a few hangers-on were joking." Or again in a single phrase, Yvonne contemplates a "little church that had been turned into a school with the tombstones and the horizontal bar in the playground."

Two other themes are emphasized in the chapter. Speaking of Hugh, the Consul explains that his half-brother has remained in Quauhnahuac, among other reasons, "to play Theodore Watts Dunton. To my Swinburne." ("Mute Swinburne," the nonartist Consul adds—for more purpose than to indicate familiarity with Gray's "Elegy.") Swinburne's intemperance at once adds him to that list of "unstable" poets to whom reference suggests something about the Consul; more pertinent, however, is the concept of Samaritanism, since Swinburne lived under Watts Dunton's solicitous eye for some thirty years. The theme, already labeled in the naming of the gunboat, is again underscored on this still introductory level when the Consul remarks that after a certain number of drinks Laruelle has been prone to "play the Good Samaritan" also.

Second, in a virtually parenthetical passage, the Consul refers to one William Blackstone: "The man who went to live among the Indians. You know who he was, of course?" Chances are the reader does not know—Blackstone the jurist being someone else again—but for the moment the matter is dropped. In Chapter V, drunk, the Consul will identify the man:

> "He's a character I've always liked. . . . Anyway, one day he arrived in what is now, I believe—no matter—somewhere in Massachusetts. And lived there quietly among the Indians. After a while the Puritans settled on the other side of the river. They invited him over; they said it was healthier on that side, you see. Ah, these people, these fellows with ideas . . . old William didn't like them—no he didn't—so he went back to live among the Indians, so he did. But the Puritans found him out. . . . Then he disappeared altogether—God knows where . . . "135

The Consul's description holds to the recorded facts, which are few; Blackstone died in 1675 in either Rhode Island or Connecticut, having maintained a bookish isolation throughout life. In a long poem entitled "The Kid," Conrad Aiken has written about the same figure, calling him "in many respects the true prototypal American." Aiken sees Blackstone as symbolic ancestor not only of the pioneers of an untracked continent, but also of such as Melville and Henry Adams whose explorations concerned "the darker kingdoms of the soul"—i.e., as Lowry intends him to be seen in regard to the Consul.

But even this early a relationship is implicit between Blackstone and another Lowry "character" altogether—meaning the Consul's father, who himself in effect "went to live among the Indians." The connection is subtle, however. Unlike most prototypal identities in the novel, that with Blackstone will be almost consciously adopted by the Consul—which is to say that in a deliberate manner he himself will often equate his position to Blackstone's. But since he will never once make that other obvious association, it will develop that Lowry is showing us the Consul's *unconscious* in operation also; romanticizing himself as another Blackstone, unwittingly the man will be identifying with his father after all.

In this respect the Blackstone theme will correspond with that involving Oedipus, although in Chapter II Oedipus hints are still minimal. In most recitations of the story, a first clue to the Theban king's fallibility lies in his limp, and the Consul is marked by this same flaw. Similarly, in anticipation of the tyrant's ultimate fate, on one occasion Yvonne here finds her ex-husband "poking at the dust with his stick, making little patterns for a minute as he went along, like a blind man." If only out of their intensity, references to the "little corpse" to be transported, and the child's funeral, might recall Oedipus also. In Chapter III, however, where a cat is named "Oedipuss," Lowry becomes less coy—additionally since the name Oedipus means "swollen foot," and there we read that the Consul's own feet are "swollen and sore."[73]

In the same scheme, Yvonne naturally becomes Jocasta, wedded to her own son. Thus again in Chapter III the Consul not only sees the woman as "youthful and ageless," but informs us further that from an earlier marriage she has had a child, now dead—"strangely named Geoffrey too."[72]

But the Consul's half-brother also "shares" much of this same mythic immortality. (Eventually it will be understood that the two are to be read as halves of the same representation, or alter egos in a polar balance between characterizations.) Additionally then, while talking to Hugh in a conversation which takes place in his mind only, the Consul will shortly proclaim: "There has been all too little opportunity to act, so to say, as a brother to you. Mind you I have perhaps acted as a father."[78] Considering Hugh's adultery with Yvonne, the Consul thus becomes both Oedipus *and* Laius in Lowry's conglomerate mythic arrangement—usurper son *and* murdered parent—whereas Hugh in turn has likewise bedded his father's wife. The Consul will actually think of himself as the "murdered man" in that same passage concerning the adultery in Chapter III, but the point will be made more delightfully once Hugh appears—and repeatedly calls the Consul "Papa."

On another plane the Consul's habitual avoidance of the light is also relevant here, or at least to the Oedipus as drawn by

Sophocles. In the play, the supreme dramatic irony lies in the blinding; after the last terrible moment of revelation—of "vision"—Oedipus tears out his eyes, yet in a metaphorical sense he has been "blind" throughout—as is the Consul to his own impending ruin.

In Goethe, Faust is also blinded at a time of vision—there a vision of salvation like Dante's own—and both analogies will come to mind when the Consul is literally without sight for a moment at the novel's climax. Simultaneously, as the Consul's identities on an occult level come into focus, a concept like that of tracing "patterns" with a stick will recall Tiresias, still another sightless creature who "sees"—and who indeed foretells the doom Oedipus cannot.

But as suggested earlier, these Oedipus parallels must first of all remind us that Lowry's characters are headed toward no playful end—though certain generalizations about the Consul's "political" status will have already begun to indicate how they enhance the signal meaning of that tragedy also. In the unrecognized crime of his life, Oedipus is responsible for the plague which visits Thebes. In his own crime, or man's—neglect of love, of brotherhood—the Consul will be seen as equally responsible for the "plague" in the modern world.

Moreover, as in "The Waste Land," this same scheme of the "dying king" will be made to recall humanity's oldest death-and-regeneration rituals, fertility rites, the Eleusinian mysteries, etc. —again, however, a cluster of meanings too prodigal to be discussed this early.

CHAPTER THREE

As in all of those sections written from the Consul's point of view, even the *syntax* at given moments in Chapter III can become inordinately complex. The opening lines are a case in point:

> The tragedy, proclaimed, as they made their way up the crescent of the drive, no less by the gaping potholes in it than by the tall exotic plants, livid and crepuscular through his dark glasses, perishing on every hand of unnecessary thirst, staggering, it almost appeared, against one another, yet struggling like dying voluptuaries in a vision to maintain some final attitude of potency, or of a collective desolate fecundity, the Consul thought distantly, seemed to be reviewed and interpreted by a person walking at his side suffering for him and saying: "Regard: see how strange, how sad, familiar things may be. Touch this tree, once your friend: alas, that that which you have known in the blood should ever seem so strange! Look up at that niche in the wall over there on the house where Christ is still, suffering, who would help you if you asked him: you cannot ask him. Consider the agony of the roses . . . You do not know how to love these things any longer. . . ."[65]

Insofar as it circles back to Chapter I, the new invocation of Marlowe is perhaps most assertive here:

> See, see, where Christ's blood streams in the firmament!
> One drop would save my soul, half a drop: ah, my Christ!—

More familiar, of course, is the echo of the Sermon on the Mount: "Consider the agony of the roses," "Consider the lilies of the field." This same horticultural misery, along with the "desolate fecundity," newly suggest abandoned Paradise, while the juxtaposition of the crucifixion and the Dantean rose is patently occult; and since the Consul will later talk of having lost his "knowledge" of such mysteries, the tree "once your friend" is again not only Edenic but Cabbalistic. The image of plants struggling "to maintain some final attitude of potency" is prophetic of the Consul's effort to do so sexually some pages hence, and the reference to the "person walking at his side," while in context implying Christ, is possibly a first echo of Eliot as well: "Who is the third who always walks beside you?" (In his note on the line in "The Waste Land," Eliot comments that such hallucinations, common evidently among Antarctic explorers, occur at "the extremity of their strength," the condition in which the Consul will most often endure variants on the sensation.) The reference to "unnecessary thirst," like Yvonne's recent comment that the grass isn't "as green as it should be," will later remind us of Eliot's pervasive symbolism of aridity also, as Lowry's scheme of fertility ritual unfolds.

Meanwhile one variant on the notion of hallucination which manifests itself quickly is that of certain "voices" prone to intrude upon the Consul's private speculations, among them a "pleasant and impertinent fellow, perhaps horned." By another the Consul is admonished against drinking now that Yvonne has returned, which he nonetheless does, in spite furthermore of what he calls Hugh's efforts to "straighten me out." Hugh has "almost literally succeeded right off with some malevolent strychnine compound he produced," the Consul has explained in Chapter II. Strychnine being poisonous, the concoction then becomes an even more obvious instrument of the self-destruction inherent in the drinking itself; thinking of it as "bella donna," the Consul admits to himself that "poison has become your daily food." Offering Yvonne a drink which is refused, he adds: "Not even a straight wormwood?" And then in a different context altogether he thinks of Lucretius, another "mad" poet who, according to legend, was a suicide.

But of the many themes adumbrated in the opening paragraph, that of Lost Eden is most immediately reasserted. After his garden is dismissed as "an indescribable confusion of briars from which the Consul averted his eyes," he hears Yvonne put it in a word: "Geoffrey, this place is a wreck!"

The same note of abandonment, or more properly of devastation, is also marked by new reference to inundation. Approaching the house Yvonne has sensed "the rising waters of possible catastrophe." Now the Consul tells her that the place was "broken into one night when I was out. And flood: the drains of Quauhnahuac visited us and left us with something that smelt like the Cosmic Egg till recently."[66] Further, speaking about his book, on which he "might get down to work again," he adds, "I might even work in something about Coxcox and Noah."

Later, the Consul will be more directly equated with Noah himself. Here, however, in bracketing the Biblical figure with this obscure hero of an Aztec deluge myth, Lowry might once more be implying something about the very reason for his all-inclusiveness—meaning that where Noah remains the classic deluge prototype, such figures are common to virtually every recorded mythology. But these same overflowing "drains" are probably intended to suggest another sort of flood as well, that "drainage" of sin wherein Dante freezes Satan in the deepest circle of hell—or, perhaps, in the abandoned iron mine here remarked beneath the Consul's garden, one more abyss ready at hand. But again the polarity, since there is a universal symbol of rebirth in the lines too: the Cosmic Egg, from which all of creation is said to spring, is another concept indigenous to such disparate mythologies as the Greek, the Vedic, the Egyptian—from all of which, when adequate detail has been recorded, Lowry will be seen to have borrowed.

But the crucial problem in Chapter III remains communication. Nearing the house the Consul speaks "amiably" to the dog which has followed them. Like Faust, if also like St. Francis, he will talk to more creatures than this during his day; in this case, however, he finds that "the animal cowered back down the drive," and as it happens his attempts at conversation with Yvonne are little more fruitful. "This was the moment then, yearned for under beds, sleeping in the corners of bars, at the

edge of dark woods . . . but the moment, stillborn, was gone."[70]
He and Yvonne embrace, "or so it all but seemed, passionately,"
yet a moment later they confront each other "like two mute
unspeaking forts." Gazing at his swimming pool the Consul
wonders: "Might a soul bathe there and be clean or slake its
drought?" (Lowry is quoting Marvell's "Clorinda and Damon."
Since the theme of the poem is the repudiation of such worldly
pleasures as the Consul's own "thirst," the usage is more ironic
than hopeful.) "Stuffed Quixotes tilting their straw mounts on
the house wall" further proclaim the human condition, and even
a bird in the garden is made to reiterate the isolation theme
(with echoes of William Blackstone's): "He's a solitary fellow
who probably lives way off in the Canyon of the Wolves over
there, away off from those other fellows with ideas."[74]

Such reflections are interrupted by the ringing of a telephone.
Answering it in a manner which anticipates a more significant
use of a phone later (the Consul is here "afraid of the furious
thing"), he returns to discover that Yvonne has entered the
bathroom. Then after an ellipsis—a device Lowry repeats to
indicate the alcoholic's more disjunctive transitions—the Consul finds himself "guiltily" mounting the street before his house.
"Never had it seemed such a long way to the top of this hill. The
road with its tossing broken stones stretched on forever into the
distance like a life of agony." While the Consul intends only "a
couple of necessary drinks unspecified in his mind," Lowry is
here making his first fairly explicit statement of the theme of life
itself as "climb." (The road is still Dante's, however, being also
"hot as a furnace.")

Then a new evocation. The Consul's destination is "a little
cool nameless cantina," which he describes as lying off a "leafy"
lane, isolated and bucolic. As he visualizes it, he admonishes the
heat: "Away! Away!" Whereas when Keats similarly desires to
"fade away into the forest dim": "Away! away! for I will fly to
thee. . . ." Ironically, the latter's ambition is to be effected "*Not*
charioted by Bacchus and his pards," though other segments of
the poem must come to mind: cf. the poet's cry for a "draught
of vintage," the wish to drink and "leave the world unseen," the
concept of being "half in love with easeful Death," etc. In lieu
of a nightingale, on the other hand, the Consul is forced to

complete his own "ode" with a recollected paean to a tom-cat: "He ah work all night mistair and sleep all day!"[77]

But the Consul has been out "all night" on his own part, and now collapses in the empty street—as he will collapse amid imagery of climb at the time of his death. Prostrate, under an illusion that Hugh is "lending the old boy a hand," it is here that he holds his imaginary conversation with his half-brother, concerned first with Hugh's infidelity and perhaps suggesting Oedipus in more ways than those mentioned above: "What you did . . . will begin to strike you in a new and darker light." And after which, despite his personification as Laius: "How shall the murdered man convince his assassin that he will not haunt him. . . . Yet does this help, what I am trying to tell you, that *I* realise to what degree I brought all this upon myself?"[79]

The illusion of Samaritanism then becomes a reality when the Consul is offered assistance, and more to the point given a drink, by an Englishman in a passing automobile. The incident itself is inconsequential, but in it Lowry is pointedly foreshadowing a moment when a failure of reciprocal Samaritanism on the Consul's part—in a situation demanding it far more urgently than this—will become the climactic symbolic act of the novel.

Returning to the house the Consul then enters Yvonne's bedroom as "innocently as a man who has committed a murder while dummy at bridge"—the accumulating Orlac-murder imagery has its own eventual point—but the barriers between the pair remain insurmountable. Yvonne almost immediately suggests that they go away together, here planting the seed from which will grow her dream of a new life in Canada, but at the same time assumes their difficulties a result of the alcoholism alone: "All right, Geoffrey: suppose we forget it until you're feeling better: we can cope with it in a day or two, when you're sober." When "the enormity of the insult" has "passed into his soul," the Consul tells himself:

As if, as if, as if, he were not sober now! Yet there was some elusive subtlety in the impeachment that still escaped him. For he was not sober. No, he was not, not at this very moment he wasn't! But what had that to do with a minute before, or half an hour ago? . . . And even if he were not sober now, by what fabulous stages,

comparable indeed only to the paths and spheres of the Holy
Cabbala itself, had he reached *this* stage again . . . this stage at
which alone he could, as she put it, "cope," this precarious stage,
so arduous to maintain, of being drunk in which alone he was
sober![84]

Lowry's occult design will be discussed at length presently;
meanwhile this new comparison between the Consul's drunken
"progressions" and those of the Cabbalist must be noted, as
must the new allusion to "balance." Some pages earlier, the
Consul speaks of an ability to "dodge about in the rigging of the
Cabbala like a St. Jago's monkey," and shortly after the above,
while "thinking or saying" something about his book—presumably thinking it, since when he finishes Yvonne is seen to be
reading—he then mentions Chicago, which leads him to remark
how "not far enough below the stockyards to escape altogether
the reek of the porterhouse of to-morrow, people can be living
in cellars the life of the old alchemists of Prague! Yes: living
among the cohabations [Lowry's word] of Faust himself, among
the litharge and agate and hyacinth and pearls."[86] He also puns
on alcohol and "alkahest," an alchemical solvent, strengthening
the association between drink and the occult, and a moment
after this again replaces his dark glasses.

"Vague images of grief and tragedy" next pass through the
Consul's mind, among them a vision of Oscar Wilde under
arrest—Wilde readily taking a place in Lowry's "cuckoo poet"
syndrome, and perhaps additionally because it was in prison that
he wrote his own *De Profundis*. The frustrations of the hour are
further epitomized by the recollection of a missed appointment
before Yvonne's departure—to have occurred on a street named
the "Via Dolorosa"—after which the Consul remembers having
been in a bar when "suddenly a man with the look of an execu-
tioner came from the street dragging two little fawns shrieking
with fright into the kitchen. . . . And you thought: better not
remember what you thought."[88] A more specific reference to
this latter theme in Chapter II has been considerably less som-
ber, however; passing an outdoor public scribe en route to the
house the Consul has offered: "I am taking the only way out,
semicolon . . . Good-bye, full stop."

But all of this has been prefatory to the more absolute frustration in the Consul's poor effort to make love. His thoughts during the attempt, at first newly occult as he puns on "that jewelled gate the desperate neophyte, Yesod-bound, projects for the thousandth time on the heavens to permit the passage of his astral body," revert almost at once to the cantinas. The vision is anything but appealing—"the debris from the night before, the dead matchboxes, lemon peel, cigarettes open like tortillas, the dead packages of them swarming in filth and sputum"—yet the desire to "go," and to do so "now," drives all else from his mind. "Ah none but he knew how beautiful it all was."[90] The passage actually terminates with an image of procreation, but of a mytho-Faustian sort, as he visualizes sunlight "falling in a single golden line as if in the act of conceiving a God, falling like a lance straight into a block of ice—" and the effort fails totally: "Sorry, it isn't any good I'm afraid." When he closes the door behind himself one of the straw Don Quixotes tumbles from the wall: for all of their larger implications such episodes are sadly human first of all.

On that fundamental level, the failure here can of course be laid to the Consul's alcoholism, though in Freudian terms the man's limp, or "wound," which becomes more vitally symbolic in other terms elsewhere, would imply "castration" to start with; which is to say that the drink, *and* the failure, are then self-imposed "punishments" for the Consul's death wish and/or desire to return to the womb. Later, Lowry associates the barranca, to which the Consul literally "returns" at death, with the caverns of that classic Freudian primer, "Kubla Khan." In such a reading the two volcanoes then become maternal—Yvonne has thought of them as "her volcanoes"—but with perennial snow at their peaks must suggest the same frigidity as the "block of ice." Like Pygmalion in reverse, in fact, before the attempt at intercourse, touching Yvonne the Consul feels "her body stiffen, becoming hard and cold."

Irrelevant to a symbolic "reading" of *Under the Volcano* as such terminology might be, it can also serve as a point of departure for another incidental connection which must somewhere be made, between the limping Consul and the perhaps equally "castrated" Captain Ahab. Where the Consul must substitute tom-cats for nightingales, his monomania correspondingly concerns bottles instead of any white whale, but mania it remains. Direct reference will occur when Hugh recalls having once felt, "for a moment asleep, like Melville, the world hurling from all heavens astern," and again when we are told that he has read the man. Less in terms of deliberate parallel, however, *Moby Dick* must assert itself as "influence," surely in such matters as Melville's genius for surrealistic foreshadowing, configurations of darkness and superstition and doom, even for such weighted symbols as funerals and devils. And at one point in the present chapter the Consul finds the summit of Popocatepetl lifting above the clouds "like a gigantic surfacing whale"—whereas in the original short story version of the novel (published for the first time in the Winter 1963/64 *Prairie Schooner*) the mountain is categorically recorded as "a sort of Moby Dick."*

At all events, after his embarrassment with Yvonne the Consul is then scolded by the voices of his "guardian angels," who question him about the missing letters. (A passing reference to Parián somewhat before this is the first in what will become that fatefully mounting succession of them.) And as always, a good deal of such "trivial" detail continues to pile up in ways that can well pass unnoticed. When the Consul remarks that he had once compelled himself "to learn the philosophical section of *War and Peace* by heart," only later will we see that Lowry has been making plausible a scene in which the man will quote from such passages. Too, the Consul here recalls learning from the same book that "Napoleon's leg twitched," and, as promised, even limps will multiply with mythic significance. Or again, when the volcanoes "remind" the Consul of the Himalayas, and he decides that a watercolor of "Nanga Parbat might well have passed for old Popo," we are not only being prepared for the moment in a dream when he will make that transposition of Popocatepetl

*Melville references outnumber those to any other author in Lowry's correspondence with the present writer—including one to "Ahab's search for his great white socks"—though he also suggests somewhere a larger "identity" with the man's life than with his work.

to India, but are also being given a new hint of that "intercourse" between East and West later to develop along more studied lines.

But the mythic chords echo also, some of which have been ignored here in passages quoted as more relevant to other topics. The moment of Yvonne's return, for example, "yearned for," among other places, "at the edge of dark woods," is of course the omnipresent Dante. The same is probably true of the "Canyon of the Wolves," wolves in the *Divine Comedy* representing that same sort of political "enemy"—so real in the life of the exiled poet himself—by whom the Consul believes himself beset. Likewise when the Consul notes in an astronomy book of Yvonne's that the Mayans "did not suspect a Copernican system," to which he remarks, "Why should they?" what might be implied is that neither did Dante—who nonetheless got on adequately with his own archaic cosmology. And in another area entirely, the Consul once compares certain of his eccentric actions with those of "Don Quixote avoiding a town invested with his abhorrence because of his excesses there."

There is added foreshadowing as well. The Englishman who assists the Consul then drives off "up the hill, waving his hand"; the one other character who makes this gesture, likewise mounting a hill, will become the key figure in that later Samaritan scene so crucial to Lowry's moral allegory. Similarly, an hallucination the Consul endures of an "object shaped like a dead man and which seemed to be lying flat on its back . . . with a large sombrero over its face,"[91] is prophetic of a moment of harsh reality to follow. (In his long letter to Jonathan Cape explicating the novel, Lowry insists that this vision "is" the dying man to be seen later: "This can happen in really super D.T.s. Paracelsus will bear me out.") And less dramatically, the Consul also here discerns Yvonne's "history" in the labels on her luggage—while as that history unfolds, those labels will be seen to have given not only a complete geographical biography but also a chronological one.

The chapter closes—as the Consul is about to fall asleep "with a crash"—with what might appear symbols of calm. Overhead, vultures seem "more graceful than eagles," and the Consul finds that "Ixtaccihuatl and Popocatepetl, that image of the perfect marriage, lay now clear and beautiful on the horizon." The irony is obvious enough with Yvonne "crying" inside the house. But in the *Inferno,* before crossing into the first circle of hell, Dante also suddenly falls "like one who is seized with sleep," and similarly after an image concerning birds—only there it is the dead streaming toward the abyss who look like them. Moreover while the Consul here decides that "the will of man is unconquerable. Even God cannot conquer it," the last spoken words before Dante's own swoon have to do with "God's wrath" and the power of "Divine Justice." And yet again, where the presence of some pretty clouds suggests that the Consul might unconcernedly drink all day—"This is life!"—Dante is overwhelmed "that death had undone so many."

On the other hand neither of the volcanoes, at least, will ever appear quite so deceptively benign again. By twilight they will have "drawn nearer . . . massive interests moving up in the background."

CHAPTER FOUR

In Chapter I, Laruelle recalls his first meeting with the Consul's half-brother: "In half an hour he'd dismissed him as an irresponsible bore, a professional indoor Marxman, vain and self-conscious really, but affecting a romantic extroverted air." In Chapter IV, written from Hugh's point of view, the reader's first impression may be much the same; like Laruelle's, however, it will change. If it is typical of Hugh's naivete that he might envision himself guiding the world "out of the Western Ocean of its misery," at the same time he is compelled sincerely by "the desire to be, to do, good, what was right." Similarly, where the Consul reduces his Loyalist sympathies to a question of "wearing a very popular front indeed these days," the truth remains that the ship which, even a year later, Laruelle believes to have been but "providentially awaiting him at Vera Cruz," is in fact bound for Spain, where she will "discharge her cargo of T.N.T. for the hard-pressed Loyalist armies and probably be blown to smithereens—"[103]

There is a good deal of Don Quixote in him, in the flesh as well as in symbol. When he returns from Mexico City after sending his "final dispatch" to a London newspaper, about a subject as grave as anti-Semitism, he is absurdly costumed in ten-gallon Stetson, high-heeled boots, bandolier and gun, and is "secretly enormously proud of his whole outfit." Not looking where he is going, he stops himself at the edge of a deep pothole thinking, "eyes in my feet, I must have, as well as straw." Later in the chapter he notices a "toy windmill," and at a time further along when he attempts a rash yet essentially "chivalrous" act, in restraining him the Consul will remark: "Never mind, old boy, it would have been worse than the windmills." To which, as deeply engrossed in his own realities as the original Gentleman of La Mancha, he will be able to reply only: "What windmills?"[248]

Again, however, his larger actions are by no means to be disparaged. Hugh has already in fact been to Spain, also to China. And while he dismisses the former venture by joking that he "fell out of an ambulance with three dozen beer bottles and six journalists on top of me," and the Chinese excursion similarly, it remains fact that in both countries very real wars have been in progress.

The chapter begins in Eden. Approaching the house Hugh is startled by a vision in which Yvonne, "working in the garden," appears "clothed entirely in sunlight." Whereas from Yvonne in turn, after she again labels the place a "wreck": "My God, this used to be a beautiful garden. It was like Paradise."[98]

Conversely, it characterizes Hugh's essential outlook that the same garden "looks quite beautiful to me, considering Geoffrey hasn't had a gardener for so long," though that lack is itself suggestive. (It becomes infinitely more so when the Consul later meets a "gardener" of transcending symbolic importance.) In the same vein, while offering Yvonne her "old room" earlier, the Consul has said that Hugh is "in the back one with the machine," meaning a lawn mower, and doubtless meaning something about the inextricableness of modern man and his mechanization, but also meaning that the tool, too, isn't in use where it ought to be. And again, when they soon decide to ride together, Hugh notes that Yvonne sits "cowboy-fashion, jammed to the saddle, and not . . . 'as in gardens.' "

The concept broadens—Mexico itself is no longer Paradise either—when Hugh finds that "in the distance the latticed watchtower of the Alcapancingo prison had just appeared with little figures on top gazing east and west through binoculars." To Yvonne, with an indifference echoing Laruelle's of Chapter I, these figures are "just playing. The police here love to be mysterious." But in a context of Hugh's predominantly political orientation Lowry's meaning is quickly made explicit: "The world was always within the binoculars of the police."[106]

Because of that orientation, several of such themes are here drawn into clearer focus. After first referring to the Consul as "our ruddy monarch"—and incidentally strengthening the identity with Oedipus in the process—Hugh then wonders if it isn't "rather indefatigably English or something of Geoff to be asleep." Whereupon: "A snore . . . was wafted to his ears: the muted voice of England long asleep."[98]

Thus too then, as the Consul now decisively comes to represent this political apathy, what he has called Hugh's effort to "straighten me out" must be seen to concern more than the drink; the fraternal relationship itself becomes politically symbolic. Regarding Hugh's "identity" as political animal, in fact, in practically his first words about his brother the Consul has spoken of his "fine Italian hand." Lest this slip by, in the present chapter a goat accommodatingly fixes Hugh with a "Machiavellian eye" of its own.

In the same general context Hugh next mentions a man named Weber, with whom by chance he had flown part way across Mexico—"one of these American semi-fascist blokes, been in the Foreign Legion . . . Parián was where he really wanted to go." When Hugh recalls something Weber had said en route, the repetition of a prophetic cliché indicates that the character is not new to the novel: "Quauhnahuac! That's where they crucified the women in the bull rings during the revolution and set the bulls at them. . . . They shoot first and ask questions later!"[99]

For the moment, however, Hugh is aware that "there was no revolution in Quauhnahuac now and in the stillness the purple slopes before them, the fields . . . seemed to be murmuring of peace, of paradise indeed." Yet as with each of Lowry's characters—cf. Yvonne's own sensation of "peace"—such illusions are to be short-lived:

> . . . it is all a bloody lie . . . we have fallen inevitably into it, it is
> as if, upon this one day in the year the dead come to life . . . this
> day of visions and miracles, by some contrariety we have been

allowed for one hour a glimpse of what never was at all, of what
never can be since brotherhood was betrayed, the image of our
happiness . . . [107]

Meanwhile a rather different "glimpse of what never was" is
had during their ride, when Hugh perceives the Consul's house
from a distance: " . . . the long garden below descending steeply,
parallel with which on different levels obliquely climbing the
hill, all the other gardens of the contiguous residences . . . also
descended steeply toward the barranca"[105]—all of which sounds
like nothing so much as the terraced architecture of the *Purgatorio.* But for the most part the chapter hews the line of Hugh's
preoccupations ("they are losing the Battle of the Ebro").
Elaborating upon that indifference ultimately to prove tragic,
Yvonne comments that "Geoffrey used to say there was far too
much sentiment about this whole business of going to die for the
Loyalists. In fact, he said he thought it would be much better if
the fascists just won and got it over with—"[101] After which she
herself is constrained to add: "There's one point where I do
agree with him, these romantic notions about the International
Brigade—"
Since this again recalls Laruelle's attitude, it is something
more than enchantment with his own symbols that brings Lowry
to repeat several from Chapter I. At the local theater—where
she recalls that "the lighting is *always* failing," as it does a year
later—Yvonne mentions having seen before her departure "a
travelogue, *Come to Sunny Andalusia,* by way of news from Spain."
Then Hugh describes the Orlac film as "all about a pianist who
has a sense of guilt because he thinks his hands are a murderer's
or something and keeps washing the blood off them. Perhaps
they really are a murderer's but I forget."[110] An irony occurs
here in that it has been Laruelle, rather than Hugh, who reads
an inference of personal guilt into this last; in either case the
relevance of the symbolism will be understood when those
"bloody hands" materialize shortly as one further abstraction
made real.
New historical parallels emerge also, here via passing reference to Bernal Díaz and W. H. Prescott—chronicler and histo-

rian respectively of the Cortez expedition—and to Winfield Scott, connected with a later "intervention" in Mexico. Earlier, too, seeing Hugh's telegram, Yvonne has asked if it is a "new message from Garcia," in that case recalling Spain again, if in a war pre-dating Hugh's—and incidentally in which we will later be informed that Yvonne's own father had been an officer. But in equally familiar fashion such themes become currently apposite once more when Hugh hears a sound, "unpleasantly familiar, as of a thousand carpets being simultaneously beaten in the distance"—this the target practice of the local police—and after which he regards a cigarette "that seemed bent, like humanity, on consuming itself as quickly as possible."

Mexico itself then again becomes microcosmic as Hugh thinks:

> Juarez had lived and died. Yet was it a country with free speech, and the guarantee of life, liberty, and the pursuit of happiness? . . . It was a country of slavery, where human beings were sold like cattle, and its native peoples . . . exterminated through deportation, or reduced to worse than peonage, their lands in thrall or the hands of foreigners. . . . rurales everywhere, jefes políticos, and murder, the extirpation of liberal political institutions, the army an engine of massacre, an instrument of exile.[108]

In terms of much modern Mexican history, Lowry is not guilty of exaggeration here; conversely, however, he also allows Hugh to remember an individual Mexican in a different light:

> Juan Cerillo! He had been one of the fairly rare overt human symbols in Spain of the generous help Mexico had actually given. . . . Trained as a chemist, he worked for a Credit Bank in Oaxaca with the Ejido, delivering money on horseback to finance the collective effort of remote Zapotecan villages; frequently beset by bandits murderously yelling *Viva el Cristo Rey,* shot at by enemies of Cárdenas in reverberating church towers, his daily job was equally an adventure in a human cause . . . [107]

This figure too is then made paradigmatic as Hugh goes on: "For man, every man, Juan seemed to be telling him, even as

Mexico, must ceaselessly struggle upward. . . . Revolution rages too in the tierra caliente of each human soul."[108] Here the climb motif is being expressed through close parallel with Goethe, from another of the epigraphs Lowry has allotted the novel: "Whosoever unceasingly strives upward . . . him can we save." And that Lowry has not been speaking of Mexico alone becomes further evident when Hugh makes an extension of "place" much like the Consul's involving India: "For that matter they might have been in England, exploring some little-known bypath of Devon or Cheshire. There was little to contradict the impression save an occasional huddled conclave of vultures up a tree."[110]

Crossing a river, Hugh then finds that "there derived a certain sensation of lightness, as if the mare were swimming, or floating through the air, bearing one across with all the divine surety of a Cristoferus."[109] Thus on this "day of visions and miracles," itself suggesting eternal renewal, Lowry here repeats that less verifiable miracle intimated in the Consul's adolescent crossing to the island in the estuary; and if the concept of "upward struggle" must now be read as involving redemption in the highest sense, Hugh's own thoughts will henceforth be very literally connected with "atonement." First, however, a polar prototype of guilt before salvation:

> Christ, how marvellous this was, or rather Christ, how he wanted to be deceived about it, as must have Judas, he thought . . . how joyous all this could be, riding on like this under the dazzling sky of Jerusalem—and forgetting for an instant, so that it really *was* joyous—how splendid it all might be had I only not betrayed that man last night, even though I knew perfectly well I was going to, how good indeed, if only it hadn't happened though, if only it were not so absolutely necessary to go out and hang oneself—[111]

"And here indeed it was again," Hugh understands, if assuming a yet more ancient guilt in the process, "the temptation, the cowardly, the future-corruptive serpent: trample on it, stupid fool." Hugh does so. For all his renewed attraction toward her, in what remains of the chapter he is to encourage Yvonne in her own hope of salvation through that "new life" with the Consul, and thus even at this juncture Lowry permits him to ride over an actual reptile on the trail. While in addition: "Have you not passed through the river?"

When the subject is first broached, on the other hand, neither of them is remarkably enthusiastic about the chances for that Consular "rebirth." Taking his symbols where he finds them, Lowry divertingly summarizes the problem by having Hugh dissuade Yvonne from the purchase of an armadillo: "If you let the thing loose in your garden it'll merely tunnel down into the ground. . . . It'll not only never come back, Yvonne, but if you try to stop it it will do its damndest to pull you down the hole too."[113] And then again the political equation: "Just sobering him up for a day or two's not going to help. Good God, if our civilization were to sober up for a couple of days it'd die of remorse on the third—"

But illusion will out, if briefly, and within moments Hugh is able to convince himself: "At this moment the best and easiest and most simple thing in the world seemed to be the happiness of these two people in a new country." They discuss Canada in terms which recall the Consul's vision in the letter—"I can see your shack now. It's between the forest and the sea"—and finally both succumb. "They were galloping . . . Judas had forgotten; nay, Judas had been, somehow, redeemed."[122]

Politically, of course, Hugh's intended self-sacrifice in Spain implies a greater redemption than the personal—in effect, man's own. Yet here as well, once more the sense of the "lie." The chapter ends at Maximilian's palace, where for reasons Hugh cannot understand, Yvonne seems "ill at ease"—but in Chapter I Laruelle has remembered a day when "he'd stumbled upon the Consul and Yvonne embracing there," doubtless now recalled by Yvonne in turn, and in Hugh's presence reminding her of *both* infidelities. Too, while Hugh recalls having entertained "a quite serious notion of finding time to climb Popo," then actually connecting this symbol with the motif of spiritual climb by regarding what he names the "affirmation" of the soul, he does so only with the qualification that it remains "so nearly always hypocritical." And again, when he finds that he can nevertheless feel, "in his heart still, the boundless impatience, the immeasurable longing," as always the polar note of warning: "But behind the volcanoes themselves he saw now that storm clouds were gathering."

Certain other incidental solemnities have found their way into the chapter before this, however. As their conversation about the Consul begins, Hugh and Yvonne notice a bus. "That's one way to get to Parián," Yvonne comments, apropos of Hugh's statement that Weber had been headed there, and again, "it's the easiest way." Hugh himself manages to perceive "something sinister" about the town, but is reassured that it is "a very dull place actually." To this last Yvonne adds that "there used to be a monastery there. . . . Some of the shops and even the cantinas are part of what were once the monks' quarters." "I wonder what Weber sees in it," Hugh muses, whereupon the matter is dropped.

This is of course the Parián of the Farolito once more, which we now understand to have been described in the Consul's letter where he speaks of "the shadow of old monasteries" and "the misericordes of unimaginable cantinas." Lowry is getting dual service out of "misericorde," in fact, since the word not only means refectory but also that medieval dagger used to apply the so-called "mercy stroke"—as near the monks' quarters of the Farolito one will be applied to the Consul, if with bullet instead of blade. What Weber "sees" in the place is the presence of a fascist headquarters later to be mentioned. Where it occurs this talk could not be more idle. Yet as the Consul finds his own inevitable "easiest way" of getting there—in part via this same bus—much of that inevitability will have sprung from the gradual intensification of just such detail.

Similarly, approaching a tavern Hugh sees an Indian sitting with "his broad hat half down over his face," then a horse tethered nearby with "the number seven branded on its rump."[109] Here again the matter is immediately dropped. But it is this same Indian, also to be remarked by the Consul beforehand, who will become the central if passive actor in the Samaritan scene at the heart of the novel, and with his hat "over his face" there also—though for reasons other than the present midday indolence. In fact it is characteristic of Lowry that our first picture of the man, "with his back against the wall . . . resting outside in the sunshine," is perhaps *the* visual Mexican cliché. Yet the entire passage of no more than six lines actually anticipates considerably more of the scene to come, since it is here that Hugh sees the toy windmill, along with another Orlac poster, and in the later episode both the novel's most obvious Don Quixote allusion *and* the real "bloody hands" will materialize. Moreover it will develop that the Indian is by no means so "passive" at all, but is very likely involved in that same "human adventure" of delivering money to collective farms only now mentioned in regard to Juan Cerillo.

Through all of this the sleeping Consul has been out of sight— if rarely out of mind. And at one point:

> "Yes," Hugh said, "how much does he really know about all this alchemy and cabbala business? How much does it mean to him?"
> "That's just what I was going to ask you. I've never been able to find out—"
> "Good lord. I don't know . . . " Hugh added with almost avuncular relish: "Maybe he's a black magician!"[118]

Some moments before, speaking of journalists, Hugh has commented: "There's no punishment on earth fit for them. Only the Malebolge . . . And here is the Malebolge." Hugh means the barranca, which he is labeling with Dante's name for the eighth circle of hell. While considering it from a small stone bridge, all too casually Hugh interrupts himself to ask, "—by the way, is that the moon up there?—" Lowry is again being obscure, but the arrangement leaves no doubt that the Consul is indeed the "black magician" mentioned above. In the *Inferno*, when Dante and Virgil stand on a similar bridge over a chasm in the original Malebolge, and at a time when the moon would be setting in daylight, they are in the realm of the soothsayers and necromancers—including such as Tiresias—who have pried into the Mysteries. (The episode occurs in Canto XX. When Laruelle's own thoughts of the Consul lead to the extensive Faust parallels of Chapter I, he is waiting for Dr. Vigil in a cantina named the "Cervecería XX.") "It *isn't* drinking, somehow,"

Yvonne here adds—deliberately being made to tell us more than she herself can know.

Yet this whole question of the occult is probably the most elusive in the novel, if only by definition—though a first clue to its nature lies in Lowry's surface portrait of the Consul himself. "I think I know a good deal about physical suffering," the man ventures in his letter, and we either come to accept this or we can scarcely accept the novel at all. Or again: "But this is worst of all, to feel your soul dying." But as the Consul endures these agonies of spirit, so too, if he is to attain self-knowledge, must the occultist suffer. And in occult or mystical lore, this tormented probing of the spirit is virtually always equated to a descent into the abyss.

On a level of essential meaning then, an equation between the Consul and the mystic will function no differently from that between the Consul and Dante; the *Divine Comedy* means very little if not that man must achieve an understanding of suffering before the way to deliverance can be made clear, or for that matter worth seeking. But a more viable analogy can perhaps first be drawn with the less intimidating work of someone like Rimbaud. Seeking his own mystic "illumination"—a cosmic or divine vision—Rimbaud underwent a very real spiritual ordeal in the slums of Paris and Soho. Failing to achieve the vision, he described the ordeal instead—and not for nothing was his poem entitled "A Season in Hell."

Indeed, while Lowry will be seen to establish only one or two deliberate parallels, the larger Rimbaud echoes assert themselves too emphatically to be overlooked. "C'est l'enfer, l'éternelle peine!" cries the younger drunkard, and the line is more than once paraphrased by words of the Consul's: "This is what it is to live in hell." In fact, "Une Saison en Enfer" is rife with images—of alienation, the Fall, anguish, funerals, unattained Paradise, dead souls, visions of redemption, even death by horses—which appear in *Under the Volcano.* Nor can we quite ignore Rimbaud himself, addict, expatriate, nonwriting writer who, in 1873, burned his last manuscripts on a date which happened to be All Souls Day, the Day of the Dead, and then to all intents and purposes "went to live among the Indians"—before finally losing a leg.

But of course Lowry's mysticism involves substantially more than any solitary new "literary" parallel. In his own curious occult compilation, *A Vision,* William Butler Yeats informs us quite matter-of-factly that his wife was wont to hear mysterious voices—or, more exactly, that she was visited by anonymous creatures which (the Consul would say "who") guided her pen during sessions of automatic writing. Like the Faustian ability to communicate with animals, such phenomena are said to be characteristic of the adept—even if the best poet of his time must run up against skepticism when he mentions them in print. (Auden's reaction, on record, is a sigh of "nonsense.") Yet the point here is one that Yeats was careful to indicate: "We have come," he says his instructors declared, "to give you metaphors for your poetry."

If nothing else, the presence of similar metaphors in *Under the Volcano* would corroborate statements the novel makes in other ways about the spiritual nature of the age, since mysticism in its assorted guises is always most prevalent in periods of weakness of the church. Thus when the Consul reads several newspaper headlines announcing "Es inevitable la muerte del Papa," they signify more than that Pius XI is dying—and more too, after Hugh refers to the Consul himself as "Papa," than that the death of Oedipus is ordained. But at the same time it follows that Lowry's more specific occult references, such as those to the Cabbala, will function precisely as do references to any other body of metaphor. But here is Lowry himself on the subject (again from his French preface):

The Cabbala is used for poetic ends because it represents man's spiritual aspirations. The Tree of Life, its emblem, is a kind of complicated ladder whose summit is Kether, or Light, while somewhere in its midst an abyss opens out . . .

In the Jewish Cabbala the abuse of magic powers is compared to drunkenness or the abuse of wine, and is expressed, if I remember rightly, by the Hebrew word *sod.* Another attribution of the word *sod* signifies garden, or neglected garden, and the Cabbala itself is sometimes considered as a garden (naturally similar to that where grew the tree of forbidden fruit which gave us

Knowledge of Good and Evil), with the Tree of Life planted in the middle. In one way or another these matters are at the base of many of our legends regarding the origins of man, and William James, if not Freud, might be in agreement with me when I affirm that the agonies of the drunkard find a very close parallel in the agonies of the mystic who has abused his powers . . .

Lowry goes on to mention mescal, a drink to become closely connected with the Consul's downfall, also equated to the drug mescaline. But already several new symbolic interrelationships become evident. The Consul's actual garden is not only Eden but a garden out of Cabbalistic esotericism also; allowing the original to grow to weed, by implication he is not only expelled from the second but denied occult attainment of the third. Similarly, the symbolism of climb gains a shading of mystic aspiration, as does the abyss of an additional despair.

And here the novel's configurations of light and dark can be put into occult perspective also—connected, as Lowry points out, with the summit of the Cabbalistic Tree of Life. Long before Rimbaud spoke of his own visions as "illuminations," or before Dante made of the sun a representation of the divine, as the primary source of "life" it was naturally germane to uncounted early religions. For Lowry's purposes, however, it is perhaps serviceable to look to its meaning as found in Swedenborg, a prototypal mystic to whom the Consul makes several passing references. For the latter, the sun appears as a personification of God, and like Dante he also sees it as a symbol of divine love; as the real sun yields natural growth, in Swedenborgian corollary so divine love yields spiritual growth. The occultist who achieves "illumination" becomes an independent, godlike creator capable of sublime visions and insights—the Consul's hallucinations, as interpreted in this framework.

Thus in a letter he is later to read, Yvonne will have stated the Consul's position at length: "You are one born to walk in the light. Plunging your head out of the white sky you flounder in an alien element. You think you are lost, but it is not so, for the spirits of light will help you and bear you up in spite of yourself."[364] Similarly, in a dream at the start of Chapter V, the Consul will find himself insatiably drinking "lightness, and

promise of lightness"—once more the occultism and the alcoholism conjoined—and the word light will appear no less than
eight times in a single sentence, an ultimate illuminist outcry.

But Lowry's moon demands attention here also. After discussing its appearance in Chapter IV, Hugh and Yvonne then speak
of place names on it; the Consul regards "lunar" potholes in a
street; Hugh later compares their bus trip with "riding *over* the
moon"; etc. Affording man's first opportunity for measuring
time, as well as his most dramatic visible cycle of death and
rebirth, the moon has its own age-old place in mystery cult—
probably also connected with its parallels to the menstrual cycle
—though here again Yeats is perhaps most immediately relevant. In fact the bulk of *A Vision* is concerned with a table of
mystical "incarnations" or "types" contrived by the poet, symbolized by positions on a Great Wheel and based on the moon's
phases: different individuals, wills, psyches fall under specific
lunar "bodies of Fate" in a complex scheme of cones and vor-
texes, finally part of a time-space continuum of consciousness
itself. We have already had mention of something akin in the
Consul's reference to the "spheres" of the Cabbala; later, Lowry
will once deliberately nod to Yeats, again implying such "spiral"
connotations for his own cyclic patterns, in having the Consul
observe "the pure cone of old Popo." (In "Through the Panama," the sight of mountains "peaked like cones" leads Lowry's
narrator to think of the Yeats book by name.)*

In fact the Consul himself can be readily placed in this centrif-
ugal Yeats wheel. In his seventeenth "phase" Yeats situates

---

*From a Lowry letter of August 25, 1951: "Re the Cabbala . . . and the whole
business of the occult . . . your rationalisation is an illusion. As a matter of fact
you could with some justice 'rationalise' the Cabbala itself (roughly speaking
a system of thought that creates a magical world *within* this one that so far as
I know has no pretense of being anything but an illusion—you may send it
flying out the window if you like, though perhaps it's not wise, it might come
back by another one) but you can't rationalise or anything else the unknown
depths of the human psyche . . . [James Joyce's] only regret re Yeats's *A Vision*
. . . was that he did not use all that tremendous stuff in a work of art." Lowry's
comment on the world as illusion will prove relevant on its own terms elsewhere. (All letters quoted, save when the long Jonathan Cape document is
indicated, are to the present writer.)

those whose will is "falling asunder" and who are "subject to nightmares," as well as those who are able, as Yeats has it, to see "the devil leaning against a tree"—which will happen in Chapter VIII when Hugh records that the Consul seems "calmly to have accepted the devil" (in reality someone in costume for a native fiesta). Interestingly enough, it is in this same category that Yeats places Shelley, whom the Consul admires and later twice quotes, and more suggestively, Dante. Conversely Yeats himself might become one further poet-avatar of the Consul, having been drawn more and more with age to both the Cabbala and to such writers as Blake, Swedenborg, Thomas Burnet, Berkeley, and Jacob Boehme, in whom the Consul's interest has been or will be remarked.

But to return to the "function" of such materials in *Under the Volcano:* speaking further of the Cabbala in his preface, Lowry comments that the "spiritual domain of the Consul is probably Qliphoth, the world of husks and demons, represented by the Tree of Life turned upside down and governed by Beelzebub, the God of the flies." In a manner of speaking Lowry is here then placing the Consul in this traditional occult scheme as he can be placed in Yeats's design—but more importantly is supplying a key to pertinent textual subtleties. As was noted, when viewed "spatially" the reference in Chapter I to images projected "upside down" must connote Oedipus inverted on the "Infernal Machine"; now we see that the same phrase alludes to the Consul's Cabbalistic "domain" as well. Too, since the Consul himself remarks in his letter that he is at Qliphoth, its overlord Beelzebub would also then join Moloch in that chapter as another cosmic exemplar of "fall." Nor is it, as ever, but "poetically" appropriate that when Laruelle burns the letter, in effect obliterating the last trace of the Consul—this man from "the world of husks and demons"—the sheets are finally described as "a dead husk now."

Meanwhile the question of occult "number" must be broached here also. As noted some pages above, that horse which itself is to serve as an occult "agent" of sorts in the novel's final pages is branded with a seven on its side, and the figure is repeated with pointed insistence throughout the novel—most memorably, of course, in the hour of day at which it begins and ends. On one hand, it will recall aspects of Lowry's mythic parallels— the seven days of Dante's pilgrimage, the seven years in Eden, etc. In occult doctrine, and in contrast with Dante's version, there are seven tabernacles in hell as usually described. Seven is the occult number for "total reality" (as indicated, the Consul's own reality will prove rather different from, say, that of a Snopes). And in one of the volumes to be listed in the Consul's library, *Dogme et Rituel de la Haute Magie,* the occultist Eliphas Levi discusses the rule of the world by the Seven Genii of the Cabbala.

Here again, the usage is immemorial—seven seals, seven heavens, seven sacraments, seven years of famine—as we will. Insofar as it played a role in much primitive religion, the number's magical attribution presumably sprang from man's first awareness of an order in the heavens, i.e., five known planets plus the sun and moon.

But Lowry is also preoccupied with the number twelve. Like the *Aeneid,* shortly to be quoted from, or like *Paradise Lost,* the novel is comprised of twelve sections. Its central action occurs in twelve hours, these in turn enclosed in the twelve months which include Laruelle's appearance. The twelve signs of the Zodiac are named, reference is made to the Apostles, the twelve labors of Heracles will be paralleled, twelve reverberates as a reminder of Faust's midnight. According to tradition there are twelve steps in the alchemist's transmutation of base metal into gold, and the number is significant in regard to Cabbalistic progressions. In the preface Lowry states that "the deeper layer of the novel" and the Cabbala are "linked" through this usage.

Another facet of such concerns, already somewhat familiar, is one which has led certain readers to question an excess of coincidence in *Under the Volcano.* It is by now superfluous to suggest that Lowry is possessed of far too much elemental "craft" not to have written out such episodes—though most are subtly substantiated as they stand—had he not had something else in mind. What Laruelle dismisses as a "trick of the gods"—his unplanned Mexican reunion with the Consul—in the latter's eyes is a specifically Baudelairean or Swedenborgian "correspondence," an interaction between the comprehensible and the unknowable of Hermetic proportions. Hugh, in fact, will describe a variant on the process when he imagines the Consul's window shades swaying "as to another control," and then the Consul will be seen in effect to exert that control—in a word, to "practice" his Faustian arts—when he considers, first, how "all-permeating" his influence has been upon Laruelle, and then when he speculates on the possibility that he has "willed" Laruelle's presence in Mexico "for obscure purposes of his own." Admittedly, those purposes remain obscure, although Lowry perhaps intends an intimation of their nature where Laruelle broods on the Consul in Chapter I: "Without knowing quite why M. Laruelle felt he might actually have proved a great force for good." The notion would correlate with at least the Swedenborgian impulse underlying such pursuits, meaning the attainment of a certain "divinity."

More of the pattern will unfold as this study advances—although there is undoubtedly more still. Indeed, in limiting her own explication of *Under the Volcano* to what might be termed the *clinically* occult, Perle Epstein is ready to pinpoint a Cabbalistic implication in virtually Lowry's every gesture; but in this less single-minded interpretation, "looser" questions must be asked. For example, is the Consul any *particular* black magician? Among others, he may be Merlin, who will come to mind when Lowry's Grail scheme is discussed subsequently, or again when the Consul believes trees to be "closing over him" in the last moment of his life, since Merlin is disposed of in just this way. Or is he Thomas Burnet, later to be named and borrowed from, who, like the Consul, resigned a government post because, like *Lowry*, he wrote a book treating the Fall as allegory? Is he Jacob Boehme, the famous shoemaker also later to be mentioned, whose concept of reality was one of ceaseless polarity and whose ontology proclaimed the inability to understand good without an awareness of evil? (Even before so significantly reading Marlowe, Laruelle glances into "Dekker's comedy" in that same Modern Library volume—viz., *The Shoemaker's Holiday*.) Is he Paracelsus, a fellow drunkard and the first alchemist to mention "alkahest"—which he also drank, to "sustain and fortify" his liver? At one juncture the Consul on his own part will as-

sociate himself with Aleister Crowley, a more recent flower-
ing of the species. None of this, as Lowry himself asserts
about the occult in the preface, is "essential" for an understanding of the novel: "I mentioned it in passing so as to
give the feeling, as Henry James said, 'that depths exist.'"

CHAPTER FIVE

The fifth chapter of *Under the Volcano* opens with the Consul's illuminist dream—*"of light, light, light, and again, of light, light, light, light, light!"* The italics are Lowry's. The dream begins:

> *Behind them walked the only living thing that shared their pilgrimage, the dog. And by degrees they reached the briny sea. Then, with souls well disciplined they reached the northern region, and beheld, with heaven aspiring hearts, the mighty mountain Himavat.*[125]

The origin of the dream can perhaps be laid to the Consul's conscious *thought* of India not long before falling asleep, where it was noted that this transposition of Popocatepetl was being prepared for; but one of the first of Lowry's *specific* Indic parallels may occur here also. In the greatest of Hindu epics, the *Mahabharata,* the last surviving heroes make their own pilgrimage to a symbolic holy mountain, likewise accompanied by a dog. The *Mahabharata* will in fact later be named in passing—though not without reason are the dogs in the Consul's waking life called "pariahs" either.

Insofar as it is approached with "heaven aspiring hearts," however, "Himavat" would similarly correspond with the Mountain of Purgatory evoked in other passages concerning climb, while the occult note of movement "by degrees" and with "discipline" evinces the climb toward Kether—light—at the summit of the Cabbalistic Tree of Life as well. Simultaneously, in the very archaism of the passage we can possibly also read a hint of *Pilgrim's Progress,* in which the Delectable Mountains serve as an essentially parallel symbol—and in which Christian's own "pilgrimage" takes place in a dream. The well-known conclusion to Part One of the Bunyan would summarize a major Lowry premise: "Then I saw that there was a way to hell, even from the gates of heaven, as well as from the City of Destruction." (The "City of Destruction" is itself later named by Lowry —which is to insist again, as with the *Mahabharata* above, that all such speculations continue to be less tenuous in a knowledge of the full text.)

At the same time there is a new echo here of Eliot, who in one of the more abstract sections of "The Waste Land" describes "black clouds . . . over Himavant." (The spellings differ as quoted.) If the dream in its totality makes any one point, it is that the Consul needs a drink, and with its spiritual overtones that thirst might equate with the drought in Eliot again then also. Eliot's whole underlying framework of fertility ritual, with its debt to Frazer and Jessie L. Weston, is itself recalled only a moment after the Consul's awakening when he contemplates "the metamorphoses of dying and reborn hallucinations"—a first irrefutable clue to such usage in Lowry himself.*

When the Consul does awaken, he finds himself "almost running" into his garden. In quest of a hidden bottle of tequila, he endeavors to check his haste by "plunging his hands, with an extraordinary attempt at nonchalance . . . deeper into the sweat-soaked pockets of his dress trousers." Lowry writes:

> Might he not, then, be reasonably suspected of a more dramatic purpose, of having assumed, for instance, the impatient buskin of a William Blackstone leaving the Puritans to dwell among the Indians, or the desperate mien of his friend Wilson when he so magnificently abandoned the University Expe-

---

*Concerning a more immediate meaning in allusions to Eliot: "Margerie suspects me sometimes of suffering without there being any proper 'objective correlative' for it . . . but one overlooks the fact that the most hellish kind of suffering of all can be simply because of that lack—the Waste Land type. One may suffer because one *can't* suffer, because after all to suffer is to be alive." (Letter postmarked May 20, 1954.)

dition to disappear, likewise in a pair of dress trousers, into the jungles of darkest Oceania, never to return?[126]

Here then, as promised, the Consul's unconscious at work. Surely, following a dream about—literally—"walking up into the Himalayas," such speculations must call to mind the Consul's father. And so they do, for the reader—whereas the Consul himself diligently blocks that more logical association with not one but two separate substitutions. Thus the Consul obviously loses no love for the man—which is to say that where he is already an Oedipus via mythic parallel, Lowry has arranged that he might be so accused on a Freudian's couch as well.

It is now that the Consul finally identifies Blackstone at length —as quoted *supra*—if drunk enough to make part of that identification for the benefit of a neighbor, one Quincey, and the rest, in his best Faustian manner, to Quincey's cat. Meanwhile Quincey himself proposes a better-known exemplar of the isolation theme when he greets the Consul with a cliché typically greater than itself in Lowry's context: "Dr. Livingstone, I presume."

But exile of this Blackstone sort is of secondary consequence in the chapter to that of man after the Fall. Retrieving his tequila, the Consul endures a "strangely subaqueous view" of the volcanoes, then finds nearer at hand that "the spectres of neglect . . . refused to disguise themselves." A garter snake appears, and in a garden adjoining his own he perceives "certain evidences of work left uncompleted." Then he comes upon a sign:

¿LE GUSTA ESTE JARDÍN?
¿QUE ES SUYO?
¡EVITE QUE SUS HIJOS LO DESTRUYAN![128]

Literally, this seems to mean: "Do you like this garden, which is yours? See to it that your children do not destroy it!" But because of his drunkenness, the Consul mistranslates the words in a way more forcefully suggestive of Lowry's thematic admonition to the age: "You like this garden? Why is it yours? We evict those who destroy!" Indeed, when the Consul does realize he has made an error, he decides that his interpretation is "near enough." (He also notes that the sign seems to have "more question marks than it should have," which it does, Lowry in effect allowing the reader to view it in the Consul's own "subaqueous" perspective; it reappears with proper punctuation elsewhere.)

Such implications are further stressed when the Consul considers the barranca in terms remindful of Laruelle's earlier comparison of it to the pitfalls of "the times": "One was, come to that, always stumbling upon the damned thing." Not to lose sight of its other meanings, however, Lowry also permits him to speculate about its role of "general Tartarus," and to decide that "one might even climb down, if one wished, by easy stages of course . . . to visit the cloacal Prometheus who doubtless inhabited it." (Conversely, the Consul also mentions "a tiny fifth side" to his estate. In much early architecture, the apex of a four-faced pyramid or spire was considered a fifth "side"—closest to God.)

At this point the Eden symbolism is expanded into one of the novel's more detailed parallels of "episode." To précis the literal events:

Drinking, the Consul discovers that he has been observed by Quincey, who is first seen "watering flowers" and is then referred to as "that apparition." After a passing thought of England leaves him "overwhelmed by sentiment, as at the same time by a violent attack of hiccups," the Consul steps "behind a gnarled fruit tree." "In this curious way he imagined himself hidden from Mr. Quincey."[131] Quincey approaches nonetheless, confronting the Consul "over the top of the watering-can as if to say: I have seen all this going on; I know all about it because I am God." Next Quincey is found "fixing him with a steady gaze that seemed . . . directed at a point rather below the Consul's midriff," after which, punning on a term from chess— "Pardon me. J'adoube"—the latter adjusts his "open fly." Then, when Quincey asks about Yvonne's return (he is forced to repeat the question) the Consul replies: "In the garden? Yes—that is, no. How do you know? No, she's asleep as far as I—"[134]

If only for the record, we are of course in Genesis, where behind the tree—and a "fruit tree" at that—the Consul is hidden "from the presence of the Lord God amongst the trees of the garden." The discovery of the "open fly"—rare synecdoche— is Adam's realization of a larger breach of the proprieties, etc.

Yvonne's identity here as "the woman whom thou gavest to be with me" is further verified when Quincey informs the Consul of Hugh's return, adding gratuitously: "I think he went out with your wife." Thus it follows that the Consul finds himself "not sorry to leave the tree, to which he had noticed clinging the sinister carapace of a seven-year locust"—Eden's own seven years are over. The parallel is rounded off some pages later when the Consul greets his brother, once again with the cliché transformed: "Hi there, Hugh, you old snake in the grass!"[141]

But more intrudes in the interim. Explaining to Quincey that he is "out inspecting my jungle," the Consul adds: "I'm afraid it really is a jungle too . . . in fact I expect Rousseau to come riding out of it at any moment on a tiger." Unquestionably the Consul is speaking of Le Douanier here; but in larger context, and particularly once we note Quincey glowering with "the cold sardonic eye of the material world," thoughts of the lost innocence bemoaned by the other Rousseau will prove equally relevant.

Mention of the garter snake then leads the Consul to *think* about Eden, in fact, explicitly relating the theme to the novel's political level by suggesting that "perhaps Adam was the first property owner and God, the first agrarian, a kind of Cárdenas, in fact—tee hee!—kicked him out. . . . for it's obvious to everyone these days—don't you think so, Quincey?—that the original sin was to be an owner of property."[133] The specific Cárdenas reference is to the expropriation of foreign oil interests, only short months before the date of the novel; the notion is perhaps to be taken more for its wit than its meaning, however, since it is actually a play of sorts on an attitude expressed quite seriously by Hugh in Chapter IV: "I wouldn't have thought it exactly a good point in history to begin to prosper as the landed gentry."

On the other hand the Consul voices several more meaningful conjectures also. "What if Adam wasn't really banished from the place at all?" he asks. "What if his punishment really consisted . . . in his having to *go on living there,* alone, of course—suffering, unseen, cut off from God . . . "[133] And again: "And of course the real *reason* for that punishment . . . might well have been that the poor fellow, who knows, secretly loathed the place! Simply hated it, and had done so all along." At first here, the Consul is talking about himself, like Faust granted in effect the equivalent of a worldly Paradise, but with the difference that it is not God's. The subsequent implication, however, would seem to be that given God, but given original Edenic innocence also, man would remain equally discontent—or again to distill the theme from Dante, that grace without a previous knowledge of sin is pinchbeck.

Meanwhile the Consul has a vision of salvation at that, personified, happily enough, by another kind of Eden: "Would it happen at the end, and would this save one, that . . . that mighty Johnsonian prospect, the road to England, would stretch out again in the Western Ocean of his soul?"[131] The Johnson reference is to the famous pun that the road in question is the "noblest prospect" ever afforded a Scot; unpunningly here, however, the Consul is really concerned with a prospect of another kind: "You do not wish merely to drink," he admits, "but to drink in a particular place and in a particular town." He adds: "Parián! . . . It was a name suggestive of old marble and the gale-swept Cyclades. The Farolito in Parián, how it called to him with its gloomy voices of the night and early dawn."[130] Reality interrupts such reveries when Quincey mentions Laruelle:

> "Laruelle?" The Consul's voice came from far away. He was aware of vertigo. . . . Mr. Quincey's words knocked on his consciousness—or someone actually was knocking on a door—fell away, then knocked again, louder. Old De Quincey; the knocking on the gate in Macbeth. . . . Of course, he should have known it, these were the final moments of the retiring of the human heart, and of the final entrance of the fiendish, the night insulated—just as the real De Quincey (that mere drug fiend . . .) imagined the murder of Duncan and the others insulated, self-withdrawn into a deep syncope and suspension of earthly passion . . . [136]

The reference to De Quincey's commentary, and an actual borrowing from the play when the Consul thinks of himself "murdering sleep," suggest an obvious parallel for Lowry's most common guilt symbol, *Las Manos de Orlac:* "Will all great Neptune's ocean wash this blood/ Clean from my hand?" The more general *Macbeth* parallels, of insanity, betrayal, supernatural incantations, derivations of "the heat-oppressed brain," etc., would be legion—if not to mention those in the De Quincey "knocking" scene itself, with its porter who likens Macbeth's gate to "hell-gate," who curses in the name of Beelzebub—and who then declaims on the apposite Consular discovery that drink "provokes the desire, but . . . takes away the performance." More subtly, though, it happens that such phrases as "the retiring of the human heart," "the entrance of the fiendish," and "a deep syncope and suspension of earthly passion," essentially "Consular" as they may be, are actually direct quotations from De Quincey's essay. De Quincey also speaks of the "transfiguration" of Macbeth and Lady Macbeth into "the world of devils," seeing them "cut off by an immeasurable gulf from the ordinary tide and succession of human affairs," or again in a "world of darkness"—i.e., as Lowry's unobtrusive "theft" means that we are to see his own characters.

As for the actual knocking in the world of the novel, it has been done by Dr. Vigil—whose appearance allows the Consul to indulge his paranoia anew. He believes Vigil has come "with the object, naturally, of spying on him," and is certain that the doctor's newspaper is full of new revelations about the "Old Samaritan Case." When the illusion passes he discovers that the real headlines seem "entirely concerned with the Pope's illness and the Battle of the Ebro," though the "Papa" has already reappeared in reference to Quincey's cat as "my-little-Oedipusspusspuss." The Consul also playfully turns the cat into a phallic god—"little priapusspuss"—and puns on one of the primary mytho-symbolic acts of the novel likewise: "Katabasis to cat abysses."

At their meeting, Vigil curiously bows to the Consul no less than three times—or perhaps less than curiously if we read in Bernal Díaz that all Aztec chieftains and sacrificial priests greeted Moctezuma in just this way, and that such priests were called "Papas." Christ then makes a shadowy appearance also, when Vigil, worried that his patient Quincey might learn of his drinking at the ball of the night before, confides that he must "comport" himself "like an apostle." He is present more obliquely when the Consul hears Yvonne talking about bougain-villea—"careful, Hugh, it's got spikes on it, and you have to look at everything carefully to be sure there're no spiders." While in context the line again recalls the Consul's own "spiders," it also anticipates a moment when these same "spikes" will imply a crown of thorns.

With Vigil's presence, occultism then joins the several other themes elsewhere moderately deflated through Lowry's self-satire, in this case as the two men arrange to raise a glass to-gether subsequently. Because of Quincey's hovering disap-proval, the ploy is accomplished through "the obscure language known only to major adepts in the Great Brotherhood of Alco-hol"—"a barely perceptible exchange of signals, a tiny symbolic mouthward flick of the wrist on the Consul's side as he glanced up at his bungalow, and upon Vigil's a slight flapping movement of the arms extended apparently in the act of stretching."[139] Comic as this may be, in naming Vigil an "adept" Lowry is again reminding us of Virgil, if in this case the original Latin poet instead of his Dantean shade. Such was Virgil's reputation in the Middle Ages that he was held to have been a magician, St. Augustine and others having believed that in his Fourth Eclogue he had foretold the birth of Christ. Indeed, when Laruelle is "shaken" in Chapter I by pressing his finger down at random in a passage of Marlowe's, he is playing what Lowry labels "sortes Shakespeareanae"—and a millennium earlier it was most often the text of the *Aeneid* used for such oracular "sortes." But an actual pun on Virgil occurs here too, where another playful tag for the cat is "my-little-anguish-in-herba," the original (in this instance from the First Eclogue) reading, "Latet anguis in herba," or "a snake lurks in the grass."

Once more alone, meanwhile, after a moment of acute con-sciousness during which he becomes aware of "the extraordi-nary activity which everywhere surrounded him . . . a lizard going up a tree, another kind of lizard coming down another tree . . . while from above, below, from the sky, and, it might be, from under the earth, came a continual sound of whistling, gnawing, rattling, even trumpeting,"[139] the Consul newly con-fronts Quincey's cat in a vignette which again recalls the epigraph from Goethe. The cat holds an insect between its teeth. "Finally the cat extended a preparate paw for the kill, opening her mouth, and the insect, whose wings had never ceased to beat, suddenly and marvellously flew out, as might indeed the human soul from the jaws of death, flew up, up, up, soaring over the trees."[140]

But the Consul is also "soaring." With him, we endure another of his abrupt jumps in consciousness, this time to a point roughly an hour later when he finds himself "getting ready to go to Tomalín." Evidently he has appeared "sober enough" to the others, but it is only when a "progression of thoughts like little elderly animals" begins to file into his mind that he is able to recall any of the lost interval. This last image may or may not newly suggest Noah; if it does, it would make of the Consul's bathroom a sort of ark—in which, indeed, he will now sit for some pages contemplating visions of havoc. The association is at least probable in that the Biblical Noah himself "drank of the wine and was drunken," and would be doubly rich in that certain readers, among them again St. Augustine, have perceived in that Old Testament drunkenness an allegorical prophecy of the passion of Christ—by no means unlike the parallel between the "agonies of the drunkard" and those of the mystic suggested in Lowry's preface. Thus we would again meet with that ubiquity of interrelationship in myth which remains Lowry's reason for such profusion of analogy to begin with. The reference to Prometheus amid the intensive Eden imagery earlier in the chapter works in much the same way. For the most part an equation between Prometheus and the Consul must imply mutual suffering—but by now the former's punishment must be read at least indirectly as paralleling Adam's for his own theft of a certain "knowledge," also.

Before leaving the garden, the Consul has asked Dr. Vigil the solution to "a case of chronic, controlled, all-possessing and inescapable delirium tremens." But where such disabilities will now draw the man to a near breaking point, after his first moment of total confusion—"Was he asleep? dead? passed out?" —he nonetheless next experiences a relative calm. Resurrecting the missing period, he recalls Vigil "magnificently giving the

whole show away" by announcing in front of Yvonne and Hugh
how sick he, the Consul, had been at the Red Cross ball, and
adding: "I think even to send a boy after you this morning to
knock your door, and find if drinking have not killed you already." In a context suggesting his identity as Virgil, the doctor
repeats this last bit of information to Laruelle a year later. In
Lowry's Oedipus scheme, however, the line can also recall the
"boy" traditionally assigned to lead the blind Tiresias. Thus
Lowry would again have a polar contrast at work, that of Vigil-
Virgil's *concerned* guidance on one hand, and on the other the
"guidance" toward ruin which, as in Sophocles, follows after
Oedipus "sends" for the prophet.

More immediately, what the doctor's lack of tact leads to is
forlorn Consular resignation: "Why couldn't people hold their
liquor? . . . In the final analysis there was no one you could trust
to drink with you to the bottom of the bowl. A lonely
thought."[143] Yet this too may recall Virgil, if again via Dante; for
all of the latter's tribute to him in the *Divine Comedy*, as a pre-
Christian "pagan" Virgil is permitted to lead the later poet
through Hell and Purgatory only, not into Paradise. (Then
again, Virgil does get to "the bottom of the bowl"—i.e., the
lowest core of the abyss.)

The sense of isolation is reiterated when the Consul next
recalls "hovering over the parapet, gazing down at the swimming pool. . . . Thou art the grave where buried love doth live."
(He is quoting Shakespeare, Sonnet 31.) More obliquely, taken
by Hugh's appearance, he has also thought "how amazingly
well, after all, those cowboy clothes seemed to suit his erect and
careless bearing!" Since the Consul has previously concluded
his biography of William Blackstone by tapping his chest and
remarking, *"Now,* little cat . . . the Indians are in here," and with
the additional explanation that he is talking about "just the final
frontier of consciousness, that's all," Lowry is here setting up
one more balance of complementary opposites—between this
private, psychological "frontier" on which the Consul's lonely
battle is waged, and that more secular one for which Hugh is
dressed to do combat. (One might also again recall William
Blake, however: "All deities reside in the human breast.")

A contrast of another sort emerges when the Consul next

remembers "lifting his face towards the volcanoes and feeling his desolation go out to those heights where even now at mid-morning the howling snow would whip the face, and the ground beneath the feet was dead lava, a soulless petrified residue of extinct plasm in which even the wildest and loneliest trees would never take root."[144] No Himavat or Mountain of Purgatory here; in fact since Lowry speaks of an "infernal" beauty only a few lines later, and since the most emphatic use of that adjective in the novel will concern Cocteau's Oedipus machinery, the symbolic mountain may well suddenly have become Cithaeron, where the infant Oedipus is put out to die—if to be rescued for his more horrendous later fate.

Discussing the Consul's difficulties meanwhile, Vigil has gone on to make another remark we have heard in 1939, that "sickness is not only in body but in that part used to be call: soul." And again this sickness is shown to infect more psyches than Geoffrey Firmin's, when the doctor compares it to something already seen as suggestive of man's general disorders:

> "The nerves are a mesh, like, how do you say it, an eclectic systemë." "Ah, very good," the Consul said, "you mean an electric system." "But after much tequila the eclectic systemë is perhaps un poco descompuesto, comprenez, as sometimes in the cine: claro?" "A sort of eclampsia, as it were," the Consul nodded . . . [144]

The Consul himself projects the concept further when he envisages "a picture of his soul as a town . . . ravaged and stricken in the black path of his excess" (in Swedenborg the ruined city is a frequent metaphor for hell). He then goes on to speculate about a gratuitous declaration by Vigil that he is "very much interested in insanes," wondering:

> Could it be Vigil considered his practised eye had detected approaching insanity. . . . Yet how interested would the doctor have been in one who felt himself being shattered by the very forces of the universe? . . . The Consul wouldn't have needed a practised eye to detect on this wall, or any other, a Mene-Tekel-Peres for the world, compared to which mere insanity was a drop in the

bucket. Yet who would ever have believed that some obscure
man, sitting at the centre of the world in a bathroom, say, thinking solitary miserable thoughts, was authoring their doom, that,
even while he was thinking, it was as if behind the scenes certain
strings were pulled, and whole continents burst into flame . . . [145]

In a sense the latter notion here establishes even one more
polarity in the chapter, if abstractly: as the sign in the garden
indicates that each man may preserve his Eden—and by extension the world's—so too can each man destroy it. The new
suggestion of occult "control," to be discussed in other contexts
subsequently, would be the obverse of that coin also, "black
magician" as opposed to godlike Swedenborgian "creator."
This is repeated when the Consul next remembers having mis-
quoted Shelley: "Ah, that the dream of dark magician in his
visioned cave, even while his hand—that's the bit I like—shakes
in its last decay, were the true end of this so lovely world."[147]
Shelley writes "true law" rather than "end"—this in "Alastor"
—the substitution being a logical result of the Consul's preoccupations; but thus he is almost consciously identifying himself
with a Faust figure precisely as he does with William Blackstone,
in effect imputing to Shelley's magician powers like those he has
only now metaphorically allotted himself. Stressing the Faust
association, even while quoting the lines the Consul notes that
it is "twelve o'clock"—not midnight to be sure, but not without
point will the man several times confuse day and night either.
    Meanwhile Lowry's source is again a good place to seek his
meaning. This from Shelley's preface to the poem: "Those who
love not their fellow human beings live unfruitful lives, and
prepare for their old age a miserable grave."

All of this is still being reconstructed in the bathroom, and it is
there also that Vigil's Dantean identity is ratified by the aforementioned invitation to Guanajuato. "Isn't Guanajuato the
place where they bury everybody standing up?" the Consul asks.
Actually, Lowry does not elaborate on the reference, and as in
the case of the "great tree" in Oaxaca the symbolism is perhaps
less effective without prior knowledge of the tomb and its mum-

mies; in fact less than a catacomb, it was long a very genuine "abyss." Conversely we can be sure that *something* Dantean is under foot when, apropos of little more than seems levity—if also close on the heels of another mention of the Farolito—Vigil presently exclaims: "Whee, es un infierno."

But Vigil's offer is refused, the choice for the others being the more accessible Tomalín. And again the step closer toward finality: "Tomalín's quite near Parián, where your pal was going," the Consul tells Hugh. "We might even go on there." As ever, the talk is almost painfully innocuous—but by now the reader does not miss the significance of the target practice erupting with a "sudden terrific detonation," or of the vultures "tearing through the trees" at the sound.

"And now the Consul was in the bathroom getting ready to go to Tomalín." But for all the relative clarity of his recollections, his condition is as desperate as it will become at any time during the day:

Suddenly the Consul rose, trembling in every limb. But it wasn't the scorpion he cared about. It was that, all at once, the thin shadows of isolated nails, the stains of murdered mosquitoes, the very scars and cracks of the wall, had begun to swarm, so that, wherever he looked, another insect was born, wriggling instantly toward his heart.[148]

Firmin, vermin. Fleeing the "appalling" vision, the Consul stumbles into his bedroom. Instead of the "terrible visible swarming," what persists now is "a kind of seething, from which, as from the persistent rolling of drums heard by some great dying monarch, occasionally a half-recognizable voice dissociated itself." The chapter concludes:

—Stop it, for God's sake, you fool. Watch your step. We can't help you any more.
—I would like the privilege of helping you, of your friendship. I would work you with. I do not care a damn for moneys anyway.
—What is this with you, Geoffrey? Don't you remember me? Your old friend, Abe. What have you done, my boy?

—Ha ha, you're in for it now. Straightened out—in a coffin!
Yeah.
—My son, my son!
—My lover. Oh come to me again as once in May.[149]

"Abe," in the third of these, is Abraham Taskerson, a poet
known by the Consul in his youth, introduced in Chapter I but
also thought of briefly in Chapter V. The interpolation of
David's lament for Absalom serves as an ultimate unconscious
refusal by the Consul to directly recall his father, who manages
to assert his presence after the talk of Blackstone nonetheless.
The others here are of course the Consul's "voices," Dr. Vigil,
the banal Mr. Quincey, and Yvonne by words from the Strauss
song quoted in Chapter I, in that order.

The careful delineation which leads to this instantaneous recognition is paralleled by other sorts of "care" to be marked in
the chapter as well. For example, it would hardly be out of
character for the Consul to cache a bottle in his garden—but
well before this (in Chapter III) his voices have parenthetically
reassured him of just this one's whereabouts. Nor does even so
casual a circumstance as that of the "open fly" but "happen" at
a moment of symbolic exigency; the Consul has slept straight
through since the hasty retreat after his sexual overtures to
Yvonne.

The word here is "craft"—though presumably Lowry would
have found a better one. As when Vigil suggests that the Consul's "eclectic" system is functioning erratically—the very last
thing that may be said of Lowry's own.

CHAPTER SIX

"Nel mezzo del bloody cammin di nostra vita mi ritrovai in . . ."

Lowry's sixth chapter opens with Hugh thus modifying Dante. What he elides of the poet's second line is of course the image of the dark wood, but by now the point would take some effort to miss: like the Consul, Hugh has lost the "straight way."*

While he quite literally entertains this idea that he has achieved "the middle of the bloody road of our life," actually Hugh is twenty-nine, six years shy of Dante's age in the poem. But with the Consul at forty-one, together the brothers give us the Biblical "threescore years and ten," and a mean which does then match Dante's. And since both go to that same metaphor to express their estate, it becomes evident that they are to be read as alter egos. Later in the chapter Hugh in fact conceives of the Consul as "some ghostly other self," and elsewhere has already named himself "Potato Firmin"—potato in Spanish being "papa."

But if such speculations are now to serve Hugh as a point of departure for a protracted look into his past, he quickly intimates another "shared" identity when he considers the future also, realizing that in "less than four years . . . one would be thirty-three"—the generally accepted age of Christ at Calvary. Nor does the equation remain this indirect (italics added):

*An indication of the symbol's meaning for Lowry personally: "For no wonder Dante found the straight way was lost. There is no straight way. Dante's wood was an abyss. Psychological . . . but true. Fortunately Virgil—since we all stand together in this world—was standing near and he had the common sense to make use of him. Dante didn't grow much happier, it is true, but perhaps that was his fault; and at least he finished his book." (Letter of August 25, 1951.)

And yet is it nothing that I am beginning to atone, to atone for
my past, so largely negative, selfish, absurd, and dishonest? That
I propose to sit on top of a shipload of dynamite bound for the
hard-pressed Loyalist armies? Nothing that after all I am willing
to give my life for humanity, if not in minute particulars? *Nothing
to ye that pass by?*[152]

Once again then, this quest for salvation predominates—but
once again Hugh will embody Don Quixote as well. Contemplating the romantic impulses of his youth, he recalls having "imagined himself a cross between Bix Beiderbecke, whose first records had just appeared in England, the infant Mozart, and the
childhood of Raleigh." Summarizing his background in book-
jacket fashion—"So and so . . . has been riveter, song-writer,
watcher of manholes," etc.—he leaves room for the possibility
that "far from having acquired through his experience a wider
view of existence, he has a somewhat narrower notion of it than
any bank clerk who has never set foot outside Newcastle-under-
Lyme."[154] And in the same passage he names himself both saint
and clown.

Nor is the paradox to be resolved. "Because of you," he imagines the wind telling him, "they are losing the Battle of the
Ebro." And while he *is* going to Spain, he is also aware that "the
whole stupid beauty of such a decision made by anyone at a time
like this, must lie in that it *was* so futile, that it *was* too late, that
the Loyalists had already lost." And again: "My disillusionment
is once more a pose. What am I trying to prove by all this?
Accept it; one is a sentimentalist, a meddler, a realist, a dreamer,
coward, hypocrite, hero, an Englishman in short, unable to follow out his own metaphors."[182]

Thus Hugh also now *is* England. And if he himself is unable to "follow out" his metaphors, Lowry immediately does
so with several. Tuning a radio Hugh hears, first, news of a
flood being delivered "with such rapidity one gained the impression the commentator himself was in danger of drown-
ing," after which another station tells of "misery blanketing a
threatened capital, people stumbling through debris littering
dark streets, hurrying thousands seeking shelter in bomb-
torn darkness"—earlier symbolic abstractions now turned

into a remote but more genuine fictional reality.

But several of Hugh's personal metaphors are strengthened also. In Chapter IV it is remarked that Hugh is reading *Valley of the Moon;* now he recalls that at the time of his first sea voyage "he had been reading too much of Jack London even then." Thus, as sailor-journalist-socialist, if not to add suicide, the latter supplies Hugh with the beginnings of a prototype-author syndrome much like the Consul's; for that matter Sir Walter Raleigh, just named, was finally executed because of interference in *Spanish* military affairs. (Hugh has also twice casually quoted Cicero—"Cui bono"—still another executed politician —and another "consul" to boot.) The London comparison runs deepest, however, since when Hugh here recalls that first sea adventure at length, his narrative can almost be read in part as a satire on London's kind of "social realism." Hugh goes to sea mainly to gain publicity for songs he has written. Because of that publicity he finds himself on "a false footing with his ship-mates." Some of them, indeed, are even "spiteful and malig-nant, though in a petty way never before associated with the sea, and never since with the proletariat."

Equally colored by politics are Hugh's recollections of his music, and of the guitar he had once played "without bashful-ness wherever I went." He is able to decide that the guitar "had probably been the least fake thing about him," yet understands also that like "Oedipus' daughter it was my guide and prop"— meaning that while preoccupied with it he too was "blind" to more significant realities. The symbolism turns explicit when he recalls passing out in a bar and "awakening" to hear his friends singing "revolutionary" songs: "But why had one never heard such songs before? . . . Perhaps because at any given gathering, one had always been singing oneself."

On the other hand while Hugh will now dismiss the guitar, by way of First Corinthians, as "certainly a childish thing to be put away," jazz figures like Beiderbecke, Lang, Trumbauer, etc., still hold meaning for him (and for the novel) on a different plane:

Hugh thought he heard Joe Venuti's violin suddenly, the joyous little lark of discursive melody soaring in some remote summer of its own above all this abyssal fury, yet furious too, with the wild

controlled abandon of that music which still sometimes seemed
to him the happiest thing about America. Probably they were
rebroadcasting some ancient record . . . and it was curious how
much it hurt, as though this music, never outgrown, belonged
irretrievably to that which had to-day at last been lost.[154]

Hugh goes on to recall his numerous instruments, all discarded, one of which has been left in a bar "long since become
a convent." This deliberate reversal on the situation of the
Farolito, a monastery now a bar, must suggest a minor "religious" dimension in the music like that in the Consul's drink.
Similarly, while Hugh even thinks of himself as having once
been destined to the life of the "eternal troubadour," like that
"mute Swinburne" the Consul he is now labeled "songless." Yet
in the same sentence in which the guitar is likened to "Oedipus'
daughter," Lowry also equates it to "Philoctetes' bow," going
on to describe Philoctetes as "a figure in Greek mythology
. . . whose cross-bow proved almost as proud and unfortunate
a possession as Hugh's guitar." Since this pause to *identify* a
classical reference is unusual in Lowry, in context we can perhaps read into it an allusion to the Freudian notion popularized
by Edmund Wilson, through analysis of this same myth, of the
artist's psychological "wound" for which he compensates with
his creative "bow." In the myth itself, Philoctetes suffers from
his foully suppurating injury for ten years before he is recalled
from isolation on Lemnos to the siege of Troy, where his
weapon then makes him a hero of the Greek conquest—as
Hugh, equally late, is bound for the siege at the Ebro. And if the
latter's own "bow" has now literally become political action
instead of music, nonetheless in his continued discontentment,
and surely in his desire to "change the world," Hugh must
embody the artistic personality. References to Venuti, in fact,
more expansive than the rest, enhance the motif also—the
"bow" of any violinist, in jazz, being as rare as was Philoctetes'
in combat.

At the same time, Lowry's description of the "fury" in
Venuti's music, with its "wild controlled abandon," too closely
parallels an earlier picture to be chance—meaning that of the
drunken horseman Laruelle sees as a "vision of senseless frenzy,

but controlled, not quite uncontrolled, somehow almost admirable." Since it is this vision Laruelle decides somehow *is* the Consul, the repetition would seem to suggest that Hugh likewise is of a piece with the jazz he once created—man *is* what he builds. Aligning the parallel more closely with the Consul's less common "artistry," in fact, Lowry also has Hugh think of himself as a "magician of commotions."

Other motifs recur in passing. Where the Consul has been described as a "pseudo" Lord Jim, it is now remarked that when he first went to sea Hugh had "nothing in his mind" of the character—meaning, of course, that now he does have something in mind. Thus again isolation, but even more vividly atonement, since Jim goes to a deliberate death in expiation of his overriding guilt. Too, Conrad's final judgment on the character is that he has been "excessively romantic," succumbing to a "shadowy ideal of conduct"—Hugh Firmin in a nutshell.

Similarly, Hugh here recalls his "passion for helping the Jews." "And somehow only a Jew, with his rich endowment of premature suffering, could understand one's own suffering, one's isolation, essentially, one's poor music." He also decides that the Jews had once seemed "the only people *old* as oneself"[177]—true perhaps as personal metaphor, truer in terms of Hugh's mythic "age."

Meanwhile virtually nothing "happens" in the chapter. At its start Hugh is reclining on the porch daybed; subsequently he helps the Consul shave and dress, after which they and Yvonne leave the house. But in the midst of this a new and quite detailed parallel would appear to be unfolding. As Hugh himself sees, for all its "stupid beauty" his gesture in regard to Spain remains only that, a gesture; to strain the Venuti metaphor, Hugh has been fiddling while Spain burned. Nevertheless the act is Promethean enough in its way, and an indirect comparison may come to mind when we learn that during his first voyage Hugh had "not yet read Melville either"—again meaning that now he has. A classic "gesture" more emphatically at hand than Captain Ahab's, however, is recalled when Hugh thinks of Mexican postage stamps showing "archers shooting at the sun." In myth it is Heracles, mentioned by name in the chapter, who attempts such a feat, and with the same bow later handed on to Philoctetes. Heracles, one more figure who harrows hell, who endures a lifetime of punishments in expiation of his habitual excesses, who suffers madness, is destroyed by magic and poison, is reborn a god. And who performs twelve immortal labors:

—The Nemean Lion. Heracles loses a finger before choking it to death. Recalling the extent of his involvement with the guitar, Hugh thinks: "Once the worst possible thing that could befall me seemed some hand injury. Nevertheless one dreamed frequently of dying, bitten by lions . . ."

—The Lernaean Hydra. The creature grows two heads for each one destroyed. Apropos of helping the Consul shave, Hugh here speaks casually of "strength obtained by decapitation."

—The Mares of Diomedes. These are man-eating. Mentioning an episode in which the Consul had been accused of "riding into college on a horse," Hugh adds: "A pretty ferocious horse too. Apparently it took thirty-seven gyps and the college porter to get it out."

—The Cretan Bull. Heracles bests it in weaponless combat. Leaving the house near the chapter's end, Hugh records that he and the others are "going to a bull throwing." (Much of a subsequent chapter is devoted to the act itself, when Hugh literally wrestles one.)

—The Stymphalian Birds. They attack humans. In a passage shortly to be quoted in another context, Hugh recalls freeing a trapped bird which "attacked me" in the process.

—The Cattle of Geryon. Once he achieves them, they are stolen from Heracles in turn, by someone who drags them tail-first to obliterate the hoofprints. En route from the house Hugh sees a boy "driving some cows . . . steering them by their tails."

—The Apples of the Hesperides. These are secured by Atlas, while Heracles substitutes for the latter in holding up the earth. One of the headlines the Consul has imagined in Vigil's newspaper reads: "Firmin innocent, but bears guilt of world on shoulders." In the present chapter Hugh watches a peon carrying something on his head—"so burdened as to be unable to look from side to side."

—The Erymanthian Boar. Thinking of life in Canada, Hugh wonders how Yvonne will feel "the first time she sees someone stick a pig." (This particular trophy is discarded by Heracles in his haste to join Jason and the Argonauts, as Hugh is essentially abandoning his own "labors," including those of getting the Consul *to* Canada, to board ship for Spain.)

—Hippolyta's Girdle. Hippolyta actually makes Heracles a gift of the garment. Late in the chapter Hugh notes that Yvonne— who has in effect previously surrendered him her own—appears "unsuitably girded" against the future.

—Cerberus. Heracles carries him up from Hades. Here the Consul remarks that he does not "believe" a headline, "Town counts dog's noses," not believing it because, as the apostrophe stands, there is only one dog and consequently one nose— except when the dog is Cerberus, who has three heads.

—The Augean Stables. Among shipboard duties, Hugh re- calls "cleaning out . . . the petty officer's bathroom."

—The Ceryneian Stag. Earlier, Hugh has seen cows that "re- semble" stags, and the Consul will note a painting of them shortly. Too, both the animal and Artemis, to whom it is sacred, will be evoked meaningfully elsewhere.

While some of this may be unconvincing, enough is verifiable to suggest that *something* of the kind is intended. Much as the brothers "share" such identities, meanwhile, Lowry can perhaps here be accused of playing a favorite—when he sums up by describing the Consul as "this man of abnormal strength and constitution."[184]

Early in the chapter, looking for something in his past "which will come to your aid against the future," Hugh recalls the above-mentioned hostile bird:

The seagull—pure scavenger of the empyrean, hunter of edi- ble stars—I rescued that day as a boy when it was caught in a fence on the cliffside and was beating itself to death, blinded by snow, and though it attacked me, I drew it out unharmed, with one hand by its feet, and for one magnificent moment held it up in the sunlight, before it soared away on angelic wings over the freezing estuary.[151]

Whereas in recollection of a humorous rock-climbing incident:

> . . . I am going back to sea again: perhaps these days of waiting are more like that droll descent, to be survived in order to repeat the climb. At the top of the Parson's Nose you could walk home to tea over the hills if you wished, just as the actor in the Passion Play can get off his cross and go home to his hotel for a Pilsener. Yet in life ascending or descending you were perpetually involved with the mists . . . [181]

The actor image is ironic in more ways than the literal, since there will be no walking off from the cross after the "Passion Play" with which Lowry's own narrative ends. Meanwhile the cyclic themes inherent here—and continually crucial—are then set off in quotation marks when Hugh's idleness is interrupted by the Consul, like Shelley's dark magician now suffering a very real case of the "shakes." "You mean the wheels," Hugh tells him. "The wheels within wheels this is," the Consul insists.

The wheels turn in a different manner as Hugh next considers the Consul's bookshelves—where in addition to Cabbalistic and alchemical volumes he notices Gogol, Blake, Berkeley, Spinoza, Tolstoy, the *Mahabharata,* the Upanishads, the Rig Veda, Shakespeare, etc. Also in evidence is *Peter Rabbit.* " 'Everything is to be found in Peter Rabbit,' the Consul liked to say," presumably meaning that even disaffected rabbits are apt to commit excesses and be driven from the Garden—or in a larger sense implying that "everything" is to be found in myth and folklore, the nuclear Lowry premise. But on another level "everything" is to be found on the Consul's shelves also, insofar as Lowry is here cataloging for us a number of his most pertinent sources (though several have yet to be discussed).

It is here also that Hugh finds the Consul's curtains swaying "as to another control," and when he brings his brother a drink it is "as if absentmindedly obeying the other's wordless instruc-

tions." The occult tone continues in Blakean terms when the
Consul indicates a sunflower that "stares into my room all day.
. . . Fiercely . . . like God!" Then when Hugh opens one of the
esoteric texts—*Sub-Mundanes, or the Elementaries of the Cabbala
. . . wherein is asserted that there are in existence on earth rational creatures
besides men*—the Consul cheerfully proceeds to name these:
"Erekia, the one who tears asunder; and they who shriek with a
long drawn cry, Illirikim . . . Effrigis, the one who quivers in a
horrible manner, you'd like Effrigis . . . " At which point: "Perhaps you would not call them precisely rational. But all of these
at one time or another have visited my bed."[185]

Against this general background, it presently occurs to Hugh
that the Consul "might be, finally, helpless, in the grip of something against which all of his remarkable defences could avail
him little." Hugh is righter than he knows, and indeed, Lowry
then brings him unwittingly close to specifying the case when he
thinks further of "this man . . . whom Hugh would never know,
could never deliver nor make agreement to God for, but in his
way loved and desired to help."[184] Hugh cannot "make agreement" for the Consul because, in the pact allotting Faust his
earthly powers, Mephistopheles has already done so—not with
God but with Lucifer. (Satan too loses out briefly to the Lowry
dialectic, however, in that moments before this the Consul and
Hugh have shared a drink specifically labeled "communal," a
Eucharist to follow Hugh's "baptism" in the morning's river. On
the other hand he will return when Hugh shortly passes some
goats like the "Machiavellian" billy which has chased him earlier, goats being a standard occult symbol for the devil.)

Otherwise the bathroom conversation, superficially, appears
trivial: where we have earlier had a "Cuckoldshaven," meaning
cuckolds' haven, now Lowry presents the cuckold shaven. But in
his letter to Jonathan Cape he reminds us more soberly that
Hugh here "shaves the corpse," and other wheels still turn. The
Consul is reading the English page of a Mexico City newspaper
—significantly enough named *El Universal,* although again the
symbol was there for the taking in Mexican reality—and as implied it is marred with typographical errors. "Kink unhappy in
exile" suggests the fate of Oedipus, although the Consul's comment, "I don't believe it myself," is doubtless a restatement of

his own attitude toward exile: the "Johnsonian prospect" has not yet beckoned. An essentially irrelevant reference to the Guelphs a few pages later, above and beyond affording a new historical equivalent for the internal political strife in Mexico, parallels this other by recalling Dante's own exile—before which, indeed, the poet had occasionally fulfilled certain ambassadorial duties, i.e., as a kind of "consul." (Interestingly, so too, some few decades later, did *Geoffrey* Chaucer.) And again recalling Dante is the Cerberus allusion which occurs here: in traditional mythology Cerberus guards the further shore of the river Styx, but in the *Comedy* Dante sets him to tearing at the gluttons —among these the drunkards.

An equally unappealing dog who will come to mind shortly with Lowry's use of Cocteau is Anubis, Cerberus's counterpart in Egyptian myth. Traditionally the "watcher of the dead," in *La Machine Infernale* Anubis hovers over the sleeping Oedipus and Jocasta whispering of doom—as the pariah dogs symbolically bespeak the Consul's own. And that this whole grotesque menagerie has its place in Lowry's all-inclusive symbology is made plain when the Consul, who like his creator has also been reading Bernal Díaz, informs Hugh that "Moctezuma, courteous fellow, even showed stout Cortez around a zoo. The poor chap thought he was in the infernal regions."

Nor are such beasts restricted to single areas of meaning. The same cows suggesting the Cattle of Geryon are also described as something out of "a dream of a dying Hindu," recalling moreover that in his own essentially Indic dream the Consul has found himself at one moment "standing, amid cattle, in a stream." And meanwhile another dumb creature altogether, in this case a scorpion, like armadillos and insects before him becomes one more symbol for the Consul himself: "Leave him be. He'll only sting himself to death anyway."

By this time Hugh and the others have left the house—or again, the ark. In fact the novel is just that. Tigers, anteaters, whip-poor-wills, condors, deer, fish, wolves, coppery-tailed-trogons, lions, bulls, sharks, swallows, seagulls, kingfishers, herons, seals, vultures, eagles, frogs, turtles, swans, elephants, pigeons, parrots, gila monsters, boa constrictors, goats, turkeys, rabbits, cocks, cats—a complete listing would overflow the page. Nor is it without significance, in terms of Lowry's universality, that for all of the weighted "intellectual" imagery in the novel, so too would a listing of plants, flowers, trees, etc. (It is something else again, though also typical, that an enumeration of the alcoholic beverages mentioned would do the same.)

Departing tangentially from previous talk about Cambridge, meanwhile, as they walk the Consul refers obscurely to the fact that "no angel with six wings is ever transformed"—an additional allusion, whatever its occult implications, to the *Inferno*, where Satan in his frozen impotence perpetually beats his own six. But it is here also that the Consul finally begins to speak of "Thomas Burnet, author of the Tellurus Theoria Sacra," who has had to be noted several times *supra*. The Consul is interrupted and his remark remains forever unsaid, though as it happens Burnet has appeared in the present chapter prior to this. Characterizing Hugh's innocence of years before, Lowry writes: "Maybe he did not know himself what he thought about; bells struck, the engine thrummed . . . and far above was perhaps another sea, where the soul ploughed its high invisible wake—"[163] The concept is Burnet's: that the Biblical "fountains of the great deep," shattered at the time of the deluge, flow now and until the Last Judgment as a vast ocean overhead. Typically, however, if the borrowing affords yet another cyclic image—that of a truly cosmic "return"—at the same time it must imply the certain mild heresies noted in regard to Burnet elsewhere. Yet in the very breath in which he now brings up Burnet by name, as an airplane swoops near them the Consul invokes the "Virgen Santísima!" and cries, "Ave María!"

Aleister Crowley makes his entry now also, when Hugh notices "obscure yellow tin plates at the bottom of walls," which, "to the quiet delight of the Consul," advertise an insecticide named "666." The advertisements are "obscure" only insofar as Lowry means that he himself wants to be, since the signs were long commonplace in Mexico. What "delights" the Consul, on the other hand, is the fact that Crowley adopted this same number as his occult "signature," unquestionably its most famous modern usage. Crowley took it from Revelations: "And I beheld another beast coming up out of the earth . . . and he doeth great wonders . . . and deceiveth them that dwell on the earth by means of those miracles which he has power to do . . . and his number is six hundred threescore and six." For Crowley's purposes the text was meant to signify his own miraculous "powers," so that he indeed styled himself "the Great Beast." But in this same context it is worth note that Revelations itself, constructed on an esoteric pattern of sevens, is an allegory of the fall of Rome—as *Under the Volcano* must eventually be seen of Western Civilization. Through an ingenious reading in *The White Goddess,* Robert Graves shows that an authentic "beast" meant by the number was Nero; thus when several actual references to Rome later occur in Lowry, the Consul himself will also prove to have been "fiddling" while things burn.

In the midst of all this—or perhaps because of it—Lowry makes another of those unobtrusive asides calculated to define his own purposes. Earlier, the Consul has noted the "collective desolate fecundity" of plants on his lawn; here, when the three leave the house, Hugh in turn broods upon their "collective distraught soul." Especially concerning souls, two "collectives" have to imply Jung, the "collective unconscious" with its archetypes common to all humanity—or to Lowry's characters. If such theories remain in a *scientific* limbo, as with Lowry's occultism, or Yeats's, their *poetic* validity is another matter—though Jung's very renegade status might be an amusing secondary reason why, when the aforementioned goats now appear, Hugh conceives of them as saying: "Father is waiting for you though. Father has not forgotten." Considering Hugh's political views, on the other hand, after two "collectives" Father could be Marx as well as Freud.

For that matter Hugh's friend Juan Cerillo delivers money to genuinely "collective" farms, which explains a basically silly question Hugh has asked Yvonne much earlier: "You probably wouldn't have expected a communist to have a dog named Harpo, or would you?" In *Under the Volcano,* the anthropomorphic counterpart to a Marx—is a Marx.

But in the interim again the sobering note. Before they leave the bedroom, and after new reference to the Consul's disguised World War I gunboat the *Samaritan,* the latter brings up the

Union Militar, the fascist party led by General Almazán. He explains that because Mexico's Inspector General is a member, the organization is "throwing their weight about a bit." It is here too that he mentions their headquarters in Parián—"if you're interested, I'm not personally."

For Hugh himself, if he can scarcely be aware of the irony, the future is more specifically seen as "beginning to unwind." But where he compounds an earlier ominous perception of Yvonne's by noticing "the school with the grey tombstones and the swings like gallows," at the same time his spirits are buoyant enough for him to become "involved with a fit of laughing."

Then an odd thing occurs. The trio meets Laruelle, and as he confronts them it appears to Hugh "as though the whole of this man, by some curious fiction, reached up to the crown of his perpendicularly raised Panama hat, for the gap below seemed . . . still occupied by something, a sort of halo or spiritual property of his body, or the essence of some guilty secret perhaps that he kept under the hat but which was now momentarily exposed, fluttering and embarrassed."[190] The "guilty secret" here would be Laruelle's affair with Yvonne, about which Hugh knows nothing; with so much mysticism in the air Lowry would seem to be permitting Hugh a partial extrasensory perception of his own. But the question of the "halo or spiritual property" itself is too explicit to be passed over as mere illusion. Earlier, when the Consul sees Vigil approaching in the garden scene, the situation is equally peculiar. Quincey has simultaneously disappeared, and with him the watering hoses have "suddenly failed as if by magic." The Consul wonders "what on earth" Vigil is doing there, the two acquaintances groan aloud before they speak, and soon thereafter Vigil makes his declaration that "I think you must have killed yourself with drinking." Was "what *on* earth" another of that chapter's several redeemed clichés?— and, with the departure of "God," were the groans those of Dante's sinners—*in* earth? Something of the sort. But might we also read into the scene an inference that the Consul's abyss is somehow a fictional *actuality*—that a Dantean "Virgil" might belong in it but the living Dr. Vigil does not? The doctor's very name would imply the keeping of a literal "vigil"—or wake among the dead—and the "collective souls" have been Gogol's dead ones all along. In other words the "curious fiction" here might be Lowry's own: since, like the doctor, Laruelle is alive a year hence to discuss these three people he now faces—*ex*-Consul, *ex*-wife, *ex*-journalist—he too is now out of place in Lowry's necropolis.

At all events, after Laruelle is explained to Hugh—who considers the renewed friendship an "unusual bloody miracle"— the Consul for a change is too annoyed to impute any occult significance to the matter at all. Preoccupied with "saying something cloacal very quietly to himself over and over"—what else to say in the abyss but something cloacal?—he acknowledges merely, "Yeah. It was a great coincidence our meeting here."

After which the long delayed postcard is given to the Consul by a passing mailman—still another "coincidence." The Consul's reaction now becomes more subtle: "Strange—" This same brief conjecture occurs in several thoughtful moments elsewhere—always a decisive clue that deeper spiralings are implied.

Lowry closes the chapter with a description of the picture on the card, of the road to Carlsbad Cavern—one more path, and to a very real abyss. But here too the polarity, if not to say the novel in miniature: the card shows a mountain as well.

CHAPTER SEVEN

Should any doubt still linger, the opening sentence of Chapter VII testifies anew that the symbolic ailments of Geoffrey Firmin are contagious. Here, the world itself is described as "drunken" and "madly revolving."

As he and the others approach Laruelle's house, which Laruelle has insisted they visit, the Consul remarks its towers painted "as if camouflaged . . . almost like the *Samaritan.*" In contrast, also on the facade is "that phrase of Frey Luis de León's the Consul did not at this moment allow himself to recall," the same one Yvonne earlier "did not want to see": "No se puede vivir sin amar." (De León, 1528–91, was an Augustinian, a poet and mystic; it was he, returning to the University of Salamanca after five years in prison, who began his first lecture with the words: "As we were saying . . . ") The inscription is ill-painted, its letters "merged together most confusingly"—which is to say, like its meaning in contemporary life.

The line remains the central thematic declaration of the novel. Read most broadly—as implying brotherhood, charity, faith—it is also the common thread unifying Lowry's diverse mythic patterns. Only a few moments hence, when he finds himself too drunk to cope at all with a telephone, asked by an operator what he wants the Consul shouts: "God!"[208] Here Dante, Faust, Adam, Christ "forsaken"—all are one.

"One cannot live without love." Yet, earlier, Yvonne has envisaged "their love . . . wandering over some desolate cactus plain," and now the Consul perceives that his own "seems so far away from me and so strange too . . . as though I could almost hear it, a droning or a weeping, but far, far away, and a sad lost sound." While as for the rest of the "madly revolving" world little reassurance can be offered either, since it develops that Laruelle himself, a year later still able to dismiss the inscription as the work of an "estúpido," is of all people sometimes called upon to "come out and explain" its meaning.

On the other hand the Consul decides that the postcard, at least, "ought to have been a good omen"—or might have been "if only it had arrived yesterday or at the house this morning. Unfortunately one could not now conceive of it as having arrived at any other moment." This renewed sense of the occult is given an extra twist when he then slips the card beneath Laruelle's pillow. He does this impulsively, thinking of it himself as "an odd thing," yet in Chapter I we find Laruelle speculating that it was "as though the Consul had calculated it all, *knowing* M. Laruelle would discover it at the precise moment when Hugh, distraughtly, would call from Parián."

It is here too that the Consul thinks at length about the notion of having "willed" Laruelle to Mexico "for obscure purposes of his own." An earlier line of Hugh's has actually broached the same kind of possibility, if somewhat more moderately: "Try persuading the world not to cut its throat for half a decade or more, like me, under one name or another, and it'll begin to dawn on you that even *your* behavior's part of its plan. I ask you, what do we know?"*[103]

Remaining alone in Laurelle's bedroom, the Consul is then arrested by what "amounted to a prohibitionist poster," quite old, in which drunkards are shown plunging "headlong into hades . . . into a tumult of fire-spangled fiends, Medusae, and belching monstrosities," while "up, up, flying palely, selflessly into the light toward heaven . . . shot the sober."[199] The Consul is amused: "It was ridiculous, but still—had anyone ever given

---

*While the line will stand without gloss, it happens to contain a private allusion for Lowry. In a letter of August 25, 1951, discussing a series of occult "correspondences" between himself and the Norwegian author Nordahl Grieg, he quotes Grieg as having remarked: "Another spiral has wound its way upward. Reason stands still. What do we know?" Grieg's forgotten novel *The Ship Sails On* was a key book in Lowry's life, though its influence is limited mainly to the early *Ultramarine*. A later incident in the present chapter, however, where certain of Christ's words are declaimed to a dog, is patterned on a similar episode in the Grieg.

a good reason why good and evil should not be this simply delimited?" Here also he discovers a number of "stone idols," some of them chained together, and "in spite of himself," continues to laugh at the thought of "Yvonne confronted in the aftermath of her passion by a whole row of fettered babies." Following reference to Medusae the concept is less than funny, however, particularly since the Consul will shortly cry out in genuine despair: "Yvonne and he should have had children, would have had children, could have had children, should have . . . " But the Medusa turns humans to stone, as when Perseus uses its severed head to transform his enemies into a row of statues very like these—which a Gorgon of alcohol has done to what offspring the Consul might have produced. The idea recurs when he next imagines that "one of the little Mayan idols seemed to be weeping," obliquely suggesting Niobe who is also turned to stone yet weeps nonetheless, in this case *because* of the loss of children. Some pages later on, as if he himself has been brooding unconsciously over the same interpretation for such symbols, the Consul mistakes a painting on a carousel for a representation of "Medea sacrificing her children."

A more familiar topic intrudes when Hugh, using binoculars, announces, "I've got Parián in pretty good focus"—abruptly the end is literally "in sight." For the moment the Consul remains caught up in his own abstractions: "Suddenly he felt something never felt before with such shocking certainty. It was that he was in hell himself."[199] But he is also "possessed of a curious calm," since Parián has naturally brought to mind the Farolito. "The Lighthouse, the lighthouse that invites the storm, and lights it!" The prospect of getting there fills the Consul with "the greatest longing he has ever known," and there follows the first really detailed picture of that perilous cantina:

At first it had appeared to him tiny. Only after he had grown to know it well had he discovered how far back it ran, that it was really composed of numerous little rooms, each smaller and darker than the last, opening one into another, the last and darkest of all being no larger than a cell. These rooms struck him as spots where diabolical plots must be hatched, atrocious murders planned; here, as when Saturn was in Capricorn, life reached bottom. But here also great wheeling thoughts hovered in the brain; while the potter and field-laborer alike, early-risen, paused a moment in the paling doorway, dreaming . . . He saw it all now . . . the beggars, hacked by war and covered with sores, one of whom one night after four drinks from the Consul had taken him for the Christ, and falling down on his knees before him, had pinned swiftly under his coat-lapel two medallions, joined to a tiny worked bleeding heart like a pincushion, portraying the Virgin of Guadalupe . . . He saw all this, feeling the atmosphere of the cantina enclosing him already with its certainty of sorrow and evil, and with its certainty of something else too, that escaped him. But he knew: it was peace. He saw the dawn again, watched it with lonely anguish from that open door, in the violet-shaded light . . . the oxen harnessed to their carts with wooden disc wheels patiently waiting outside for their drivers, in the sharp cool pure air of heaven . . . [200]

About as clearly here as anywhere then, the mystic-religious fatality in the drink, if not to add the "piety" prefigured elsewhere. The reference to the Virgin of Guadalupe, Mexico's patron saint, gives us as it were an historical parallel for the "miracle" occurring in the scene itself: as the Christ-Consul appears before the beggar, so the Virgin appeared to a converted Indian some ten years after Cortez. There is a characteristic irony in the Consul's "certainty" of peace, but as part of the overall picture it nonetheless heightens the Indic motif which emerges almost as vividly as the Christian. The "violet-shaded" dawn with its archaic ox carts, and with its "sharp cool pure air of heaven," is assuredly that in which Buddha achieves enlightenment, a transcendent version of this same "peace." Later in the chapter, in fact, Laruelle will speak of a certain "release" the Consul seeks, this by far the most common translation of the Sanskrit for Buddha's attainment. In the same passage the Consul will be reminded also of "the wheel of the law," a reference to the wheel of *dharma,* or moral law, set into motion by the former— adding meaning to the "great wheeling thoughts" in the above as well. And predictably, the novel's most detailed Buddhist evocations will occur *at* the Farolito.

Similar themes recur on a less profound level when from Laruelle's porch the Consul next imagines the countryside as an enormous golf course. He names a "Golgotha Hole," after which the word golf is transposed into the French "gouffre = gulf"—or of course abyss. Naturally enough, it follows that Prometheus "would retrieve lost balls"—which the Consul decides directly after again quoting "Alastor," here changing Shelley's "this so lovely world" to this "so lousy" one, but perhaps remembering in the process that Shelley wrote a Prometheus drama of his own. Then Geoffrey (gouffre) is jarred back to adolescence by a recollection of the pub named in the golf course anecdote of Chapter I, "The Case is Altered." The case is altered rather differently today, however, or at least another kind of "innocence" has been lost: "Was it some figment of himself, who had once enjoyed such a simple healthy stupid good thing as golf?" No longer able to play (Firmin, infirm) the Consul becomes instead "a sort of Donne of the fairways." "And who, upon that last and final green, though I hole out in four, accepts my ten and three score . . . Though I have more."[203]

Typically, Lowry is *quoting* Donne there, the last phrase being a refrain in "A Hymn to God the Father"; what Donne has "more" of is sin. But after the play on "threescore and ten," like a recent line of Hugh's that same usage can probably also be taken as an allusion to symbolic "age." The concept is additionally relevant to the Consul as magician or "seer," insofar as figures like Tiresias or the sibyls are said to live on inordinately, usually too in punishment for some transgression. Presently the Consul will conclude that it "was already the longest day in his entire experience, a lifetime"—though in that instance he is perhaps meant to be describing the novel itself.

Shelley himself then becomes one more symbolic forebear of the Consul's: "The story I like about Shelley is the one where he just let himself sink to the bottom of the sea—taking several books with him of course—and just stayed there, rather than admit he couldn't swim."[204] (The books were Keats and Sophocles; the Consul is going under with a five-foot shelf, though both are included.) But at the same time the poet is also equated to precisely those people from whom another of the Consul's counterparts has fled, when he is next labeled "another fellow with ideas." Rather than evoking William Blackstone, however, the phrase here might serve to point out a wholly new motive behind Lowry's use of the "Alastor" quotation. Since a good number of any "ideas" connected with Shelley are Platonic, the "visioned cave" where he places his dark magician would then be that of Plato's famous metaphor, in which shadows on the wall are all we know of the real. And while discussion of what the Consul's letter calls "ultimate reality" must still be withheld, other hints of Lowry's interest in that cave begin to assert themselves even more sharply in the chapter. "Can't you see it?" Yvonne asks at one juncture, meaning that they are together once more, and not only is it said that the Consul "couldn't see," but that he can "feel, feel the unreality"—and this while *holding* his wife in his arms. Likewise Dr. Vigil, only an hour absent, is completely "unreal" when the Consul has reason to think of him.

For a time, meanwhile, the Consul is alone on the mirador. "And yet not alone. For Yvonne had left a drink . . . Jacques' was in one of the crenels, Hugh's on the side parapet." Conscious of the irony, and unlike Shelley now, he considers the possibility of "admission that one couldn't swim," after which he puns on "admission indeed . . . into a sanitorium." His voices, pointedly now called "demons," are "in possession." And thus the sun again also: "Like the truth, it was well-nigh impossible to face; he did not want to go anywhere near it, least of all, sit in its light, facing it."[205]

Something else the Consul finds it difficult to face is "the abominable impact upon his whole being" of the sight of Laruelle undressed for the shower after the others depart; at the thought of Laruelle's "pleasure in his wife's body" he repudiates reality as "incredibly loathsome," still another clue that something may exist to be sought in its stead. In his mounting distress it is here that the Consul cries into the phone for God, actually having intended to seek a doctor, whereupon a different "reality" does intrude. Two names come "starting" out of the directory at him, Zuzugoitea and Sanabria. Both will have been long forgotten when they reappear some 150 pages later. Zuzugoitea and Sanabria are two of the three fascists instrumental in the Consul's murder.

Cattle reappear here also, although in this case hardly suggesting anyone's vision of heaven: as the Consul gulps down "all the drinks in sight,'' he endures an hallucination in which ''about three hundred head . . . dead, frozen stiff in the postures of the living,'' spring onto the hillside. A moment before, considering Laruelle's library, he has again quoted Marvell in deciding that a soul might after all ''bathe there or quench its draught'' [this is Lowry's spelling, as opposed to the earlier ''drought,'' perhaps a pun], though he adds that ''in none of those books would one find one's own suffering.'' But now in point of fact he does find his own: ''Oui, mon enfant, mon petit enfant . . . les choses qui paraissent abominable aux humains, si tu savais, de l'endroit où j'habite, elles ont peu d'importance.''[209]

This is the Cocteau, the drama of Oedipus caught up in the diabolical mechanisms of the gods as the Consul shortly will become entangled in a very real ''Máquina Infernal.'' First, however, he and Laruelle walk together to the central plaza of the town. En route, he motions to a man ''also in dark glasses who seemed familiar,'' assumably the same ''spider'' he has ''enigmatically'' greeted in the morning. The Rivera murals on the Cortez Palace, which Lowry uses as it exists in Cuernavaca, connote to Laruelle ''the gradual imposition of the Spaniards' conquering will upon the Indians,'' although to the Consul, noting ''who paid for them,'' they symbolize ''the gradual imposition of the Americans' conquering friendship''—at last a pleasant polar obverse to symbols of oppression in 1938. Then the Indian passes on his horse with its number seven brand. Saddlebags are mentioned, and the Consul records that they ''chinked,'' later suggesting a question of money to become vital. At the top of a hill the man waves a hand, recalling the gesture by the English Samaritan earlier, looking ahead to the failure of Samaritanism to come. As in Chapter IV, the man himself is on stage only briefly, but here the Consul dwells on him for a time. First, fleetingly, a vision of riding ''into the heart of all the simplicity and peace in the world'' strikes him as akin to ''the opportunity afforded by life itself.'' And then: ''The Consul wanted to raise his head, and shout for joy, like the horseman: she is here! Wake up, she has come back again! Sweetheart, darling, I love you!''[214]

Since this same horse will ultimately become a vehicle of destruction, a severe irony underlies such affirmation as it stands, but the usual dialectic occurs to make the point as well. " . . . Es inevitable la muerte del Papa. . . . this time, an instant, he had thought the headlines referred to himself. But of course it was only the poor Pope whose death was inevitable."[213] Of course. The Medea horror intrudes here, and then the holiday fiesta itself suddenly becomes "transcendentally awful and tragic . . . carried over into an obscure region of death, a gathering thunder of immedicable sorrow." (Dante writes of a "dolorous valley of the abyss, which gathers the thunder of ancient wailings.") And when they stop at a cafe called the "Paris"—which the Consul in fact finds "reminiscent of Paris," another extension of place—within a moment he is drinking tequila which Laruelle calls his "poison."

Venus then reappears conversationally, but to have its meaning inverted as the Consul calls it a "horned star." Upon first meeting Laruelle earlier, the Consul has told Hugh: "I really think you two ought to get together, you have something in common." With corresponding ambiguity insofar as Laruelle is concerned, he here declares: "Cabrón. You too, perhaps . . . " This is a pun, however, since the word means both cuckold and male goat; thus as the real cabrón the "horned" Consul himself again becomes a devil.

The two men talk past one another, the Consul preoccupied with his "battle for the survival of the human consciousness"— it is significant that he does not say merely his own—while Laruelle in turn accuses him of bringing his disasters down upon himself. "Your Ben Jonson, for instance, or perhaps it was Christopher Marlowe, your Faust man, saw the Carthaginians fighting on his big toe-nail. That's the kind of clear seeing you indulge in."[217] The use of "your" here, in regard to both writers, means of course in the Consul's volume of Elizabethan plays, presumably already misplaced by Laruelle (only moments ago, the Consul has noted its absence from Laruelle's rooms). Too, since the Carthaginian fantasy *was* Jonson's, as with Yvonne's spurious Dantean translation for Quauhnahuac Lowry is ringing in Marlowe for the sake of new Faust emphasis only. More to the point, however, we are back at the reality question, compounded throughout by frequent mention of the Consul's sunglasses; and what with Hugh already having quoted Corinthians, another line from Paul might apply: "For now we see through a glass, darkly." Or since Goethe is also named in the chapter:

> Ah, me! this dungeon still I see . . .
> Where even the welcome daylight strains
> But darkly through the painted panes.

Meanwhile the comparison between the Consul and Jonson is curious—and not only because a forgettable Jonson play, based on changed identities, disguises, etc., is entitled *The Case Is Altered.* If the Consul's description of the "standing" mummies at Guanajuato doesn't recall the popular anecdote about Jonson's burial, in a poem called "At the Bar" Lowry verifies the connection by speaking of drunkards "buried standing up like Ben Jonson." (By way of guaranteeing entry into Westminster Abbey, Jonson contrived assignment of a plot beforehand—too small to permit more than this.) Obviously, the Consul himself is already buried standing up—or, as in a legend about another author on his shelves not otherwise mentioned here, Duns Scotus, buried alive. But too, the Jonson identity is perhaps the first to place an actual "murderer" among his poet-ancestors as well.

It is in this same outdoor cafe that Laruelle speaks of the Consul's mystical "release," and where the Consul is reminded of Buddha's wheel. Guilt then reintrudes when the Consul mishears a word in a Spanish song: "It had sounded like Samaritana." Whereupon the Consul next proceeds to outdo Stephen Dedalus in the learned naming of his regrets: "Consider the word remorse. Remord. Mordeo, mordere. La Mordida! Agenbite too . . . And why rongeur? Why all this biting, all those rodents, in the etymology?" One answer, perhaps, is because it brings Christ into the etymology; punning on his own use of "Agenbite," Joyce refers to Christ as the "Agenbuyer," implying the "buying again" of souls for redemption—though the inverted echo here of Gogol would not escape Lowry either. Yet again reality also: "Why do people see rats? These are the sort of questions that ought to concern the world, Jacques."[218]

To which Laruelle: "Facilis est descensus Averno . . . It's too easy." And once more the original (non-Dantean) Virgil then: "Easy is the descent into hell; all night and day the gate of dark Dis stands open; but to recall thy steps and issue into the open air, this is the task, this the burden." We are in the *Aeneid,* of course—but as it happens Lowry's Mexico has been a peculiarly Virgilian hell from the start. The lake of Avernus lies in the crater of a volcano. In passing, the Consul here refers to a trip once taken to the town of Cholula; in Chapter I, while recalling the same trip, Laruelle makes a point of describing "the Mexican lake-bed"—i.e., the country's central valley, still under water at the time of Cortez—as "itself once the crater of a huge volcano."

Aeneas, then: last of the embattled Trojans, victim, but more importantly survivor, of another Fall—if not to add a fall brought about by a truly prototypal "horse." Too, a figure whose descent into hell reveals the promise of a truly extraordinary rebirth, since it becomes his destiny to found Rome itself.

But in regard to all such "descents": in addition to palingenesis, or the by no means alien dimension of access to hidden mysteries, there is again here that Dantean concept of the initiation into sin prerequisite to salvation, not unlike what St. Augustine calls the *felix culpa,* or happy fault, which brings the greatest redemption. Thus with each repeated visit to the underworld we spiral back upward to the Consul's Jonsonian toe-nail—a circumscribed vision perhaps, but by implication far more profound than Laruelle's unimaginative one.

Meanwhile the full quotation from Virgil may call to mind its equally relevant echo in Milton: " . . . long is the way/ And hard, that out of Hell leads up to the light." Or again, Dante: "The way is long, and difficult the road." But still the insistent Laruelle has other ideas: "Je crois que le vautour est doux à Prometheus et que les Ixion se plaisent en Enfers." Hence even another new prototype—cum wheel also, if of an unregenerative sort—though as the Consul indicates, the concept itself is anything but new: "Yet what about that belated postcard . . . ? It proved the lonely torment unnecessary, proved, even, he must have wanted it." While in a climactic moment he is to put it more succinctly yet: "I love hell."

For the moment, however, if still Bunyan's Chief of Sinners who does not "desire deliverance," the Consul also finds that he has been left alone in something of a stupor, "talking to himself." "I can see the writing on the wall," he decides, whereupon it occurs that some very real writing has been posted near him:

¿LE GUSTA ESTE JARDÍN?

Thus now even familiar signs come to reappear in archetypal form, insofar as the Consul has earlier envisioned a Biblical Mene-Tekel-Peres "on the wall" of his bathroom—though de León's vital thematic declaration is also literally "the writing on the wall." (Thus too, Lowry's use of such paraphernalia—public notices, posters, newspaper headlines—must finally be seen as immeasurably more organic than in those fictions where they afford a certain authenticity of background merely, at last dated.)

Leaving the cafe the Consul realizes he is in "a state of drunkenness, so to speak, rare for him." He is headed toward a cantina: "But he simply could not steer a straight course there." The cantina is the aforementioned El Bosque, in fact. By now, however, in addition to Dante the generalized path symbolism might also be intended to suggest the Tao, which itself means road or way, viz., life's own. As noted previously, the same concept can be said to underlie the Yin and Yang of Lowry's unending dialectic: "Just for one moment, one horrible moment in the Paris, he had thought it night."[220] (Nor, in turn, is Lowry about to let us forget what *that* means: "Dies Faustus," the Consul declaims while walking.)

The man then finds that he has wandered to "the final frontiers of the fair." And with the phrase deliberately echoing his earlier reference to "the final frontiers of consciousness," again his psyche is mirrored by externals: here "it was the day of the dead indeed . . . not so much asleep as lifeless, beyond hope of revival. Yet there were faint signs of life after all, he saw."

It is now that the Consul comes upon the actual "infernal machine," "struck by some coincidence" in its name. The loop-the-loop suggests "some huge evil spirit, screaming in its lonely hell." Nonetheless, like Dante mounting Geryon for the journey into the Malebolge, he finds himself "boarding the monster."

Unsurprisingly, several of his mythic alter egos board it with him. Situated in "a little confession box," he is first Prometheus again: "The Consul, like that poor fool who was bringing light to the world, was hung upside down over it."[222] But by virtue of the "coincidence" of the Cocteau, the otherwise unmentioned Oedipus analogy has to be taken as primary; as Hugh has felt, the Consul is now "in the grip of something" indeed. Simultaneously, however, he is also newly in that Cabbalistic realm represented by the Tree of Life turned "upside down," nor have we really needed Lowry's preface to tell us so—since at the Paris the Consul has remarked that "the d.t.'s are only the beginning, the music round the portal of Qliphoth . . . conducted by the God of Flies."

Nor are the two recusant Greeks and Beelzebub his only companions. "And it was scarcely a dignified position for an ex-representative of His Majesty's government to find himself in," he tells us, "though it was symbolic, of what he could not conceive, but it was undoubtedly symbolic." Undoubtedly. The Consul's next comment is a terse "Jesus." Symbolic of an "ex-representative" of Christ also? Peter crucified upside down? Certainly a crucifixion of sorts.

In anticipation of the "parting of the raiment" in a much more detailed crucifixion scene at the novel's end, the Consul also finds objects falling from his pockets, or rather being "wrested from him, torn away." Most in this case are returned, although not his passport, a matter to be of as much consequence as the discovery that he is carrying "some telegram of Hugh's." (The Consul is wearing a jacket Hugh has been using when the telegram is noted earlier.) Once he alights, his dizziness then contrives to make a reality of the metaphor with which the chapter opened—the world *is* now spinning "madly." He takes a seat on a bench, and when he does he comes upon a child's notebook: "No one loves Scrooge and Scrooge loves no one . . . He is alone in the world." From armadillos to Shelley to Scrooge: "Bloody old Scrooge; how queer to meet him here!" Scrooge, who is devoid of "charity," who is visited by spirits.

Still seated the Consul watches a madman flinging a bicycle tire ahead of himself, "repeating the process, to the irreducible logic of which he appeared eternally committed," an Ixion-Sisyphus type now made flesh. In the same thematic vein he is also made to note a man, seen earlier, climbing a pole—"still halfway up . . . neither near enough to the top nor the bottom to be certain of reaching either in comfort."

When he achieves the Bosque, where it is "so dark that even with his sunglasses off" he is forced to pause, like Hugh the Consul now recites his penny's worth of Dante, concluding, despite his confusion of "selva" with "bosca," that "the cantina was well named." It is, since the darkness remains a dominant motif in the scene which follows—and which is not always easy *to* follow. An elusive note is struck at once when the Consul remarks that the barroom, "facing east, became progressively darker as the sun, to those who noticed such things, climbed higher into the sky," meaning that we *are* to notice it, an odd new polar balance wherein darkness intensifies because light does. The effect is patently lunar, and Yeats's Great Wheel may be turning. As for the east itself, in the Consul's vision of "some northern country" he describes a scene in which he and Yvonne "face east, like Swedenborg's angels." Most obviously, to face east is to face the reborn sun. The garden is "eastward in Eden," and Buddha faces east beneath the Bo Tree. Too: "For as the lightning cometh out of the east, and shineth even unto the west, so shall the coming of the Son of Man be." Which is Matthew—but may not solve the problem.

A more readily apprehended motif emerges as the Consul's voices appear to inform him: "Geoffrey Firmin, this is what it is like to die, just this and no more, an awakening from a dream into a dark place."[226] Señora Gregorio, the proprietress, seems "dead" also, at least evincing "the most extraordinary waxen pallor." Yet the conversation which ensues could not be more explicitly affirmative, despite the old woman's faulty English: "If you har your wife you would lose all things in that love."

Certain of Lowry's intentions do become evident when the woman departs momentarily and one of the pariah dogs appears, whereupon the Consul stands to declaim: "Yet this day, pichicho, shalt thou be with me in—" On one level, this is an awful foreshadowing of plot alone, since when the Consul dies a dead dog will be flung into the ravine after him. Yet on another, of course, it is an ultimate association with the crucifixion:

"Verily I say unto thee, 'Today shalt thou be with me in para-dise.' " The dog itself flees at the words, yet within a moment the Consul finds that the cantina "seemed to have grown very much lighter."

But if Christ has brought light, there remains darkness enough for Dante. Murals materialize on the cantina's walls, showing a sleigh being pursued by wolves and reminding the Consul of a wolf hunt in Tolstoy, but at the same time leading him to recall "having been told that wolves never hunted in packs at all"—perhaps meaning that what he really remembers is the first canto of the *Comedy* where there *is* only one wolf, a symbol of avarice. (As noted *supra,* used plurally in Dante wolves become the Florentines who caused his exile.) But then again Christ: "Yes, indeed, how many patterns in life were based on kindred misconceptions, how many wolves do we feel on our heels, while our real enemies go in sheepskin by?" (Cf. the Sermon on the Mount: "Beware of false prophets, which come to you in sheep's clothing, but inwardly they are ravening wolves.")

When Señora Gregorio returns, for an instant the Consul thinks he "is looking at his own mother," actually possessed of an urge to "embrace" the woman, while she in turn tells him: "I have no house only a shadow. But whenever you are in need of a shadow, my shadow is yours."[230] This again is hard going. Like Yvonne's shadow cast by starlight, this one too could imply a Dantean corporeality in that dismal world where the dead cast none at all—meaning that Señora Gregorio is somehow offering the Consul "life." At Lowry's climax, new thoughts of the Con-sul's mother will suggest the terrible recognition of Jocasta as such by Oedipus, whereas after a Homeric parallel soon to occur, one might also recall Odysseus embracing his own mother in Hades and clasping only shadows; indeed, Odysseus too once goes "in sheepskin by" when escaping from the Cy-clops. Certainly we are in hell, and in the same sixth book of the *Aeneid* only now quoted, as he approaches the Styx, Aeneas is told: "This is the land of shadows . . . no living body may pass." But then again Christ's mother is on the slope at Golgotha, perhaps suggesting that the Consul is not only dead but some-way "entombed" here. In fact several times when he calls out his

words echo hollowly, half spoken—and all this *after* the crucifixion on the machine, of course.

In any case the rebirth concept does prevail: "Life
changes, you know . . . I think I see you with your esposa
again soon. I see you laughing together in some kernice
place where you laugh . . . Far away. In some kernice place
where all those troubles you har now will har—"²²⁹ Since the
woman presumably has no way of knowing about Yvonne's
return, the Consul is startled here: "What was Señora Gregorio saying?" And once again then, the vision of the "new
life," strengthened a hundredfold by the old woman's substitution of "laugh" for "live," perhaps the novel's most telling
pun—but for all this, where? Despite the negation with which
the narrative appears to end, the question will be seen as
crucial to Lowry's eschatology.

Nor will it prove irrelevant that Señora Gregorio wears her
hair in a "Psyche knot"—Psyche meaning soul, and symbolized
by Yvonne's own butterflies, but who, in the old myth, after
endless trial is united with Cupid forever.

Meanwhile two minor items. Long ago, Señora Gregorio says,
when she "used to dream about kernice dreams," life was good;
"now, I don't think of nothing but trouble . . . and trouble
comes." Here too then the occult "will," that sense, so to speak,
of creating one's own destiny by the very act of consciousness
itself, one more subject which must be discussed elsewhere;
similarly, the image of death as an "awakening from a dream"
must be held in mind as another clue to the nature of Consular
reality.

A last paragraph covers the Consul's departure to meet
Yvonne and Hugh at the bus for Tomalín. Hurrying by the
cantina's door as he emerges are Dr. Vigil, Quincey, and the
theater manager Bustamente, not looking his way, although
the Consul suspects "their conversation to be entirely about
him." Wolves, hunting in packs, in sheepskins—"spiders,"
Florentines. Perhaps even the three mythical judges of Tartarus, who pass sentence on the dead; they are off "to get a
few more 'opinions' about him," the Consul is sure, and Tartarus has been his own name for the barranca. But three
more "living" characters, also, who like Laruelle with his

halo do not belong in this landscape on the Day of the Dead, who are themselves unreal: "They flitted here and there, vanished . . . "

After which, in multileveled summation: "Es inevitable la muerte del Papa."

CHAPTER EIGHT

The theme of Samaritanism overshadows all others in Lowry's eighth chapter. No longer metaphor, here it becomes symbolic "act" in parallel with the narrative in Luke:

> A certain man went down from Jerusalem to Jericho, and fell among thieves, which stripped him of his raiment, and wounded him, and departed, leaving him half dead. And by chance there came down a certain priest that way: and when he saw him he passed by on the other side. And likewise a Levite, when he was at the place, came and looked on him, and passed by on the other side. But a certain Samaritan, as he journeyed, came where he was: and when he saw him he had compassion on him, and went to him, and bound up his wounds, pouring in oil and wine, and set him on his own beast, and brought him to an inn, and took care of him . . .

In Lowry's version, however, the Samaritan is distinguished only by his absence, and as a consequence the scene becomes the moral climax of the novel. When Yvonne and the Consul die, it will be through symbolic involvement with the same wounded man seen here—and, by inescapable inference, *because* of this failure of charity.

The duration of the chapter, which is Hugh's, is that of the bus trip from Quauhnahuac to Tomalín. Something of its essential thematic nature becomes evident almost at once as a man, "drunk, or drugged, or both," boards the vehicle. The Consul comments that he is not Mexican but Spanish, while "for some reason" he is wearing two hats—"a kind of cheap Homburg

fitting neatly over the broad crown of his sombrero." Whatever
the man's own reason for the idiosyncrasy, Lowry's would be to
connote the eternal duality of Mexico's Hispanic-Indian culture.
The point emerges explicitly when the Consul further refers to
the man as a "pelado." Hugh has seen the word defined somewhere as "shoeless illiterate," but:

> According to the Consul this was only one meaning; pelados
> were indeed "peeled ones," the stripped, but also those who did
> not have to be rich to prey on the really poor. . . . Hugh under-
> stood the word finally to be pretty ambiguous. A Spaniard, say,
> could interpret it as Indian, the Indian he despised, used, made
> drunk. The Indian, however, might mean Spaniard by it. . . . It
> was perhaps one of those words that had actually been distilled
> out of conquest, suggesting, as it did, on the one hand thief, on
> the other exploiter. Interchangeable ever were the terms of abuse
> with which the aggressor discredits those about to be ravaged![235]

There is an element of foreshadowing here, considering certain "terms of abuse" to be flung at the Consul at the time of
his own murder—including "pelado." More important for the
moment is that when he considers the man, Hugh sees his hands
to be "huge, capable and rapacious"—

> Hands of the conquistador, Hugh thought suddenly. But his
> general aspect suggested less the conquistador than, it was
> Hugh's perhaps too neat idea, the confusion that tends eventu-
> ally to overtake conquistadores. His blue suit was of quite ex-
> pensive cut. . . . The shoes however . . . were full of holes. He
> wore no tie. . . . The shirt was torn and in places hung out over
> his trousers.[234]

"Despite his stupor," the pelado is significantly also "a man
on guard," and Hugh finds him maintaining an appearance of
"knowing everything that was going on." Thus when the dying
Indian is discovered it is he who moves toward him first: "His
eyes were still only half open, and they preserved a dead glaze.
Yet there could be no doubt he had already taken in the whole
situation."

As for the Indian, seen by Hugh in the morning with "his

broad hat half down over his face," he now lies with his face "covered" by it. Similarly, in his first new view of him here, Hugh is puzzled that no one else "seemed to think it peculiar a man should choose to sleep, however perilous his position, in the sun on the main road." Whereas: "Can't be all right, you were lying right down in the road there, what?"—this the Consul as admonished by the English Samaritan in Chapter III.

Stepping down, Yvonne turns away instantly: "Don't mind me. It's just that I can't stand the sight of blood, damn it." Nor do the Consul or Hugh react much more decisively: "For each knew the other was also thinking it would be better still should one of the passengers, even the pelado, examine the man." And again: "You can't touch him. . . . For his protection. Actually it's a sensible law. Otherwise you might become an accessory after the fact."[243] (This last is less "Consular" awareness than simple Mexican reality—as many a tourist has learned to his chagrin.)

The scene is then sustained through an agony of indecision, until Hugh feels an "absolute dislocation of time." Further underscoring the inactivity is the fact that both he and the Consul recognize the Indian's horse, meaning by indirection the man himself:

Though the most potent and final obstacle to doing anything about the Indian was this discovery that it wasn't one's own business, but someone else's. And looking round him, Hugh saw that this too was just what everyone else was arguing. It's not my business, but, as it were, yours, they all said . . . and no, not yours either, but someone else's, their objections becoming more and more involved, more and more theoretical, till at last the discussion began to take a political turn.[245]

Here then Lowry's latter-day Samaritanism. Obviously, after what has gone before, it is nonintervention in Spain, indifference to the dying Loyalist cause—to the "cause" of mankind itself. Only a few pages earlier, in fact, the connection has been made explicitly when the sounds of the bus have woven what Hugh dismisses as "an idiotic syllogism" into his mind: "I am losing the Battle of the Ebro, I am losing Yvonne, therefore Yvonne is . . ." The unspoken deduction is considerably less fallacious than Hugh thinks, since both losses do stem from an essential failure of love in Lowry's several uses of the word.

In the interim, the pelado has uncovered "a sum of money, four or five silver pesos and a handful of centavos, that had been placed neatly under the loose collar of the man's blouse." It is at this juncture that the Orlac "murderer's hands" materialize, the pelado's own coming away "blotched with half-dried blood." Even as the chapter opens, Hugh sees another graphic advertisement for the film, and this same blood must then be read as staining the hands of Lowry's protagonists as well; in their failure to act they are unquestionably "murdering" the Indian symbolically.

But then an extra turn of the screw. Once the fascist police arrive and the bus is moving again, Hugh and the Consul discover that "the pelado's smeared conquistador's hands . . . now clutched a bloodstained pile of silver pesos and centavos." Thus by that same failure they have permitted the theft also—an ultimate "peeling" which preys on death itself.

And meanwhile the still larger implication. As the bus first sets out, Hugh catches sight of a sign over an undertaker's: *"Quo Vadis?"* The question is asked by Peter at the Last Supper: "Lord, whither goest thou?" What follows, amid protestations of fidelity, is the declaration that "the cock shall not crow, till thou hast denied me thrice"—as will happen literally in the novel itself, but which must remind us of the abjuration of Christ here also. And of course it is Christ who tells the story of the Samaritan to begin with: "Go, and do thou likewise."

Taken as a whole, the chapter is the least subjective in the novel, almost totally devoid of any sort of retrospection—if anything but devoid of the usual undercurrents. Almost as it opens, the driver shows Yvonne and Hugh "two beautiful white tame pigeons." Later, the Consul will refer to the birds as "palomas," for which the primary meaning is dove—while in Virgil two doves lead Aeneas to the Golden Bough he must pluck before gaining entry into the abyss. Indeed, the first word of the chapter, a paragraph in itself, is the Dantean invocation: "Downhill . . ."

Similarly, as the bus progresses, Hugh in his own turn is now instructed by a sign that if he "likes" this garden, he should see to it that his children "do not destroy it." The notion is then restated by indirection short moments later when he decides that the trip seems "the best of all possible ideas," an echo which can scarcely fail to call to mind the other famous line from the same satire: "We must cultivate our gardens." (Hugh's essential optimism might suggest *Candide* more generally also, as when the Consul's garden "looks quite beautiful to me," etc.)

It is during the early part of the trip that Hugh sees the figure, in costume for a dance festival, who is "apparently the devil himself." As they pass the celebration, which they had earlier spoken of attending, he exchanges a "look of regret" with Yvonne, since it is now "too late to get out." We must take this literally, for the self-evident reason that the bus is moving—though doubtless implied is that the workings of the "máquina infernal" can no longer be halted either. A moment later, in fact, the bus crosses the barranca and Hugh sees "a dead dog right at the bottom, nuzzling the refuse"—more dire prophecy.

In this same context Hugh spies a clock which, "like the one in Rupert Brooke," says ten to three. The reference is to "The Old Vicarage, Grantchester," itself an unread remnant of Edwardian sentimentality. But the Consul's is not the only poet-ancestry to keep expanding—Brooke having died young in a war on foreign soil.

Nor does Yvonne escape either. Once the Indian has been left, Hugh informs us that with "the unerring instinct of all war correspondents," he had been "on the lookout immediately for possible clues to diagnosis such as broken ladders, stains of blood, moving machinery, and restive horses."[249] The horse, if not restive here, decidedly will be when it kills Yvonne, a death which occurs when she slips from a very real (and very Cabbalistic) broken ladder at the fallen tree she is climbing. As for the blood, it is only a page or two later that the "stains" become evident on the stolen money—while the reference to "moving machinery" would be an even more direct hint that it is "too late to get out."

More foreshadowing occurs when it is noted that a tavern from which the pelado has emerged is "another of your fascist joints." The driver has called his birds "aerial pigeons," and, in discussing the pelado, the Consul remarks, "I can tell you this much . . . He's not an aerial pigeon"—meaning that he is more likely some sort of "stool pigeon," a term to occur later. And while this again recalls the spy motif, enhanced by the idea of the pelado being aware of "everything that was going on," Lowry stresses the theme by having Hugh notice "a bald boy, with earrings, sleepily scratching his stomach and swinging madly on a hammock"—one more of those "spiders" so off-handedly listed in Chapter I. (In contrast, as they wait briefly at the same tavern, we read that from within there "came a sound of singing." The echo is slight, but it is worth note that in two separate short stories Lowry quotes a line of Conrad Aiken's: "And from the whole world, as it revolved through space, came a sound of singing.")

Too, it is stated that the police who appear are "not the pukka police anyhow, only those birds I told you about"—the "birds" being more "pigeons," specifically members of the Union Militar to be confronted in Parián. (Here, such knowledge *is* presumably a product of the Consul's diplomatic background—although the irony in his indifference deepens insofar as it persists *despite* these awarenesses.)

For all of such portentous intrusions, however, Hugh remains Hugh. It is after being restrained from argument with the police that he is told the incident "would have been worse than the windmills." But even before this he has fatuously conceived of himself as informing Christ—"who agreed"—that "the time has come for you to join your comrades, to aid the workers," while next imagining that he has "rescued Him" from "those hypocrites."

The latter notion, meanwhile, may also again suggest the familiar sense of the omniscient "they," decisively marked in the scene with the Indian. Hugh is warned to discard his cigarette because "they have prohibidated it." When he bends to touch the man it is said that "they have prohibidated that, tambien."

With the chapter's emphasis on external perceptions, Lowry's polar stresses are also particularly evident. No more than does Hugh recognize the "devil" when the man moves away—"toward a church." He broods upon such pleasantries as volcanic eruption and "encroaching flood," yet within a minute finds on the bus "a sense of gaiety, a feeling, almost, of the fiesta itself again." Just as quickly this gaiety turns out to have been "short-lived as a burst of sunlight," whereupon he considers a ruined church, "blackened with fire," and with "an air of being damned." Popocatepetl looms with "one side beautifully curved as a woman's breast, the other precipitous, jagged, ferocious." And even as they stand above the dying Indian, he hears first from among the passengers "pobrecito," a diminutive of compassion, and then an expletive of "obscene contempt."

Above and beyond their quietly "creative" effectiveness, a meaning behind some of these constructions may finally be occult. Earlier, when Hugh has contemplated his brother's books, the Consul has pointedly remarked, "Too bad . . . I left my Boehme in Paris," i.e., adding Boehme to his "catalogue" also. And as was noted briefly *supra,* for Boehme reality was a concept of ceaseless polarity; like Paracelsus before him, he held that such "contraries" were an expression of divine law. Blake, in his own turn indebted to Boehme, saw in these same contrasts the balance between good and evil, or again, between heaven and hell. But this "balance" is of course again Cabbalistic as well. (In more strictly literary terms there is probably something of the method of metaphysical poetry here also, at least in Dr. Johnson's sense of it as "a kind of *discordia concors*"—i.e., "a combination of dissimilar images, or discovery of occult resemblances in things apparently unlike.")

Meanwhile another such contrast occurs when, at one moment, the landscape becomes "so reminiscent of England one expected at any point to see a sign: Public Footpath to Lostwithiel," whereas in the next: "Dust, dust, dust—it filtered through the windows, a soft invasion of dissolution."

The latter image is newly emphasized at the chapter's end: "The three of them stood again in the dust, dazzled by the whiteness, the blaze of the afternoon." Particularly after the symbolic murder which seals the Consul's doom, at this juncture the picture may suggest Thebes parched by the curse upon Oedipus.

Too, the usual parade of familiar motifs. Passing a spot where he and Yvonne had ridden, Hugh contemplates the "twenty-one other paths they might have taken." (Discussing "something preternatural about paths" in "The Forest Path to the Spring," Lowry mentions "the twenty-one paths that lead back to Eden.") Initially, the doves are called "ambassadors of peace"; later Hugh remarks two pullets which have "signed their Munich agreement," and a turkey which looks "remarkably like Neville Chamberlain"—perhaps because there has been "appeasement" in the surrender of the Indian to the fascist police. And when the pelado leaves the bus, Hugh perceives that "his course was straight."

This last is noteworthy. Insofar as he embodies man's cultural heritage, for the Consul to lose the "straight way" is to fail in moral responsibility likewise; it is critical to a definition of Lowry's tragedy not that the Consul *should* know better, but that he undeniably does and permits himself to be destroyed nonetheless. But where the pelado walks a straight course, even when drunk, a paradox arises. Despite his overt criminality, the man knows *only* the abyss—and in a relative way is consequently innocent.

The moral status of the others on the bus is considered more directly. Once they are newly underway, Hugh catches the eye of one of several old women—"guiltily"—only to find her own face "completely expressionless." Which leads him to speculate, again with echoes of Weber: "Perhaps they remembered the days of revolution in the valley . . . those crucified and gored in the bull ring, the pariah dogs barbecued in the market place. There was no callousness in their faces, no cruelty. Death they knew, better than the law, and their memories were long."[248]

Since Hugh has been aware of "a massiveness in their movements" when the women have boarded the bus, and has remarked their "faces of old idols," we are back again to the Indian as symbol of abidance. "And yet, in these old women it was as if, through the various tragedies of Mexican history, pity, the impulse to approach, and terror, the impulse to escape (as one had learned at college), having replaced it, had finally been reconciled by prudence, the conviction it is better to stay where you are."[248]

What Hugh has "learned at college," of course, is his Aristotle, granted that Lowry is here using the latter's terms in a poetics of history rather than drama. Yet the allusion might also remind us parenthetically that in his twelve-hour time span, Lowry is also adhering, perhaps as closely as possible in a novel, to the concept of Aristotelian "unities." Moreover a mildly comic "catharsis" even follows, when Hugh turns to the other passengers—celebrants of the holiday—only to discover that "they'd all got out, apparently, and walked; since death, by the roadside, must not be allowed to interfere with one's plans for resurrection, in the cemetery."

Nor is the chapter without its own signification of rebirth, if ambiguously predicated. The Indian is found "with his arms outstretched" toward a stone wayside cross, whereas the cross itself stands "in a sort of rubbish heap," and beneath it lie "a milk bottle, a funnel, a sock, and part of an old suitcase." This far along in the novel it is difficult not to assume the latter items euphemisms, perhaps for something in the Tarot, perhaps even for elements of a distorted Mass—bottle as chalice, funnel as cup, suitcase as tabernacle, etc. Then again, the cross in a "rubbish heap" is of itself sufficient symbol for Christ's modern estate.

The chapter concludes when the three disembark near a cantina named "Todos Contentos y Yo También," which the Consul translates aloud: "Everybody happy, including me." "And including those," Hugh thinks to himself, "who effortlessly, beautifully, in the blue sky above them, floated, the vultures—xopilotes, who wait only for the ratification of death."[253]

Doubtless Hugh still has the Indian in mind; but it will be left to him, himself, to make other "ratifications" sooner than he knows.

CHAPTER NINE

When the Indian is left behind, Hugh wonders if, being "moderately case-hardened," he might somehow have "acquitted himself, have done something, have not done nothing." Though it scarcely "acquits" him, when a substitute rider is needed at the bull ring in Chapter IX, Hugh impulsively volunteers. As Yvonne sees it—the point of view is hers—Hugh is "submitting to that absurd necessity he felt for action, so wildly exacerbated by the dawdling inhuman day."[275] He is also presenting us with an immediate symbolic counterpart to his equally tardy "gesture" in Spain.

Through the events of the Samaritan scene (read "nonevents," or rather, "nonact"), the course of the tragedy has been set; the present chapter, contrastingly marked by an excessive introspection, is in effect an hiatus, the lull before the storm. Pointedly, it contains the one moment of authentic *calm* in the novel, an exchange between the Consul and Yvonne of the tenderness neither has elsewhere been able to communicate.

Predictably, however, that calm is illusory. "What a wonderful time everybody was having. . . . How merrily Mexico laughed away its tragic history, the past, the underlying death!" Yet within three pages: "Mexico was not laughing away her tragic history; Mexico was bored. . . . All that had happened was that Yvonne's drink in the bus had taken effect and was now wearing off."[257]

In fact Lowry's synthesis of opposites here becomes almost Hegelian:

—While using her mirror, Yvonne notices the volcanoes:

"How sentimental one could become about them! . . . Popocatepetl seemed even more beautiful for being reflected . . ." Whereupon: "Her eyes were tired and playing tricks. For a second she'd had the awful sensation that, not Popocatepetl, but the old woman with the dominoes that morning, was looking over her shoulder."[256]

—Yvonne daydreams at length about "their home between the forest and the sea," this in Canada, where they will live "in simplicity and love." A moment afterward her attention is caught by "the man in dark glasses who'd been outside the Bella Vista this morning and then later—or had she imagined it?—standing up beside the Cortez Palace. 'Geoffrey, who's that man?' "[273] (Preoccupied, the Consul does not answer.)

—It is against the background of Hugh's ride, with its real enough element of danger, that Yvonne abruptly suggests: "Geoffrey . . . there isn't anything to keep us here any longer." When the Consul agrees she feels "as if a spirit of intercession and tenderness hovered over them," going on to envisage "Venus and the golden moon at sunrise"—an immemorial pair of mythic lovers. Yet simultaneously: "It ran in Yvonne's mind that all at once they were talking—agreeing hastily—like prisoners who do not have much time to talk." Then in the same passage she finds the Consul "leaning his damp head against her hair like a child," a concept even less salutary, on the level of the Oedipus analogy.

—Emotion builds, and midway through the only stichomythic exchange in the novel the Consul admits: "I've fallen down, you know . . . Somewhat." To which Yvonne: "Oh Geoffrey. We *could* be happy, we *could*—" But after a sudden scream: "Hugh . . . Something's happened."

—Hugh is unhurt and Yvonne begins again—"hurriedly." "I don't expect you to—I mean—I know it's going to be—" "But the Consul was finishing the habanero."

—Leaving the arena Yvonne is captured by sunlight falling on a "little silver lake glittering cool, fresh, and inviting before them." The lake is a mirage, "a broken greenhouse roof." Hope persists anyway—"their home was real." Yet: "Why was it though, that right in the centre of her brain, there should be a figure of a woman having hysterics, jerking like a puppet and banging her fists upon the ground?"[279] (The "mythic" answer to this last will unfold subsequently.)

Equally pronounced in the chapter is the dialectic between past and present. More noticeably here than elsewhere, however, past becomes less a matter of natural reminiscence than part of the *active* stuff of consciousness itself, often even dictating the form of present perceptions. For example, Yvonne watches the bull "drawn, lured, into events of which he has no real comprehension, by people with whom he wishes to be friendly . . . and by whom . . . he is finally entangled," and a moment later her dead father is able to "make his way" toward her in the stands —since it will develop that she has unwittingly been describing the man as closely as the bull.

The point, here, emerges perhaps most clearly at the chapter's conclusion. Yvonne and the others will again pass the Todos Contentos y Yo También. The doors open and "something" appears:

> Bent double, groaning with the weight, an old lame Indian was carrying on his back, by means of a strap looped over his forehead, another poor Indian, yet older and more decrepit than himself. He carried the older man and his crutches, trembling in every limb under this weight of the past, he carried both their burdens.[280]

On the surface alone, the picture is remorseless in counterpoint to the failure of Samaritanism so recently witnessed; too, it again strengthens Lowry's theme of the Indian in general, in the sense of a timeless, super-Faulknerian motif of "endurance." After the several quotations from Virgil, it must also suggest Aeneas carrying his father Anchises, to essentially that same latter thematic point, and in the Jonathan Cape letter Lowry himself defines the image as that of "man eternally carrying the psychological burden of his father," which would additionally give us another Freudian correlative to the more literary uses of the Oedipus myth. For all of this, however, and perhaps more importantly yet, this "weight of the past," labeled as it is, is the weight of Geoffrey/Yvonne/Hugh's as well—and by extension man's own burden of history which, as Ortega y Gasset has suggested, must be understood before it can be escaped. To great degree then, Lowry's subjectivity must at last be seen as a vehicle for holding the past and present of his characters in "spatial" balance much like that in his spatially mythic constructions, and to frequently corresponding thematic purpose: as through comprehension of sin the way to redemption, so too out of the past the future.

But on the personal level, the theme will here take on a more subtle hue as well, affording a new variant on the concept of cyclic repetition. Voicing it hypothetically, Yvonne speculates that "her own destiny was buried in the distant past, and might for all she knew repeat itself in the future." But in Hollywood, we find, Yvonne had been an adolescent actress, a "star." In a passage which assumes in her mind the tone of a publicity release, she remembers that because the word "had undergone some mysterious transformation" in her mind, she had subsequently taken a course in astronomy. By way of the same publicity story we are also told that in a later period she was "well on her way for the second time to becoming a star," and, when the Consul here agrees that they should leave Mexico, her previously interrupted reverie about "rebirth" in Canada breaks back across her mind in mid-sentence: "—into a wild sky full of stars at rising . . . " All of this is ordinary enough in context. But at the time of her death, amid the most affirmative rebirth symbolism in the novel, Yvonne will feel herself "gathered upwards and borne towards the stars"—physically "gathered," since there is no trace of simile in the passage at all. Obviously, this will demand later discussion; but if we read Lowry at that juncture as he will insist upon being read, Yvonne will have undergone a completely literal "transformation" of the sort joked about here. That destiny "buried in the distant past" will profoundly indeed "repeat itself in the future."

For that matter the present chapter spills over with rebirth imagery as is. Finding the bull "temporarily defeated," Yvonne sees in the incident "death, or a sort of death . . . and now, once more, resurrection," etc. Nor is that sense of cyclic "predestination" limited to Lowry's pun on the meaning of "stars" alone.

It is here that Yvonne several times notices boys "marvelously balanced" on fences, recalling the Consul's talk of Cabbalistic "equilibrium" on one hand, anticipating her death on the other. Likewise she remembers a film once seen in New York, which itself years later she learned was one of Laruelle's, in which "at her entrance . . . a shadowy horse, gigantic, filling the whole screen, seemed leaping out of it at her"—still more of that same "destiny" so soon to repeat.

The motif of shared identities is newly extended here also, although in actuality it has never been limited to an equation between the Consul and Hugh. As early as in Chapter I, Laruelle comments that "he had acquired a certain identity with Hugh" —this in the days following the tragedy—whereas while sitting with Laruelle in the Paris it seems to the Consul "as if all the desolation of the months following Yvonne's departure were now mirrored in the *other's* eyes." Now, remembering that she had once shown Laruelle old photos of herself in cowboy attire like Hugh's, Yvonne records that in Laruelle's "amazed and bewildered recognition of her this horrible morning, she had wondered was there not just an instant's faltering—for surely Hugh and Yvonne were in some grotesque fashion transposed!"[265] Less directly, but in echo of Hugh's earlier session with the radio, she recalls a night of watching "the illuminated news aloft traveling around the Times Building, news of disaster, of suicide, of banks failing, of approaching war . . . which, as she gazed upward with the crowd, broke off abruptly, snapped off into darkness, into the end of the world, she had felt, when there was no more news. Or was it—Golgotha?"[265] (Any news *after* Golgotha, of course, would be that of the Gospels, by translation the "good news.") And by way of indicating that she, too, has walked Eliot's Baudelairean "unreal city," or Dante's: "The cripples jerked themselves slowly past. Men muttered by in whose faces all hope seemed to have died."

Simultaneously, a radically new identity emerges here as well, perhaps implying another kind of "repetition" in the process, as Yvonne finds the Consul's face assuming "that brooding expression of her father's she remembered so well." Nor does this even begin to tell the story. Yvonne's father had been a consul. As in the case of the *Samaritan,* for what is described

as an "imagined disgrace" Constable had suffered the "beset-
ting illusion . . . that he'd been cashiered from the army,"
while being "strictly alcoholic in character," and dying insane.
Moreover he had run a Hawaiian farm where "the pineapples
rotted in the fields," and he had once endeavored "to harness
the volcano behind their estate to run the hemp machine."
With even the *symbols* in his biography tailored to fit the Consul's, the construction here may be extreme; but in having
married—loved—the image of her father, Yvonne is of course
thereby meant to become the obverse of the Freudian coin in
Lowry's Oedipus symbolism, not Jocasta now but Electra. By
way of enlarging the notion, she further thinks of herself as
"no child of her mother's people."

Conversely, an interesting *opposition* of character is repeated
here also. Whereas the nongolfing Consul must envy even Laruelle as someone "who could shave and put on his socks by
himself," Hugh is shown to ride the bull with a certain "expert-
ness." "One felt, even, half ironically, that this was the kind of
thing Hugh might be best fitted to do." In the Cape letter, in
fact, Lowry has it that Hugh here "conquers the animal forces
of nature which the Consul later lets loose"—i.e., when it is at
his death that the horse breaks toward the forest, and Yvonne.

Heracles to the contrary then, it is left for the Consul to fulfill
the cerebral half of the balance by declaiming about the bull: "I
christen him Nandi, vehicle of Siva, from whose hair the River
Ganges flows and who has also been identified with the Vedic
storm god Vindra—known to the ancient Mexicans as Huracán."[257] Or again, by apostrophizing the animal in felicitous
paraphrase of two poets at once: "See the old unhappy bull
. . . in the plaza beautiful . . . Waiting with a wild surmise for the
ropes that tantalise." The first lines here are Ralph Hodgson's,
whose own beast is in a "forest beautiful" rather than a plaza;
more relevant is a phrase between these in the poem which the
Consul omits, Hodgson's bull being "sick in soul and body
both." The Keats, meanwhile, is then extended to encircle an
additional motif: "Stout Cortez . . . gazing at the horrific, who
was the least pacific of all men."

The Vedic elements here will come into focus in a crucial,
essentially "anthropological" section of Lowry's next chapter,

as will the aspect of "ritual combat" in Hugh's action in the arena. Meanwhile, if Chapter IX is perhaps Lowry's "slightest," as always the minor themes intrude. There is a new element of "correspondence" in the fact that Yvonne and Laruelle unknowingly once attended the same Hollywood party. If not by outcast dogs, Yvonne nonetheless remarks a sensation of "being followed, always followed." A Miltonic deep appears in the form of Los Angeles, described as "the dark and accursed City of the Angels." And a new stand-in for William Blackstone materializes in the person of Robinson Crusoe.

The communication theme is also newly adumbrated when it occurs to Yvonne that Hugh knows nothing of her film background: "Such areas there are in one another we leave, perhaps forever, unexplored!" (In thinking this she further recalls that she had "never told him a word . . . not even that day in Robinson." Since "Robinson" has also once crossed Hugh's mind, but the Consul himself has indicated that their adultery occurred "in Paris," this would then be an obscure town some dozen kilometers to the south—which *Michelin* dismisses as having little more than a "jardin" and an exceptional view.)

Too, Yvonne here becomes Venus once again, albeit a "honey-tanned Venus" this time, in the jargon of the press release—"just emerging from the surf." According to the same source she has been "submerged in burning lakes, suspended over precipices, ridden horses down ravines"—Dante via *The Perils of Pauline*. Virgil is at last mentioned by name—the name of a Los Angeles street—and in similar reduction Golgotha becomes a question of "that daily crucifixion of the post," i.e., the mails.

Rimbaud might be alluded to also, when Yvonne remembers "seeing, as might the Consul, the sign in the Town House window 'Informal Dancing in the Zebra Room' turn 'Infernal'—or 'Notice to Destroy Weeds' become 'Notice to Newlyweds.' " Illustrations in "A Season in Hell" are different—more like the "ruined Grecian temple" Yvonne will imagine in Chapter XI— but Rimbaud proclaims himself equally adept at "l'hallucination simple."

But finally one more time the wasteland, with even the eternal "wheel" distorted now. Yvonne, Hugh, and the Consul are walking:

> Their shadows crawled before them in the dust, slid down white thirsty walls of houses, were caught violently for a moment in an elliptical shade, the turning wrenched wheel of a boy's bicycle.
>
> The spoked shadow of the wheel, enormous, insolent, swept away.[280]

Fore*shadowing* idealized: for the instant Lowry's characters themselves become as the images in Plato's cave, an ultimate unreality. Nor is it to be missed that even the shadows do not elude their "machine."

CHAPTER TEN

Occasionally, in the course of his day, mescal has been in the Consul's mind, this the drink symbolically connected with the hallucinatory drug mescaline. "If I ever start to drink mescal again," he has told Laruelle, "I'm afraid, yes, that would be the end."[216]

As the tenth chapter of *Under the Volcano* opens in the Salón Ofélia, "almost absent-mindedly" the Consul orders the drink. "What had he said? Never mind. Nothing less than mescal would do. But it mustn't be a serious mescal, he persuaded himself." If not quite the end, this is unquestionably the beginning of it; the Consul has plucked his Forbidden Fruit. As the episode of the Indian has been a climax of moral choice, the present is another in terms of basic human conflict. After the argument between the Consul and the others with which it concludes, the tragedy to follow will have become a dramatic as well as a thematic inevitability.

The chapter is inordinately complex, on its surface and below. Nowhere is the Consul drunker. At one juncture past and present merge in his consciousness into an anarchic juxtaposition outside of time entirely, while it is here too that Lowry makes his most obvious genuflection to Joyce, incorporating within some thirty-five pages his own detailed parallel with the *Odyssey*.

Fair warning of the difficulties to come is given at once, when the Consul recalls an occasion on which he had attempted to meet a train when even drunker than *this*—unable to remember what train, its time of arrival, its track. The passage is totally disjunctive, and the fact that he is meeting one "Lee Maitland" not previously named in the novel, where *everything* is generally anticipated, would further indicate the extent of his removal from ordinary reality—i.e., he is recalling an incident normally buried. (In his Cape letter, Lowry relates the scene to "Freudian death dreams.") Yet for all the chaos of the event itself, it occurs with the intensity of a "re-enduring" rather than a recollection; when the "experience" is over, the Consul is "oozing alcohol from every pore."

As other memories finally intrude, two lines of French also run into the Consul's head, both from Racine. The first, from Athaliah's dream of the ruin of her life, pertains mainly to these latter recollections themselves, since several concern a night marked by "portents of doom": *"C'etait pendant l'horreur d'une profonde nuit."* The second, however, quickly leads to something else again: *"Mais tout dort, et l'armée, et les vents, et Neptune."*[284] This is the Iphegenia story, the calm before it is ordained that Agamemnon must sacrifice the girl if the Greek armada is to achieve Troy.

A first point behind its inclusion becomes evident with the appearance of the proprietor of the tavern, the Cervantes named in Chapter I. When the man shows the Consul a fighting cock, the Consul broods: "Was this the face that launched five hundred ships and betrayed Christ into being in the Western Hemisphere?"[286] Insofar as it departs from Marlowe the line will need comment in several regards; but in the original we are of course again with Agamemnon's fleet—as is Odysseus. Odysseus, who, as every schoolboy used to know, one day meets the dreadful Cyclops. Or meets Señor Cervantes: "A shabby little man with a black shade over one eye . . . savage at heart."

Wherewith, and far more decisively than in the parallel with Heracles, the episodes of the *Odyssey:*

—The Cyclops. The eye-patch makes Cervantes *a* cyclops— enforced by a gratuitous "I love hunting"—but Lowry further identifies him with Polyphemus particularly. The latter imprisons Odysseus and his crew in a cave, its entrance blocked by a stone; here the Consul soon finds himself in a bathroom "all of grey stone," and when he requests tissue Cervantes offers him "a stone" instead. Too, Polyphemus believes Odysseus' joke about his name being "Nobody," and when blinded by the Greeks can explain only that "Nobody" has been there and done the deed; in turn the Consul recalls Dr. Vigil speaking about the church of "the Virgin for those who have nobody with," and then reiterating: "Nobody come here."

—The Laestrygonians. These are cannibals. Midway in the chapter the Consul and the others eat live shellfish. "Now you see what sort of creatures we are. . . . Eating things alive." Lest crustaceans don't count, there follows reference to the Nazi system "swallowing live struggling men and women."

—Aeolus. This the island where the winds are kept in a cave— from whence Agamemnon is already here doing obeisance to raise them. Viewing a waterfall near the tavern the Consul recalls Niagara and "the Cave of the Winds." Moreover, he will be reminded of the same place a second time, immediately after mention of the saddle-bags from which money is now believed to have been stolen from the Indian, and at Aeolus the winds are presented to Odysseus for his personal use—in a bag which his men open in their own curiosity about supposed treasure.

—Circe. She turns humans into swine. Hugh, during the argument late in the chapter: "Don't be a bloody swine, Geoffrey."

—Hades. New references would appear almost superfluous. Nonetheless: "I love hell. . . . In fact I'm running, I'm almost back there already." And since Odysseus' individual visit is made for purposes of consulting the soothsayer Tiresias, it can be added that the Consul has occasion to plead: "Give me back . . . the knowledge of the Mysteries."

—The Sirens. Early in the chapter the Consul imagines he hears voices wailing the Spanish word for drunkard—"Borrrrr-aaacho." He refers to the Bay of Biscay in Spanish also, "Mar Cantábrico," in essence a "singing sea." (In this case, however, Lowry is perhaps also reminding us of the first ship to carry American arms to the Loyalists—an S. S. *Mar Cantábrico*.)

—Scylla and Charybdis. Scylla is another who devours living creatures, and two such cannibalisms have been listed. Charybdis is a whirlpool; the Consul likens the sound of the waterfall to "the noise of the maelstrom."

—The Wandering Rocks. Cervantes passes in and out of the scene repeatedly, serving, doing errands, etc. In his earlier appearances the offer of "a stone" occurs frequently enough to become a refrain. As we read, the phrase truly does seem to "wander."

—-The Oxen of Hyperion. Odysseus' crewmen slaughter them. Later in the chapter the Consul has a fantasy about Hugh, first as Hugh has shaved him, but after which, "back in the ring, he was bearing down upon an ox: now he had exchanged his razor for a sword. He thrust forward the sword to bring the ox to its knees."

—-Calypso. When Odysseus is stranded on her island she offers him anything a man might desire, save for freedom. "I've been beguiled by your offers of . . . Paradise," the Consul tells Yvonne. But: "I've got my own piddling little fight for freedom on my hands."

—-The Lotus Eaters. " 'Mescal,' the Consul said." (A quite vivid "drugged" moment will be described in another context shortly.)

—-Nausicaä. Odysseus meets her at a stream where she is gaily washing with several handmaidens. Early in the chapter the Consul watches Yvonne swim, sees two other girls "squealing as they came down to the water"—two girls wearing "ancient" costumes.

—-The Homecoming. Odysseus is first recognized through the scar of an old wound in his thigh; the Consul's limp is newly mentioned. Odysseus finds some hundred-odd suitors paying court to Penelope; accusing Yvonne of infidelity the Consul declares it has involved "a hundred or so" others. And as for the vengeance wrought upon the latter, as his suspicions newly mount the Consul here feels an "all but irresistible, senseless onrush of wild rage" toward Hugh.

On a more general plane, we might also recall that it is Odysseus who devises the stratagem of the wooden horse—cf. the Consul's vague "responsibility" in the matter of the disguised gunboat—while in parallel with the man's prototypal "cunning" the Consul here takes great pains to fool the others about his drinking, to hide his condition, etc. At the same time it is noteworthy that unlike Leopold Bloom, whose nonmythic background Joyce restricts mainly to Dublin, both the Consul and Hugh have spent much of their lives in travel, meaning that

Lowry has long since established a *biographical* point of departure for the analogy. For that matter since the heart of the motif
is "journey"—the *odyssey*—all of Lowry's characters can be read
as veritable Wandering Jews, the Consul whom Hugh recalls
"was always in Rabat or Timbuctoo," Yvonne with her multi-
labeled luggage, etc.

The chapter remains. Near the end of the Lee Maitland passage,
several recollections occur of a gravedigger, and then of corpses
in transit, finally jarring the Consul back to the present by recalling his own prophetic words of the morning: "A corpse will be
transported by express." The area near the tavern is resortlike,
though Dr. Vigil's Guanajuato has already illustrated where
Lowry's "tourists" wind up: the waterfall drops into a reservoir
built on "levels," exactly like the falls in the Malebolge, while
the Consul decides the view "suggestive of some agonized ultimate sweat." The novel's many paths then cease to be metaphor
as he traces in his mind's eye the now highly accessible path to
Parián, which is literally that, not a road. And Parián itself meanwhile, which he categorizes as an "obscure administrative centre," strikes him as a mystery: "One met people going there;
few, now he thought about it, ever coming back. Of course
they'd come back, he had himself: there was an explanation."[285]
(Laruelle has only recently offered one of several in quoting
Virgil on the "easy" descent into Avernus.)
     In geographical actuality both Parián and Tomalín, where the
Consul still is, would incidentally seem to be Cuautla, a town in
Morelos fitting Lowry's larger descriptions of both and reached
from Cuernavaca via the same general route ascribed to the bus.
The Consul once makes the obvious play on Parián and "pariah," and has also found it "suggestive" of the Cyclades, natural enough since the original adjective derives from one of them,
viz., Paros. Virgil himself speaks of "Parian marble," source of
the island's chief fame in antiquity, which the Consul is likewise
aware of. As if to assert the fictional independence of his own
creation, however, Lowry actually mentions Cuautla in passing;
but among his poems is one entitled "Thirty-five Mescals in
Cuautla," a personal if not Consular verification of the connection, surely.

While Hugh and Yvonne prepare to swim, meanwhile, the Consul notices rainbows in the waterfall, but adds that even without them the mescal—i.e., the lotus—"would have already invested the place with a magic." And this then the beginning of a final mystical foregathering; not very differently from perceptions as described by Havelock Ellis and other early writers on mescaline, in fact, he goes on to record that "the drifting mists all seemed to be dancing, through the elusive subtleties of ribboned light. . . . It was a phantom dance of souls . . . seeking permanence in the midst of what was only perpetually evanescent, or eternally lost."[286]

This last may also be an echo of the beginning of Part Two of Goethe's *Faust,* where Faust, like the Consul earlier unable to face the sun, looks to a waterfall himself, with its own rainbow, deciding that life exists in the "reflected color." In any case it is here that the Consul salutes the cock as "the face that launched five hundred ships and betrayed Christ into being," a line from which Lowry derives remarkably more mileage than that already associated with Odysseus. Insofar as the original is spoken by Faust, first of all Yvonne then here becomes Helen, and as the latter betrays Menelaus so indeed will Yvonne's literal "betrayal" of the Consul occupy much of the chapter. But since it is scarcely Helen whose act "betrayed Christ into being," Lowry has Eve in mind also. But as a matter of fact the duality here can really only be understood as the new introduction to a complex Fall parallelism shortly to unfold, not only involving the fall of Troy, which Helen does cause, or of man, but of Rome, the Aztecs, etc. Moreover the connection of the betrayal motif with a real cock must again anticipate the betrayal of Christ as well—"The cock shall not crow," etc.

As for the actual bird, it in turn becomes a symbol of a different type when the Consul decides that "the vicious little man-made battles, cruel and destructive, yet somehow bedraggledly inconclusive . . . disgusted and bored him"—a judgment closely analogous to political attitudes he is soon to express.

Then Hamlet steps from the wings—predictably enough in a tavern named for Ophelia and following the gravedigger of the Lee Maitland passage—as the Consul broods: "To drink or not to drink." Actually, however, *Hamlet* has been paraphrased on

much the same level previously, where Hugh has recalled a
demeaning employment which followed his first sea adventure:
"So it had come to this!"

In variation on the motif of transported corpses—or of people
"buried standing up"—man is then seen as "a little soul holding
up a corpse," whereupon the soul on its own part becomes
political microcosm: "The soul! Ah, and did she not too have
her savage and traitorous Tlaxcalans, her Cortez and her noches
tristes, and, sitting within her innermost citadel in chains, drinking chocolate, her pale Moctezuma?"[287] The Consul has been
thinking of the Tlaxcalans before this, as the local "forebears"
of Cervantes. The more specific reference is to the fact that the
latter allied themselves with Cortez as he prepared for his as-
sault on the Aztecs. Moctezuma attempted appeasement—re-
enter Neville Chamberlain—and was imprisoned. The so-called
"noche triste" was the night of June 30, 1520, after a temporary
defeat which left Cortez weeping beneath a great cypress
claimed still to exist in Mexico City—yet another real tree as
counterpart to those in Lowry's forest of symbols.

Next Cervantes reappears to lead the Consul to a Virgin before which a perpetual candle burns:

Mescal tears came to the Consul's eyes, and he remembered
sometime during last night's debauch going with Dr. Vigil to a
church in Quauhnahuac he didn't know, with sombre tapestries,
and strange votive pictures, a compassionate Virgin floating in
the gloom, to whom he prayed, with muddily beating heart, he
might have Yvonne again. . . . "She is the Virgin for those who
have nobody with," the doctor told him. . . . "And for mariners
on the sea." . . . Now the Consul made this Virgin the other who
had answered his prayer and as they stood in silence before her,
he prayed again. . . . "Please let Yvonne have her dream—dream?
—of a new life with me—please let me believe that all that is not
an abominable self-deception," he tried. . . . "I have sunk low. Let
me sink lower still, that I may know the truth. Teach me to love
again, to love life." That wouldn't do either . . . "Let me truly
suffer. Give me back my purity, the knowledge of the Mysteries,
that I have betrayed and lost.—Let me be truly lonely, that I may
honestly pray. Let us be happy again somewhere, if it's only

together, if it's only out of this terrible world. Destroy the
world!" he cried in his heart.[289]

Here then the Consul's Faustian inability to achieve grace now
also becomes fictional "reality" rather than metaphor. Conversely, the reference to "mariners on the sea," while strengthening the Odysseus evocation, might finally suggest a wholly
new analogy for the concept—and particularly in conjunction
with the second of the Racine quotations, that of the "winds
asleep," etc. Several times, when the Consul entertains visions
in which things are going well for him, they are characterized by
the presence of wind—and vice versa. In passing, unquoted
here, there has also been a recent declaration that the barranca
near the Farolito reminds him of "Kubla Khan." Since he is
already an "ancient mariner" in more ways than one, and with
his own albatross of guilt, we might sooner or later connect him
with Coleridge's as well. In fact one of Lowry's longer stories,
about a voyage, makes use of Coleridgean marginalia throughout—and it is perhaps distantly relevant that the epigraph to
"The Ancient Mariner" comes from Thomas Burnet, or again,
that Coleridge once attempted to transpose some of the *Telluris
Theoria Sacra* into verse. Even prototypal "influences," as it
were, interlock.

Meanwhile the Consul's plea that he might "sink lower still"
gives us a first direct verbalization of that recurrent theme—sin
before redemption—while his "lost knowledge of the Mysteries," already performing minor service in the Homeric apparatus, on its broadest level would again imply the repudiation of
his essential "power" for life—what Laruelle has seen as a potential "great force for good." But also demanding attention is
the Consul's declaration that his "other prayer" of the night
before has been answered, i.e., by Yvonne's return, like her
forthcoming "assumption" again a proposition broached without qualification. The subject of Lowry's own "belief" will be
discussed later; but even in passing, meanwhile, the Consul's cry
for happiness if "only out of this terrible world" must be noted
as an echo of Señora Gregorio's mystical vision of the pair
"laughing together in some kernice place . . . Far away."

This endless "postponement" of discussion is hardly deliberate, again being an indication, even this late along in Lowry's
text, of how much must be held in mind *throughout* for a properly
spatial reading of the book. Indeed, the above passage illus-
trates the point on yet a different level. Far earlier in the day,
the Consul has recalled this same drunken night with Dr. Vigil,
remembering a visit to the doctor's office—"macabre with its
pictures of ancient Spanish surgeons . . . roaring with laughter
as they performed inquisitorial operations"[137]—but the episode
of the church has been out of his mind completely. Thus, a
hundred and fifty pages later, the sudden polar recollection.
More than simply completing a picture the reader cannot have
known to be incomplete, it must jolt him into a realization of the
intensity of the Consul's experience—or of Lowry's art.

The motif of dead children is newly adumbrated when Cervantes produces a photograph of one, "lying in a coffin"—the
gesture is typically Mexican—though the subject must now take
on still darker tone insofar as both of the Racine evocations
themselves reek of infanticide. Athaliah puts to death the children of the House of David, and not only is the girl Iphegenia
sacrificed, but the whole bloody saga of the *Oresteia* grows out
of an earlier murder of children and the curse upon Agamemnon's father Atreus.

On the other hand, the same gesture makes a different point
entirely. Where the Consul repeatedly fails on a more sophisticated level to "communicate" with such as Yvonne and Hugh,
as in the case of Señora Gregorio a long-standing empathy with
Cervantes is here implicit. "What magnetism drew these quaking ruined creatures into his orbit?" The same question might
be asked at the end, when two peasants—both of them strangers
—offer to aid him at risk to themselves.

Then again climb also, as Hugh and Yvonne are overheard
talking about Hugh's notion of an attempt at Popocatepetl. At
the moment, the Consul thinks of the idea as "having the significance of a lifetime together," but the symbolism shifts abruptly
when he next hears: "—at midnight, at the Hotel Fausto!"
Hugh's relish over the juxtaposition is understandable, though
the line itself may not be; Lowry simply means that climbers

intending a one-day trek frequently set out in the middle of the night.

When the others finally join him where he sits "innocent, drinkless in a booth," the Consul is forced to think of "the supper at Emmaeus . . . trying to disguise his distant mescal voice"—i.e., the Consul is now perhaps dead sitting down, or has been once more "entombed." Lowry spells Emmaus as quoted, however, perhaps intending a pun on yet another supper, that at the hut of the swineherd Eumaeus where Odysseus reveals his identity to Telemachus upon his return to Ithaca. In the King James "Emmaus" Jesus pronounces: "Ought not Christ to have suffered these things, and to enter into his glory?" —again the theme of trial before resurrection only now voiced.

With climb still in his mind the Consul next recalls his first meeting with Yvonne in Granada: "Gardens, gardens, gardens everywhere . . . and up, up, now they were climbing themselves . . . to the Moorish tomb on the extreme summit of the hill; here they plighted their troth."[292] If only in the past then, the symbolism of the ascent of the Mountain of Purgatory also now gains its worldly counterpart; once, at least, Eden was. And this, incidentally, in a Spain which here emerges in polar opposition to *itself,* so to speak, after its usage as a symbol of political disturbance. (Typically, however: "gardens everywhere"—but also a "tomb.")

Then instantly the larger antithetical note: "In how many glasses, how many bottles had he hidden himself, since then alone?" And yet again the reflexive balance across a hundred pages, since the Consul has earlier thought: "Ah, in how many rooms, upon how many studio couches . . . had they found their own love, their marriage . . .?"[201]

Whereupon a new transitional ellipsis: " . . . Cave of the Winds, seat of all great decisions . . . sanctuary bought for a penny or nothing." Only gradually do we come to understand precisely what "seat" the Consul is talking about (or what "winds"): "The toilet was all of grey stone, and looked like a tomb—even the seat was cold stone." (Actually, the British colloquialism "spending a penny" means to use a bathroom.) Since the man is inordinately drunk again, or still, it is now that voices out of the past will appear in conjunction with his own, or with those of Hugh and Yvonne from over a partition. In fact the full scene is not unlike the much shorter one in Chapter II where Yvonne hears Weber from an adjoining room, if with the added complication that the Consul also reads from a tourist folder. In any case what Hugh has elsewhere described as an "absolute dislocation of time" now happens in subjective narrative fact.

By virtue of its "frozen" or muralistic aspect, the passage will perhaps invite comparison with that more elaborate "timeless" scheme in the opening section of *The Sound and the Fury;* but since Lowry does not "waste" references, we are perhaps safest in recalling the Consul's personal selection of books and looking to Spinoza here. For the latter, any sort of psychological dependency upon an apprehension of events as past, or as coming, is contrary to reason: "Insofar as the mind conceives of a thing under the dictate of reason, it is effected equally whether the idea be of a thing present, past, or future." Only recently have we seen Yvonne's consciousness impinged upon "actively" by past events, and to all intents and purposes Lowry's repeated insistence upon occult possibility lends the future corresponding weight as well—though indeed, there will also be much talk of "eternity" in the pages that follow. Thus then a fluid dialectic of time among the many other balances, which is to say a view of life *sub specie eternitatis,* or with the ultimate of timeless objectivity—in effect the logical metaphysical correlate for the mythic perspective which also voids all common chronology. But the Consul summarizes the concept himself: "Perhaps there was no time either, in this stone retreat. Perhaps this was the eternity that he'd been making so much fuss about."[294]

But Spinoza's larger ontology is equally relevant to Lowry's approach. In seeing the human mind as part of what he names "an eternal mode of thinking," Spinoza is forced to conclude that thoughts themselves are finally somehow indestructible—a man's moment of consciousness remains part of nature's endless current. In an oblique way then we circle back to the Jungian idea of the collective unconscious, not quite the same thing, and equally hypothetical—but equally germane to the mythic novelist.

But before such complications are intimated the Consul manages to recall that the meal itself had "started well": at the arrival of the clam chowder he had proclaimed, "Dangerous Clam Magoo." (In the Service poem, Dan McGrew is shot by someone not only "crazed with hooch," but who has also "lived in hell." The McGrew fits.) Soon enough, however, and with an excruciating degree of alcoholic "truth," the Consul finds need to wonder: "Why was he here? Why was he always more or less, here?" He also decides that he "would have been glad of a mirror, to ask himself that question," though in a previously unmentioned mythic way the mirror is already at hand. Endlessly sighing "Alas, alas," Echo grieves to death over Narcissus's inability, like the Consul's own, to feel love, and Narcissus is punished by being made to die for adoration of his reflection in a pool. Regarding the "ism" alone, the Consul has once summed up by speaking of "this dreadful tyranny of self," and of course it can be said that he is pursuing his own image, and death, in drink. More to the point, the Consul smokes a brand of cigarettes called "Alas," and in his garden earlier: "The emptiness . . . filled with whispers: *alas, alas.* "[136]

It is next that the Consul does his brooding about eternity, and a passing paraphrase of Svidrigailov, regarding its likeness to "a bath house in the country full of spiders," may add a strain of Dostoevskian guilt to his prototypal bloodline. In the following single page, in fact, the word "pulquería" appears three times, this meaning an inexpensive cantina, but also being the name of Raskolnikov's mother. Lowry himself points this out in the letter to Jonathan Cape, adding that "it should doubtless not be taken too seriously"—but its very repetition must indicate the Consul's own abstract attention to it.

The Tlaxcalan tourist folder materializes at this time, in lieu finally of the "stone," or perhaps lest the Consul forget where he is: "SEAT OF THE HISTORY OF THE CONQUEST." Also at hand is a railway and bus timetable, not the same one we have seen hours earlier, though the novel's own "schedule" is to be remarked as unchanged.

As the Consul studies the folder, certain phrases catch his attention, which Lowry repeats in italics—in effect, as once earlier, arranging that we "read" with the man. One of these phrases concerns Granada, which he has only now recalled, a preoccupation to cause trouble later. Another, by this point beginning to suggest "troubles" of a more remediable sort, refers to a park where there are "seats all over." And in the same pages an echo of Hugh's Aristotelian speculations might be taken as a hint at Lowry's own aims: "Its whole gives a sight of emotional majesty, *emotional majesty* without losing the tranquillity and rest appearance."[297]

Hugh is then heard describing the "Ejidal" to Yvonne, the "bank that advances money to finance collective effort in the villages," and it is now that the Indian is connected with work like that done by Juan Cerillo. Hugh can only guess at the possibility, but Yvonne mentions one such bank "just by Cortez Palace"—precisely where we may recall the Consul and Laruelle having seen the man with his "chinking" saddle-bags.

There follow several references in the folder to altars of "a churrigueresque (overloaded) style"—which the Cape letter admits may be taken as further Spanish colonial archetypes for *Under the Volcano* itself—and one to "the famous pulpit from where was preached in the New World, for first time, the Gospel," a concrete illustration of what, intending several larger meanings to be discussed shortly, the Consul has termed "intercourse" between cultures. The theme then turns political—after Hugh's sage comment that "I still don't think the fascists have any hold here"—when a chapel is described as that "where the Tlaxcaltecan Senators, for the first time, prayed to the Conqueror's God." There has been an earlier reference to the baptism of these senators—"being their God-Fathers the conqueror Hernán Cortés and several of his Captains"—and when Cervantes next appears the Consul sees him as "the godson of the Conqueror himself." In parallel reduction the warrior-king Moctezuma materializes as the brand-name of a beer, and the conquest itself has boiled down to "the final chapter, the exploitation of everybody by everybody else"—an ultimate peladoism.

The Consul's private voices, already intruding, now take charge completely, totally disjointed in their order of intrusion though all readily identifiable, echoing such unrelated individuals as an insane man quoted in the Lee Maitland passage, the English Samaritan, Quincey, etc., along with the Consul repeating himself on assorted topics. Despite the seeming chaos of the several pages, however, if the individual lines are read in terms of their established symbolic associations—a Blackstone allusion implying isolation, Guanajuato again recalling the abyss—it becomes evident that Lowry has newly cited most of his principal themes in passing.

A more conventional narrative order returns when the Consul does, although if anything the man is more remote than ever (he has continued to drink mescal in the "stone retreat"). At once, he finds himself having a "beautiful" vision of Tlaxcala, "in many respects . . . like Granada"—i.e., like that other Eden—in which everything is "white," "one could drink forever on credit," the wind is "blowing." But since the Consul also perceives that "there was nobody there, no one," and visualizes a clock which "itself was timeless," he is obviously still concerned with eternity here, in this case that eternity he has imagined for himself and Yvonne "only together . . . out of this terrible world"—perhaps meaning the Eden again *to be*.

Then the Consul discovers that he is talking about the three of them actually going to Tlaxcala. By this time his condition is so evident—despite what he believes the secrecy in his recent "closet" drinking—that Yvonne is crying. This fact the Consul contrives to misinterpret completely:

> Did they suspect? He had adjured Cervantes to silence; had the Tlaxcaltecan, unable to resist it, betrayed him? What had they really been talking about while he was outside? The Consul . . . had not been away very long (he thought), no more than seven minutes all told . . . Et tu Bruto! The Consul could feel his glance at Hugh becoming a cold look of hatred.[303]

Here then certain of the larger "betrayals," first Cervantes suspected of an act paralleling the betrayal by his "forebears" —Lowry has switched from his earlier "Tlaxcalans" to the more historical-sounding "Tlaxcaltecans" of the folder—and after which Caesar. Actually, however, Brutus has been in the chapter from the start, nor is "Bruto" here but an incidental transposition into Spanish; in the same early paragraph where the cock evokes betrayal by Eve and Helen, Cervantes calls the bird itself "un bruto."

Through what he considers a "constructive effort," the Consul changes the subject—not that anyone has been saying a word —but he remains in a world of his own. As a political argument no more than begins: "See here, old bean . . . to have against you Franco, or Hitler, is one thing, but to have Actinium, Argon, Beryllium, Dysprosium . . . "[304]

Not without cause, then, has the man elsewhere seen himself "shattered by the very forces of the universe," these being the natural elements. Indeed, the Aeschylean point is made again as his recitation concludes: "Thunder suddenly sprang again outside with a clap and bang, slithering." Nor are most of those he names chosen at random. Argon for example occurs in *volcanic* gasses. Niobium and Tantalum are derived from their obvious mythic sources. Palladium again recalls Homer, since Odysseus is one of those who carries off the image of Pallas Athena sacred to the Trojans, a Palladium. Tellurium, in context, will recall the Burnet title. Uranium is Uranus, personification of the heavens and also suggestive of Urania, muse of Yvonne's astronomy. Ruthenium, from Ruthenia, Russia, ties in with those the Consul mentions last—Europium, Germanium, Columbium—returning us to the political argument at hand. And while its derivation will not apply, Samarium needs no comment whatsoever.

The universe to the contrary, however, the political discussion pushes on. By way of building an analogy for communism's position in the modern world, Hugh makes use of Matthew Arnold's essay on Marcus Aurelius, in which early Christianity, in the eyes of the Roman emperors, is seen as constituting "a vast secret society, with obscure aims of political and social subversion," this for reasons of being "a new spirit in the Roman world, destined to act in that world as its dissolvent."[305] Hugh is never quite permitted to complete his point, but even as it stands the comparison is less felicitous than he supposes— references to the "Conqueror's God" already having implied judgment on certain of Christianity's own predilections.

Although he is to come back to the subject with a vengeance, the Consul is first bored here, then distracted. He tries again to promote the visit to Tlaxcala, this time inadvertently bespeaking new prophecy to Hugh also: "Tlaxcala is on the way to Vera Cruz, the true cross . . . This is the last time we'll be seeing you . . ." Mention is made of the superstition concerning three on a match, ironically heeded—though the infernal machine will scarcely be restrained by any such paltry obeisance. And then:

> . . . it seemed to the Consul that, over the coffee, he had, all at once, begun to talk soberly, brilliantly, and fluently again. . . . And the Consul was talking about the Indo-Aryans, the Iranians and the sacred fire, Agni, called down from heaven, with his firesticks, by the priest. He was talking of soma, Amrita, the nectar of immortality, praised in one whole book of the Rig Veda —*bhang*, which was, perhaps, much the same thing as mescal itself. . . . The Consul was talking about the Vedic gods, who were not properly anthropomorphised, whereas Popocatepetl and Ixtaccihuatl . . . In any event the Consul, once more, was talking about the sacred fire, the sacrificial fire, of the stone soma press, the sacrifices of cakes and oxen and horses . . . how the drinking rites, simple at first, became more and more complicated as time went on, the ritual having to be carried out with meticulous care, since one slip—*tee hee!*—would render the sacrifice invalid. . . . He was talking of the immolation of wives, and the fact that . . . in Taxila, at the mouth of the Khyber Pass, the widow of a childless man might contract a Levirate marriage with her brother-in-law. The Consul found himself claiming to see an obscure relation, apart from any purely verbal one, between Taxila and Tlaxcala itself: for when that great pupil of Aristotle's—Yvonne—Alexander, arrived in Taxila, had he not Cortez-like already been in communication with Ambhi, Taxila's king, who likewise had seen in an alliance with a foreign conqueror, an excellent chance of undoing a rival, in this case not Moctezuma but the Paurave monarch, who ruled the country between the Jhelma and the Chenab?[307]

Most of the specifically "anthropological" aspects of all this will be discussed at the end of the present chapter. Of itself, the elaboration on the theme of intercourse between cultures is even more detailed in Lowry than as quoted here, while too, the religious connotations in the Consul's drink must now be seen to find a parallel in Vedic rites. The question of "one slip" equates again with the need for "equilibrium" in matters occult, the giggle of course apropos of the mescal now causing one, and the equation between mescal and soma verifies in turn that

between mescal and mescaline, soma itself causing hallucinations (it is now thought to have been a mushroom derivative).
And all of course again becomes "sacramental."

The reference to the anthropomorphism of the two volcanoes
is not new either, since we have already seen them described as
"that image of the perfect marriage," though in the next chapter
Yvonne will enlarge the concept essentially as it exists in Mexican lore: "Popocatepetl himself was . . . the dreamer: the fires
of his warrior's love, never extinct in the poet's heart, burned
eternally for Ixtaccihuatl, whom he had no sooner found than
lost, and whom he guarded in her endless sleep."[318]

Mention of Aristotle by name was due sooner or later, but
more important at that point is Lowry's equation between Alexander and Cortez, certainly a clue that he intends other such
parallels to be discerned. But the same equation must also then
again imply history itself as cyclic: events repeat on this scale
exactly as Lowry insists they do in man's individual existence.
Within a few pages, in fact, the political argument will swing
toward just this point of view—or more properly, toward Os-
wald Spengler's. Again by adhering to what might be termed the
principle of never-a-superfluous-reference, we will have had to
hold Spengler in mind from as early as Chapter IV, where Hugh
mentions him in passing. At the time, Hugh is talking of something trivial, and obviously learned secondhand, since a moment
later he quotes *the Consul* as having suggested that "a sort of
'freezing' of culture" will follow a fascist victory in Spain—i.e.,
unaware that the latter has to have been reading *The Decline of
the West* himself, in which such rigidity of cultural form is what
Spengler allows the name of civilization. It is during such "freezing" that Spengler sees the rise of totalitarianism and/or coloni-
alism amid spiritual decay—precisely the sort of "civilization"
Lowry presents in the majority of his contemporary references,
if not to say in the Rome of Marcus Aurelius, the Spain of
Cortez, or, to come full cycle, the Greece of Alexander. Or, by
implication in each case, before the Fall.

But the reference to Alexander is suggestive in another way
—and not only because the man drank himself to death. Alexander crossed the Himalayas in 327 B.C.—here then the first
significant occurrence of that very "intercourse" with which

Lowry remains preoccupied. In point of fact, however, he takes
the concept back further still through his reference to the "Indo-
Aryans," these the northern migrants into India of the second
millennium B.C., roughly contemporary with the Hellenic invad-
ers of Greece; the presumed common origin of the two groups
supplies a key to the more seminal kind of interrelationship
between Vedic and Homeric traditions in which Lowry is really
interested. (Cf. his comment in the preface, quoted *supra,* about
"the origins of man.") Moreover Lowry has actually connected
these very Indo-Aryans with the Consul *directly,* when Hugh has
humorously suggested to himself that the man's limp might pass
as the result of "an old brush with Pathans." Simultaneously,
mention of the "Iranians" would imply the Parsees, displaced
survivors of the Persian followers of Zoroaster; thus an age-old
evocation of "illumination" also, since the latter worshipped fire
as a divinity—as their descendants still do today.

But the same fecund passage continues:

> . . . The Consul was talking, like Sir Thomas Browne, of Archime-
> des, Moses, Achilles, Methuselah, Charles V and Pontius Pilate.
> The Consul was talking furthermore of Jesus Christ, or rather of
> Yus Asaf who, according to Kashmiri legend, *was* Christ—Christ,
> who had, after being taken down from the cross, wandered to
> Kashmir in search of the lost tribes of Israel, and died there, in
> Srinagar—[307]

The Consul finds abruptly that there is "a slight mistake," and
that he has "not uttered a single word." Nonetheless Lowry has
again uttered several. Later, the Kashmiri legend he summarizes
will serve to augment the final detailed Christ equation, while
implying still more "intercourse"—nor is it quite chance that
the Consul himself has spent his boyhood in Kashmir (or that
Srinagar, built upon a system of causeways and canals very like
Moctezuma's Tenochtitlán, was for centuries called "Paradise
on Earth"). Meanwhile however, "like" Browne—yet another
man of obscure learning and mystic obsessions, believer in spirits and occult numerologies—the Consul is talking about whom?
The greatest of ancient mathematicians and natural philosophers; the spiritual leader of a wandering people and giver of

their unchanging moral law; an invincible Homeric warrior, save for the single "flaw" of the heel; a figuratively speaking ageless man; the king of Spain at the time of the conquest of Mexico and history's greatest era of expansion and colonization; the procurator of Judea, *and* of Samaria, at the time of the crucifixion—and finally of the Messiah. For the point of which, Laruelle's own question might again prove relevant: "What, after all, was a Consul that one was mindful of him?"

But the sheer weight of the passage raises an altogether different sort of question. Very little of this erudition is intrusive, since it has long since proved to *be* the man; yet there is something rare here. By virtue of their essential passion or charisma, a certain few novelistic figures—fewer than one imagines—might be said to convey a quality akin to genius: Stavrogin, for example. But almost never, in such portraits, is there evidence of corresponding intellect. Ivan Karamazov's vision of the Grand Inquisitor is an isolated exception, more an expression of creative imagination than of learning, however. Wyatt Gwyon in *The Recognitions* demands mention, as might Stephen Dedalus or certain characters in Mann; but is there any "range" comparable to the Consul's? Symbolic contrivances beside the point then, the latter must be seen to represent modern man because of what he does know, which is all we mean by modern. And when he displays that awareness most conspicuously, as in the present scene, and then finds that he has "not uttered a single word," his terrible impotence becomes our own—as will his destruction.

Thus it follows that the Cabbalistic symbolism of equilibrium transcends itself also; civilization too remains astride that "fine American-style highway" which leads into Quauhnahuac on the first page of the novel and comes out "a goat track." Entire *ages* have been categorized by the adjective Dante applies to the wood.

Dismissing his protracted excursus as "all an illusion," the Consul simultaneously finds it an illusion "out of which, at last, at long last, at this very instant, emerged, rounded and complete, order." And order it is: "The act of a madman or a drunkard, old bean . . . or of a man labouring under violent excitement seems less free and more inevitable to the one who knows the mental condition of the man who performed the action, and more free and less inevitable to the one who does not know it."[308]

Re-enter Tolstoy: some two hundred pages after we have been told that the Consul once learned certain "philosophical" portions of *War and Peace* by heart, one such appears. (Actually, it has been announced in advance by a new reference to Napoleon's "twitch," also recalled from the same novel.) On the surface the Consul seems to be talking politics again, referring first to certain unknown factors in the case of the Indian. But then he broaches the subject of *ignoratio elenchi:*

" . . . Or the fallacy of supposing a point proved or disproved by argument which proves or disproves something not at issue. Like these wars. For it seems to me that almost everywhere in the world these days there has long since ceased to be anything fundamental to man at issue at all . . . Ah, you people with ideas! . . . All this, for instance, about going to fight for Spain . . . and poor little defenceless China! Can't you see there's a sort of determinism in the fate of nations? They all seem to get what they deserve in the long run."[309]

As ever, references to "people with ideas" mean that our point of view is William Blackstone's, though the connection would appear unnecessary for an understanding that the Consul is talking about himself here; in fact, before deciding that entire nations "get what they deserve," sitting in the bathroom and contemplating the shabby inevitability which repeatedly puts him *there,* he has concluded: "It is what I deserve . . . It is what I am." But thus again the intricacy: the fallacy of *ignoratio elenchi* is not only at work in the surface political argument, but at another depth altogether, which even Hugh finally perceives. Protesting against interference with history's "worthless stupid course," the Consul insists that the "heroic resistance put up by poor little defenceless peoples" has nothing to do with the "survival of the human spirit." When Hugh accuses him of talking nonsense, the Consul demands: "Why can't people mind their own damned business!" To which Hugh: "Or say what they mean?"[310]

What the Consul does mean then becomes explicit beyond recall: "You're all the same, all of you, Yvonne, Jacques, you, Hugh, trying to interfere with other people's lives, interfering, interfering . . . " And when he reaches a point which he himself sees as "vulgar," still another abstraction turns flesh, in this case Tolstoy's own on free will and necessity: "Was the Consul saying this? Must he say it?—It seemed he must."[312]

But then something perhaps even more subtle. Tolstoy speaks of a madman *or* a drunkard. Even before he quotes the former word, the Consul thinks of his long digression as "a whirling cerebral chaos." At a moment when the discussion remains at least ostensibly political, he starts to speak of Rousseau, with Lowry pointedly indicating this time that Jean Jacques and "not douanier" is meant, though the Consul's statement is interrupted and fails to make its point, doubtless something about Rousseau's own aversion to "interference"; but like so many figures alluded to elsewhere, this Rousseau, in his own acute paranoia, went mad. Leaving the others the Consul then finds himself in a room where "matter was disjunct: a doorknob was standing a little way out from the door. A curtain floated in by itself, unfastened, unattached to anything," and after this, Macbeth-like, he endures the sensation that the curtain has come "to strangle him." And when he is in the process of departing altogether, announcing that he has no interest in Yvonne's offer "of a sober and non-alcoholic Paradise," suddenly he voices one of those clichés which, in Lowry, always somehow means exactly what it says: "But now I've made up my melodramatic little mind, what's left of it."[314]

Since we also read that "an orderly little clock . . . called him back to his senses," it would appear that the Consul has been briefly "out of time" in the most absolute sense of all—and in Ophelia's tavern at that.

But more. During the Lee Maitland passage, the Consul once recalls a certain "Suspension Bridge." When he does, the word suspension is then repeated in the rush of his thoughts, set off by dashes, italicized, followed by an exclamation point. Here, when the Consul repudiates the "non-alcoholic Paradise," he proclaims additionally that "far from wanting it, thank you very much, on the contrary I choose—" He starts to say Tlaxcala, which is still on his mind, but doesn't, and then the sentence hangs unfinished through two paragraphs before he says: "Hell." During the hiatus, his state is such that images from the chaotic Lee Maitland incident reappear, and again the word catches him up: "Suspension!" Thus Lowry has at least four concentric wheels turning at once: the Consul's words hang in literal suspension; he himself wavers in this suspension of momentary insanity; the question of Cabbalistic "equilibrium" is surely at hand; and nothing less than the crucial thematic polarity of the novel waits in its own ultimate suspension as well: Hell or Paradise, both deliberately named.

Meanwhile this from Swedenborg: "For anything to have existence there must be equilibrium in all things. . . . There is a perpetual equilibrium between heaven and hell." And from the Lowry novella, *Lunar Caustic:* "Many who are supposed to be mad . . . are simply people who perhaps once saw, however confusedly, the necessity for change in themselves, for *rebirth.*"

And thus too then, with Beatrice denied, salvation repudiated, one last transformation from metaphor to reality becomes inevitable: "He was running . . . running toward the forest, which was growing darker and darker." Or to put an end to a more literal suspension in the same breath: "He would take the path to Parián, to the Farolito."

As sheer drama alone, and despite all such manipulations, the impact of these last pages is overwhelming—though still other secondary matters intrude. Accusing Yvonne of denying "the only natural and good function you have," the Consul is actually echoing something she herself has contemplated in regard to her acting ambitions, which "suffered in some sense from the dislocation of the functions . . . of womanhood itself." Describing her infidelities in terms of an alleged "hundred or so other ninneyhammers with gills like codfish and veins like racehorses," he is not only alluding to the suitors of Penelope but repeating imagery very similar to that which has entered his mind at the sight of Laruelle in the shower. And in making such accusations to start with he is contrasting yet another episode of several hundred pages before, that in which he has the illusion, lying in the road, of speaking "forgiveness" to Hugh.

Or again on a different plane, after an interruption the Consul at one point begins: "As if he plucked up kisses by the roots and then laid his leg over her thigh and sighed. What an uncommon time you two must have had . . . "[313] An accusation of adultery, even if years past—what else to borrow from but *Othello*? In fact the Consul also uses Iago's line describing Desdemona and Cassio as being "prime as goats, hot as monkeys, as salt as wolves in pride"—and none of this following by too many pages the memory of betrothal at the "Moorish" tomb.

Meanwhile it is just before his departure that the Consul confirms certain of Laruelle's suspicions by announcing flatly: "I love hell." The notion of insanity is also then newly stressed when it develops that, even as he runs, he is "calling back to them crazily," but with the difference now that "the queer thing was, he wasn't quite serious."[314] Thus a final paradox likewise, that of the absurd to be sensed even in tragedy—what Yeats implies when he writes that "Hamlet and Lear are gay." The Consul has here turned his back on love, brotherhood, redemption, and is plunging willy-nilly to his death, while, in permitting him this other insight, Lowry must be seen as "out of time" himself—viewing his own creation *sub specie eternitatis,* or in the most profound meaning of aesthetic detachment.

After all of this, meanwhile, some of the more *exceptionally* elusive threads in the novel, often hinted at throughout, can perhaps finally be drawn together.

In Lowry's eighth chapter, when his three central characters are setting out for Tomalín, the Consul makes an erudite pun on their mode of transportation: "Quod semper, quod ubique, quod ab omnibus." The quotation is taken from the fifth-century *Commonitorium* of St. Vincent of Lerins, as it were a definition of Catholicity: "What is always, what is everywhere, what is by all people believed" (Lowry omits the "creditum est"). Even by that juncture, however, it must stand to reason that any "catholicity" Lowry himself has in mind will be uncapitalized.

Stressing the point, in fact, he uses the phrase only a moment after Hugh remarks the archaic holiday festival with its Indian dancers, a sound of "clashing machetes," etc.

But a considerably broader degree of that catholicity becomes evident in the present chapter. When the meal itself begins, the Consul does a rather different sort of punning on the faulty printing of their menus. "Madre? . . . What's this madre here? —You like to eat your mother, Yvonne?" Cervantes explains that "badre," a type of fish, is meant—whereupon the Consul next asks Hugh if he would like "to wait for the fish that dies."[291]

Now on one plane, and following closely after references to the supper at Emmaus, some of this symbolism is still loosely "Christian," at least insofar as the fish was one of the earliest secret symbols for Christ. (Read acrostically in Greek, the initial letters of "Jesus Christ, the Son of God, Savior," form the word for fish.) But since as a life-symbol the fish has long represented such as Buddha, or Vishnu's first avatar Matsya, among other gods "that die," the allusion can scarcely be restricted, and all the less so in view of the Consul's subsequent digression concerning anthropomorphism, ritual sacrifice, drinking rites, immolation—that passage, indeed, which reads like nothing so much as a page out of a comparative anthropology text.

On its own terms the notion of the eating of the god is itself one to which Lowry's "omnibus" line might be applied, since, as Sir James Frazer spent a lifetime documenting, it lies at the heart of a manifestly universal primitive ritual. A priest-king whose powers are on the wane, and whose decline is believed to affect the lands, is symbolically torn apart and then eaten so that his magic may pass on to others—or, as a Freudian would have it, that guilt for his murder may be diffused among the tribe. Nor is the practice restricted to "primitive" belief—witness its residue in the partaking of the Host in Christian ritual.

But naturally such rituals gradually metamorphose into a cognate scheme of myth; again as Frazer indicates, man may attempt to control nature with his own poor magic originally, but a realization of his impotence will finally lead him to impute that control to higher powers. But a more salient point than this, at least for purposes of literary criticism, is that a substantial portion of man's literature is closely if unconsciously molded on these ancient ritual forms. So deep runs the grain in human experience—or mayhap, in the "collective unconscious"—that even so relatively sophisticated a writer as Euripides will follow it unknowingly.

Though it is doubtless rash to lay *anything* in Lowry to chance, by way of exercise the point can be illustrated in *Under the Volcano* itself. In Frazer, a classic example of the universal ritual pattern is that of the Osiris story: the Egyptian sun god and great educator Osiris is envied by a brother who desires his throne, and who chops his body into pieces; his sister-bride Isis goes seeking him, and finds all portions save the phallus, which has been cast into the Nile. After the "rivalry" between Lowry's own sun god (*or* educator) and his brother in the present chapter, when the former is subsequently being "torn apart," or in any case literally being made a scapegoat, Yvonne will simultaneously be very actively hunting for him. Before he is thrown into the barranca the Consul will also have heard waters flowing there—no Nile-cum-phallus perhaps, but when he first puns on the anthropological questions at dinner he happens to add a bawdy remark about "onans in soup." Furthermore while popular versions put it that Osiris is hacked into fourteen pieces, the most careful researcher among ancient historians, Diodorus of Sicily, says twenty-six, the exact number of "elements" the Consul has here chosen to list. (Ultimately, a tree grows from the tomb of Osiris, embodying him, as trees will "close over" the Consul at novel's end also.)

Exclusive of Frazer's own work, meanwhile—and again in a realm of literary interest—the most famous investigation into these ancient wellsprings is perhaps Jessie L. Weston's explicitly titled *From Ritual to Romance,* dealing with evidences of ritual origin in the various narratives of the Holy Grail. Our familiarity with Weston, of course, arises in good part from Eliot's acknowledged use of her insights in "The Waste Land." And where Lowry in turn has been seen to make occasional oblique "use" of Eliot, the truth is that such allusions may in fact have been to the Grail quest by way of Weston herself.

To begin, obviously, with knighthood: as early as in Chapter I, Laruelle is described as "a knight of old," replete with shield and scrip. The picture is satirical, though *any* prototypal figure must lose stature as reincarnated into an unheroic age—which is indeed much of the point behind such usages in Eliot. And thus Hugh, then, with his perhaps ambiguous yet undeviating sense of "code": Hemingway's are not the only contemporary figures who mourn the romantic order of medieval chivalry. Or again Hugh, who is first seen with a gun on his hip, who wears cowboy clothes—and who wrestles a bull in lieu of any other contemporary "joust." (While as for the Consul, perhaps: "Miniver coughed, and called it fate,/ And kept on drinking.")

It is probably unnecessary to supplement this aspect of the scheme through analogy with individual Arthurian figures, though one might recall Tristan's adultery, or Launcelot's—viz., with the wife of "our ruddy monarch"—while too, certain of Hugh's early adventures will readily equate to the prototypal bumpkinism of the young Percival. But a connection too obvious to go without mention does arise in the peculiar architecture of Laruelle's house, which Lowry designs not only with towers, observation posts, and spiral staircases, but also with battlements, crenellated miradors that he compares with bartizans, merlons, machicolations, etc. Only the moat is missing.

But the pattern becomes infinitely more detailed in the realm of the quest for the Grail itself—or, rather, through parallel with its intrinsic ritual forms as outlined in Weston. Items:

—A basic characteristic of the romances is of course that of blight upon the land, no water, no renewal. The king himself, called the Fisher King, is ill or languishing, a concept often euphemistic for sterility, and he is often maimed. We have already had innumerable symbols for the blight upon Thebes in Lowry's Oedipus scheme, and by extension for the blight upon the modern world. The Consul has been symbolically "sterile" in his attempt at intimacy with Yvonne. The Consul limps. (Mentioned *supra* has been the Consul's reference to "the metamorphoses of dying and reborn hallucinations;" in "Through the Panama," Lowry allows his narrator to put it less subtly: "God save the Fisher King.")

—The task of the Grail hero is to restore the land. Laruelle states explicitly that Hugh dreams of "changing the world . . . through his actions," and in Chapter XI he himself will sing a song in which youth is exhorted "para un nuevo mundo hacer," to make a new world. Further, the hero is younger than the king, the hero begins as the king's guest.

—If the king himself is not ill, he is then represented by a knight on a bier—cf. the dying Indian. (Via equation with Juan Cerillo the Indian's own "knighthood" is also manifest.)

—There is usually a "doctor" or medicine man in the narrative; compare Dr. Vigil, although here the Consul's initiation into the "mysteries" is more likely apposite. But certain of the heroes themselves are said to be healers, particularly Gawain—who once miraculously cures a fellow knight *wounded at the roadside.*

—The quest is almost always marked by episodes in a perilous chapel. Witness the "sombre" church recalled in the present chapter—to which Dr. Vigil in fact carries a gun. (The Consul's explanation of this last is enigmatic: "Dr. Vigil always went armed to Red Cross Balls." But then a red cross was often the shield emblem of the Grail knight.) Better, witness the Farolito, formerly a *monastery,* with its rooms where "diabolical plots must be hatched," etc.

—The quest is also pervaded by an aura of mystery frequently involving strange voices. Moreover the Grail itself is believed to appear, though unseen, behind a supernaturally guided veil—*vide* the curtain floating "by itself . . . unattached to anything."

—There is often a motif of wailing women—though it may be assumed they wail something other than "Borrrrraaacho."

As indicated, what this weight of ritual material implies about the old romances themselves is that where a Malory or a Chrétien de Troyes is writing on the surface about a profoundly Christian subject, he casts his narrative in a form man has eternally adopted to invoke fertility of the land—and which, rather more consciously, Lowry has chosen to incorporate into his own "romance." But not that Lowry in any way limits himself to the single pattern; the Rig Veda, for example, which the Consul keeps on his shelves and mentions here in regard to "drinking rites," is of demonstrably ritual origin on its own part:

We have drunk Soma; we have become immortal.
We have gone to the light; we have found the gods.

—VIII, 48

Thus any number of new relationships begin to unfold. The
Consul has only now referred to Agni, the Hindu god of fire,
and to a "nectar of immortality," but since Soma, capitalized,
is a moon god, his drink then connects not only with "light"
but with lunar aspects of his occultism also. In a footnote to
the aforementioned "Thirty-five Mescals in Cuautla," Lowry
himself points out this latter association, but adding the obvious fact that the moon in turn "controls vegetation"—i.e.,
thereby completing the circle in again equating drink itself to
fertility ritual.

Much more might be pursued. The Consul christens Hugh's
bull "Nandi"; Nandi being an embodiment of Siva, Hugh is then
wrestling a god in the classic manner of ritual combat. Normally
such ceremonies, initially communal, at last become mystery
cults restricted to the few—precisely those "secret societies" in
the time of Marcus Aurelius also mentioned herein. Mithra, for
example, wrestled a bull, or was imitated in so doing, in the
secret cults *most particularly* prevalent in Rome—not to add that
he was the son of Ahura-Mazda, god of *light,* chief warrior in the
battle against the *prince of darkness,* etc., etc.

Nor are such complexities anything less than Lowry's point.
Of itself, the Grail parallel adds one further mythic dimension
to his narrative. But by reaching back beyond it to man's primal
modes of expression, with their inescapable parallels however
separate their origins in time or place, he affords that narrative
perhaps its most telling universality of all.

All of which might explain, too, why one of the few pieces of
classical music named in the novel is the *Sacre du Printemps*—
though it is also typical of Lowry that while spanning these time
gaps he simultaneously reminds us that they do not exist at all.
Masks, sword dances, food left in the cemeteries—not Babylon
in the era of Tammuz but Mexico, 1938. In fact the Day of the
Dead is a standard contemporary anthropological citation in
several regards. (To which we might add Lowry's use of the

Pathans and Parsees also; Hugh is wrong: the Jews are not "the only people *old* as oneself.")

Thematically, of course, we are back to rebirth again, in man's most urgent apprehension of the concept—the annual renewal of the maize. The first time the holiday is mentioned in the novel, Laruelle sees mourners moving among "trussed corn-stalks"—and on its own level the Oedipus analogy has bespoken the same ritual meaning throughout. In the more limited Grail parallel, as established, Hugh is the knight setting forth to redeem the dead land—en route for that matter to Vera Cruz, which it is worth note that Lowry has paused to translate. The Grail itself remains elusive, in Lowry's allegory no Galahad attains it. Yet it is not wholly beyond sight either; once indeed the Consul records that it has "gleamed on his soul." Nor is there too much irony in the fact that he is talking about a bottle, especially since he will later say of another that "it must have been Jesus who sent me this." The bottle *is* the Consul's Holy Chalice, through which he, at least, partakes of his "eternal sacrament"—becoming as one with his strange, or not so strange, gods.*

But there remain some additional, loosely "anthropological" matters:

—Working in the inescapable shadow of *The Plumed Serpent*, Lowry seems deliberately to minimize his references, but one can scarcely avoid being reminded of the Toltec divinity Quetzalcoatl—worshipped as a god of knowledge and as the spiritual teacher who civilized old Mexico. Briefly, the story is of a chaste king prompted by evil advisors (i.e., demons) who gets drunk (*sic*) and commits a carnal act (as will the Consul in Chapter XII). In penance, he dies voluntarily by fire and his heart rises to the

---

*Something of the same general catholicity in Lowry's life will be suggested by the postscript to a letter postmarked November 14, 1953: "I wrote this Tuesday night—yesterday—didn't find out till just now, Wednesday, to our great grief, Dylan is dead . . . We drank his health, poured a libation of gin to his memory and for some reason cut down a tree, likewise dead, and an old friend . . . There is no symbolic significance attached to the tree: unless one had felt as a reaction to the black news one had to do something exhilirating lifegiving deathdealing painful and useful at once. Selah."

heavens, associated thereafter with Venus as the morning star (q.v.). Quetzalcoatl is also a famous magician, wears a beard, has a twin brother who is his enemy, visits the underworld, spends four days in a *stone coffin,* and before his death promises to return —from the east. (Indeed, the bearded Cortez was believed by the Aztecs to be he, as were his horses thought supernatural beings.) The figure was most fervently esteemed in the town of Cholula, to which the Consul and Laruelle *both* recall having made a pilgrimage.

—In thinking about Cambridge earlier, Hugh mentions one John Cornford. Cornford was the first Englishman to die for the Loyalists. Also, however, he was the son of F. M. Cornford, who along with Frazer, Jane Ellen Harrison and others formed the so-called "Cambridge School" in classics and anthropology— the fount of all such comparative mytho-ritualistic readings, and whose influence would have been all-pervasive by the time Lowry himself attended the university. (The younger Cornford was also Darwin's great-grandson—to which no significance presumably need be attached.)

—Nothing Biblical can elude similar ritual interpretation. The original "Mene-Tekel-Peres" is translated by Daniel not only as a prophecy of Belshazzar's death—one more priest-king deposed—but of the division of his kingdom. As seen by the Consul on his own wall, it would then correlate with the historical falls noted, Caesar's, Moctezuma's, and finally that of the modern world. (And what the phrase is said to mean, of course, is that one has been weighed in the *balance* and found wanting.)

—No connection except the pleasantly verbal one exists between the Fisher King and Christ as "fisher of men," the Fisher King fishing simply because he is too ill or badly wounded to provide for his people in any other way. The Consul's own "wound" has already become analogous here, connected with that of Oedipus; but the decade-long suffering of Philoctetes gains new significance in this light, as does the "scar" of Odysseus, both figures becoming "redeemers" in their separate ways. More suggestive, perhaps, is that in the Wagnerian version of the Grail legend, Amfortas, the very keeper of the Grail, and one more "magician," suffers an incurable wound also.

—Thoughts of Wagner would again perhaps suggest Hugh as

Percival—Parsifal—the Innocent Fool and/or yet another Re-
deemer. A line not quoted herein, in which a swan "plummets
to earth," might announce his arrival on a Bayreuth stage.

—The god most frequently torn to pieces in Greek fertility
ritual was Dionysus—in fact Herodotus has it that *all* tragedy
represented his sufferings and rebirth, and was shrewd enough
to point out that his story is often identical with that of Osiris.
Worship of Dionysus occurred particularly at Delphi, which the
Greeks believed the center of the earth—where the Consul has
once considered himself seated. Indeed, the site of the temple
of the Delphic Oracle, source of all magic and prophecy, was
marked by a round *stone*. The word bacchanalia, from the
Roman version of such celebrations, is hardly alien here—and
of course Dionysus was the god of wine. (He was also incidentally a "horned" god.)

—Lowry's awareness of all of this has been long since documented via uncounted allusions in his text, but is further verified
in his Cape letter where he points out "added meaning" in
Chapter XI, in which Hugh and Yvonne search for the Consul,
for "anyone who knows anything of the Eleusinian mysteries."
The mysteries themselves—where Dionysus was also worshipped—are based upon the tale of Persephone, stolen into the
underworld by Pluto and thereafter sought desperately by her
mother Demeter; through the intervention of Zeus, it is decreed
that Persephone will spend part of the year below ground, part
above. Ergo, her annual resurrection is again coincidental with
the renewal of fertility. According to Frazer, the mysteries include torchlight processions, an all-night "vigil," the passing on
of occult knowledge, drinking from a holy chalice, etc. Most of
these symbols, already overly familiar, will be re-emphasized in
Chapter XI—along with a reference to nature "out-doing itself
in extravagant fructification."

—A picture once framed in Yvonne's consciousness, and to be
repeated in Chapter XI, of a "woman having hysterics . . . banging her fists upon the ground," would also then be solved by the
above—Yvonne becoming Demeter. (As noted, she has lost a
child in biographical fact; the weight of "dead children" symbolism throughout the novel will become extremely meaningful in
Lowry's final chapter.)

—Speaking of the Eleusinian mysteries in the Cape letter, Lowry adds that "the same esoteric idea of this kind of search also appears in Shakespeare's *Tempest*"—presumably referring most immediately to the bounty promised by the "spirits" in Act IV. But at the Cafe Paris, the taste of tequila running down the Consul's spine is compared to "lightning striking a tree which, thereupon, miraculously blossoms," and where the Consul's "stick" has previously been connected only with Tiresias or, by extension, the blinded Oedipus, it must now recall Prospero's staff as well—or indeed, out of the same syndrome, the "blossoming" wand in *Tannhäuser*. Nor would it have escaped Lowry that a wand was crucial to the rites of Dionysus—in that case blossoming into the vine of the grape.

—While this on the other hand *may* be coincidence, one cannot forget that Archimedes, only recently named by the Consul, was murdered by soldiers while preoccupied with drawing configurations into the sand with a stick, almost exactly what the Consul appears to be doing when his own is first noticed.

—References to archaic ritual activities in the celebration of the Day of the Dead hardly complete the story of Lowry's modern perspective vis-à-vis the past. At least twice, we have heard Weber's comments about "crucifixion" in the bull rings during the revolution, still another essentially "contemporary" actuality which would take us back to the Colosseum itself. Similarly the oxen, and their "carts with wooden disc wheels" outside of the Farolito, must bridge an equal gap. And for that matter there are cultists in today's Srinagar who claim to be *direct descendants* of Yus Asaf.

—If only through association with the earlier allusion to Heracles and the Minoan bull, it is difficult not to connect Hugh's ritual "bull throwing"—or, as some might have it, Lowry's critic's—with the combat between Theseus and the Minotaur, which also occurs on Crete. Like Hugh, Theseus is a volunteer, and the Consul's subsequent vision, more strictly ritualistic, of Hugh "bearing down upon an ox," would strengthen the connection. (More lamely, it might also be noted that the Minotaur is bested in the Dedalean labyrinth at Cnossos, through which Theseus finds his way by unwinding and then retracing Ariadne's thread, and in setting out for the arena Hugh has thought of the future as "beginning to unwind.")

—Another "incidental" piece of information perhaps relevant here is that the most popular contemporary ritual involving bulls, the annual festival at Pamplona described in *The Sun Also Rises,* is the festival of San Fermin.

To say all of this differently, if reductively: as myth itself evolves out of rite, Greek tragedy in particular is the remnant of a rite involving the slaying of a bull, and in essence Lowry has simply put back the bull. But the very word tragedy means "goat song," and as we have seen, he has several times given us the goat as well—so it is perhaps also of interest here that the chief objects of sacrifice at the rites of Dionysus were oxen *and* goats. But the final point, of course, is that this timeless, eternally repeated pattern of contest, sparagmos, and renewal, must surely be seen as one of *Under the Volcano*'s own.

And still, one or two other tangentially relevant matters:

—Frequently, the Consul is called "Old Bean." Like many such symbols the name occurs interchangeably, but when the Consul uses it in speaking to Hugh it is significantly uncapitalized. At the Cafe Paris, Laruelle is made to add the phrase as a sort of touchstone of familiarity after telling the Consul, "I'm afraid of you," a context indicating that Lowry wants the usage taken seriously—though Laruelle cannot know just what he is afraid *of.* According to Frazer, the bean is the only vegetable ever granted the totem status accorded to animals—i.e., said to bear the reborn spirit of a god. (One more cliché, too, is resurrected simultaneously.)

—A classic figure who particularly cautioned against the eating of beans was Pythagoras, if in the less dramatic belief that they contained the souls of mere mortals. The basic Pythagorean premise of flux and synthesis, or that "all things change, nothing passes," would take much in Lowry back to its philosophical beginnings.

Then again, still another who first propounded many of these same theories was Empedocles. Empedocles—magician, self-styled god among men—who died by leaping into a volcano.

Nothing does pass; it is only reshaped into art.

CHAPTER ELEVEN

Early in Chapter X the Consul thinks about the routes to Parián, a main path and a more direct cut-off. Following him in Chapter XI, Yvonne and Hugh choose the former, which "would bring them to the same place finally, and, what was more to the point, past . . . at least two other cantinas."[318] As we know, their decision is the wrong one, since the Consul has gone by the quicker route—ironically, he has taken the "straight way."

The importance of the choice is made plain when Lowry causes Yvonne to see the two paths "stretched out before her on either side like the arms . . . of a man being crucified." But at the same time he is also providing a topographical correlative here for the novel's structure, which itself now bifurcates. The last two chapters of *Under the Volcano* occur simultaneously. When she and Hugh at last do approach Parián, Yvonne will hear gunshots, and a moment later will be killed by the horse. Only at the end of Chapter XII, after following the Consul through this same period of roughly an hour and a half, do we learn that those shots are fired at him, and that the horse bolts at the sounds.

Aesthetically, this divergence might be read as an inevitable result of the shattering of dramatic suspension just witnessed: with the novel's basic polar balance destroyed, even its unity of progression falls asunder. Yet after Lowry's many parallels across historical time, implying identities between his characters and their mythic counterparts, what is now building, in effect, is a parallel in immediate fictional time between two of those characters themselves—meaning that even as Yvonne and the Consul separate, their fates remain inextricably in conjunction.

It is in this chapter that the anthropomorphism of Popocatepetl and Ixtaccihuatl is enlarged upon. Here too, probably in echo of Ovid's tale of Baucis and Philemon, who likewise die simultaneously, Yvonne notices "a low thick tree, really two trees embracing one another," and then thinks of them as "the two tree lovers." (The same symbols might also well recall the burial of Tristan and Iseult.) Additionally, sampling mescal for the first time, she herself has several fleeting hallucinations, as if drugged, and in this same moment of ultimate identification finds herself "overwhelmed by a sudden wave through her whole being of desperate love and tenderness for the Consul."

But that inseparability is equally implicit in Lowry's final manipulation of the horse. Since it is the Consul's curiosity about the animal which involves him with the police, it thus becomes as instrumental in his own death, symbolically, as it is literally in Yvonne's.

Thematically, of course, the reappearance of the horse as a destructive agent completes the metaphor of the Samaritan. When first seen by the Consul the animal has represented nothing less than "the opportunity afforded by life itself." But in his failure to "intervene" on behalf of the dying Indian, like modern man in Spain he and the rest have permitted the horse—"life itself"—to fall into the hands of the fascists. "No se puede vivir sin amar."

But as indicated some time since, the animal must finally be understood as more than a convenient symbolic tool with which Lowry connects these separate episodes. Obviously it is not the horse as an external entity, but Lowry's *characters* who bring down that final destruction upon themselves. Items:

—Replying to a comment of Yvonne's about his health, the Consul declares: "Still strong as a horse, so to speak, strong as a horse."

—Riding with Yvonne, Hugh repeats the same cliché (n.b. that it *is* a cliché): "Geoff's strong as a horse."

—Hearing Hugh whinny to call back some foals in the same scene, Yvonne remarks: "You do sound astonishingly like a horse."

—Waiting as the horse plunges toward her at the end of the

present chapter, Yvonne finds its neigh "becoming a scream almost human."

—Responding to the Consul's statement that he is a "writer," one of the fascists at the Farolito will pronounce the word as "wrider."

—Delivering the Consul's long-delayed postcard, the mailman announces in his equally bad English that it is addressed "for your horse."

—Replying to this last, the Consul asks: "What?—nothing for Señor Calígula."

Admittedly, in this final case Lowry is again being playful, though the line makes his point even more decisively than do the others—Caligula having planned to appoint his favorite horse a *consul* in Rome.

The sum of which, then, brings us back to Laruelle's declaration about another horse that "this too, obscurely, was the Consul," if with the difference that the qualification of "obscurity" has been rendered superfluous. In the same conversation where the Consul speaks of "the fish that dies," Lowry twice uses the contraction "youn'" to indicate Cervantes's pronunciation of "young"—once, no less, when Yvonne imitates the man while suggesting that she "could eat a youn' horse." Lowry means a "Jung horse," beyond question—since he has made of the animal an archetype in the most basic sense of the word.*

For Jung, that sense is of an image occurring to all intents universally in man's collective myths, but which is an everyday product of unconscious origin also, as in dreams. Of the horse archetype specifically he would have it that it represents the nonhuman psyche, i.e., man's animal drives or unconscious impulses. But in a context involving such notions as those of the dying god or the totem animal, more pertinent to Lowry's eclecticism would again be the implication of rebirth. Yvonne and the Consul die, the horse which destroys them lives on. Presumably we are not asked to believe that the Consul *becomes* the horse—even if, as it happens, the animal has a sore on its hipbone to

---

*A Lowry letter dated August 25, 1951, remarks "the pungent aroma of frying horse, for inflation has driven us . . . to eating our archetypes too!"

further strengthen the identity. But the reminder that man persists in creating *myths* in which such things occur remains critical:
"—for long after Adam had left the garden the light in Adam's
house burned on."

The cyclic motif, which we must now note as Eleusinian as well,
is particularly accentuated in the chapter, which in fact opens
with a Dantean image of birds scattering upward "with ever
wider circlings." Like Laruelle at approximately this same hour
on another Day of the Dead, Yvonne sees mourners in a cemetery "visible only as their candle flames," and hears their "soft
cries and lamentations." (The mourners are described as
"chanting over the graves"; not quoted from the preceding
chapter is a reference to "the priest chanting from the Veda.")
A storm, itself "traveling in a circle," and unseasonal like the
one from which Laruelle takes shelter, is breaking across "the
tempestuous sky." And again as Laruelle has remarked—as he
is to remark—we are in the "night of the culmination of the
Pleiades."

A new note of archaism is struck when Yvonne sees a woman
pass, "balancing on her head, with the grace of a Rebecca, a
small light bottle," though probably this is another assertion of
her destiny as indivisible from the Consul's also; the latter has
spoken of "fate" in connection with their first meeting, which
furthermore occurred at a well—as does Rebecca's "preor-
dained" meeting with Isaac. It is here too that Yvonne perceives
the "extravagant fructification" noted *supra,* and has the sensation "one might almost have heard things growing," both notions of course newly Edenic as well as Eleusinian.

As in the previous chapter written from Yvonne's point of
view, however, contrasts predominate. Almost at once, and
again like Laruelle in Chapter I, she sees "worn-out plough-
shares." In obvious analogy with mankind, she conceives of
vultures "on earth . . . defiling themselves with blood and filth,
but who were yet capable of rising, like this, above the storms,
to heights shared only by the condor, above the summit of the
Andes—"[317] She glimpses "blood red snow" at the peak of
Ixtaccihuatl, a moment later recalls the legend making the two
volcanoes lovers. And where she is aware of "rotting vegeta-

tion" and "a smell of decay"—literally indicating the proximity of the barranca, but also again suggesting ruined Eden—almost instantly she finds the air blowing "strangely warmer and sweeter."

And as always the intimations of doom. Shortly after thinking of Popocatepetl in terms of "the fires of his warrior's heart," she herself feels "as if something within her were smouldering, had taken fire, as if her whole being at any moment were going to explode." Even as the chapter begins she spies "the moon itself, preparing to follow the sun below the horizon"—*both* sources of "illumination" and/or influence are departing—and again in parallel with a sensation of the Consul's it strikes her that "the whole precipitous bulk of Popocatepetl seemed to be coming toward them."

Similarly, a new description of the Pleiades, as "those whose culmination was at midnight tonight," must call to mind Faust's imminent "culmination" if not her own. And here too—while still another metaphor turns real—she contemplates a tavern pictured as "about all remaining . . . of the formerly prosperous village . . . which had burned."

But then in further contrast, at this first cantina Yvonne waits outside while Hugh inquires about the Consul; in a cage she finds a small eagle:

> With hurried quivering hands Yvonne began to unfasten the cage. The bird fluttered out of it and alighted at her feet, hesitated . . . then abruptly flew off through the dusk, not to the nearest tree, as might have been supposed, but up—she was right, it knew it was free—up soaring, with a sudden cleaving of pinions into the deep dark blue pure sky above, in which at that moment appeared one star.[320]

As in the description of the seagull freed by Hugh, the most immediate suggestion here is of the phoenix; in fact since the phoenix arises from its own ashes, the "smouldering" within Yvonne herself in this period is doubtless not a completely negative sign either. But more crucial in a fuller context is the poetic merging of bird into star—a direct anticipation of Yvonne's own celestial "transformation" to follow.

For the moment, however, Yvonne's connection with the heavens is remote; she is unable to "get her bearings," and the stars seem all "in the wrong place, and all the wrong shape." In point of realism, this loss of perspective would occur because of her recent journey, though thematically it also points up her general sense of displacement; after wondering why the stars seem "so far away from home," she is forced to ask: "From what home?" (Both Hugh and the Consul have been given pause by variants on the same question.) On the other hand their "very being" consoles her, and she finally does become reoriented: " . . . ah, there, here they were, after all, in their right places, their configurations all at once right, recognised":

"As Scorpio sets in the southwest, the Pleiades are rising in the northeast." "As Capricorn sets in the west, Orion rises in the east. . . . " To-night, as ages hence, people would say this, or shut their doors on them, turn in bereaved agony from them, or toward them with love saying: "That is our star up there, yours and mine"; steer by them above the clouds or lost at sea, or standing in the spray on the forecastle head, watch them, suddenly, career; put their faith or lack of it in them; train, in a thousand observatories, feeble telescopes upon them, across whose lenses swam mysterious swarms of stars and clouds of dead dark stars, catastrophes of exploding suns. . . . And the earth itself still turning on its axis and revolving around that sun, the sun revolving around the luminous wheel of this galaxy, the countless unmeasured jewelled wheels of countless unmeasured galaxies, turning, turning, majestically, into infinity, into eternity, through all of which life ran on—all this, long after she herself was dead, men would still be reading in the night sky, and as the earth turned through those distant seasons, and they watched the constellations still rising, culminating, setting, to rise again . . . would they not, too, still be asking the hopeless eternal question: to what end? What force drives this sublime celestial machinery? . . . and some would watch with a sense of fleeting, yet feeling their diamonded brightness gleam an instant on the soul, touching all within that in memory was sweet or noble or courageous or proud, as high overhead appeared, flying softly like a flock of birds toward Orion, the beneficent Pleiades . . . [322]

Has it been often enough said, all weight of "meaning" beside the point, that Lowry must be bracketed among the incomparable *writers,* pure and simple, of English prose? (Jacques Barzun to the contrary here, who informed early readers that Lowry's language was "desperately dull"—and then offered in illustration the line, quoted *supra,* which Lowry takes verbatim from Andrew Marvell.)

Meanwhile what emerges in the passage itself is first of all, of course, a cosmic extension of the novel's themes of "timelessness," if not to say an invocation of *the* cyclic "wheel" or continuum—in which the reversal on "moving machinery" is subtly memorable as well. Not indicated in the paragraph as abridged is the fact that the Pleiades are *literally* rising as Yvonne thinks of them, though at this particular moment "unseen beyond the volcanoes"; but since they will, in fact, emerge at the instant of her death, Lowry is thus preparing *realistically* for an occurrence which will serve an essentially poetic function. But also, since the one other object which has been said to "gleam on the soul" is the Consul's bottle, the stars must now be seen to afford the same mystic or religious dimension in Yvonne's life that drink does in the Consul's.

But it is at the second cantina that the more tangible parallels between them are established, epitomizing Lowry's concept of their "shared" destiny. The cantina has a "waiting character that pertains to a border at night," in reality being near the border of the state, metaphorically impinging upon a "border" of death. The place is named "El Popo," and Yvonne is thus now "in" the volcano as the Consul at the Farolito will find himself "under" it, there literally as well as symbolically. Her hallucinations commence here, as she finds the Consul "disappearing round every corner, and going out of every door," and even the restaurant takes on certain characteristics of the Farolito itself when she sees verandahs giving "an effect of cloisters," and

again, a "dark monastic archway." And when she orders the
mescal, to find out "what Geoffrey sees in it," she shakes her
head "solemnly"—this her initiation into the "drinking rites."

Earlier, meanwhile, Hugh has asked this same question about
Parián: "I wonder what Weber sees in it." From the Consul's
point of view, "seeing" something in mescal or in Parián would
come to much the same thing, yet the connection strikes an odd
note. For whatever their separate reasons, both he and Weber
are bound for the identical place, and one toward which the
Consul has looked with a longing undeniably "religious" in
character. Has the Consul turned toward Parián in "prayer?"
Weber has been in the Foreign Legion, a "Moorish" tomb has
been named. "Pilgrims going to Mecca" are mentioned in one
of Hugh's reminiscences, and in the present chapter, en route
to Parián herself, Yvonne sees "striped mysterious tents." The
Mexican town of Ameca*meca,* itself the site of an ancient shrine,
is also named, and in fact will come back into the Consul's mind
amid symbolism of spiritual "ascension" at the time of his death;
too, the most venerated object at Mecca happens to be a cele-
brated "black stone," said to have dropped from heaven at
Adam's Fall. An Islamic undercurrent would certainly enhance
Lowry's general catholicity, and worth note is that the phrase,
"Show us the straight path," forms one of the seven most common verses of prayer from the Koran. On the other hand Lowry
would have reason for not pressing the analogy—since Moslems
do not drink.

It is next that Yvonne appears, if subtly, drugged. Squeezing
lemon into her glass, she finds that "all this took her an inordinately long time to do." She is conscious for a second time of
both "laughing unnaturally to herself" and that something
within her is "smouldering." And again her mind shapes that
picture "of a woman ceaselessly beating her fists on the
ground."

In addition to suggesting Demeter, this last may also be a
further indirect evocation of the Consul, since the god Hades
learns nothing of the upper world save when called upon by this
sort of pounding; too, the intimation of hysteria in the line might
correspond with the Consul's own madness. Simultaneously,

however, and while the mescal is described as "working," Yvonne hears someone singing "La Paloma," "The Dove"— which might make her own "rites," even if Eleusinian, more strictly "Christian" than are his. In either case: "But no, it was not herself that was on fire. . . . it was their house by the sea. But where was the fire? It was the Consul who had been the first to notice it. What were these crazy thoughts, thoughts without form or logic?"[326]

It is when she takes a second drink that Yvonne's "sudden wave . . . of desperate love and tenderness for the Consul" occurs. The "logic" she herself finds missing here is conversely very much present as a logic of the novelist's craft, since Lowry is establishing a point of departure for the expansion of just such fire imagery at her death, though Yvonne also happens to be getting drunk. Her voice becomes slightly "blurred and re-mote," yet she has still another mescal with Hugh, an irony after her unfulfilled intention "not to have one drink alone but a great many drinks with the Consul." Ironic in a different way is that when she and Hugh offer the familiar toast, "Salud y pesetas," again as in Chapter I the word for love is omitted.

Through much of the foregoing Hugh has been away from the table; when he returns he has purchased a guitar from a musi-cian seen earlier at the Salón Ofélia. The incident is minor but telling, particularly since the presence of the instrument almost immediately sets him to singing certain Loyalist songs—i.e., the very "revolutionary songs" he had not known in his youth. In other words Hugh's own history is now beginning to repeat itself, but this time as he goes back to sea the guitar is no longer a symbol of innocence. Here too Eden has been lost.

Also, here, is an echo of Lowry's concern for those areas "in one another we leave, perhaps forever, unexplored," since for all the inevitability of the appearance of the guitar, Hugh has once recalled that Yvonne "doesn't know I ever played." In the interim, meanwhile, he has been given an old chit written by the Consul on the reverse of a menu. On the same card there is also "a poem in the process of composition," likewise the Consul's and about a man obviously himself, "Hounded by eyes and thronged terrors"—i.e., again in the abyss, perhaps specifically in the realm of Typhoeus, of whose "hundred heads and . . . fearful eyes and voices" he will later think. The fragment concludes:

> There would have been a scandal at his death
> Perhaps. No more than this. Some tell
> Strange hellish tales of this poor foundered soul
> Who once fled north . . .[330]

We can probably do with "scandal" what we will, though an interesting possibility occurs in Matthew: "All you shall be scandalized in me this night. . . . But after I am risen again I will go before you into Galilee." Too, according to St. Augustine, the Incarnation was a "scandal to the Gentiles." But of more consequence would seem to be the final elided phrase, which Yvonne repeats to herself no less than five times as she and Hugh are leaving the tavern. Superficially, of course, the reminder of Canada would be what causes her preoccupation; in fact a secondary motif in the poem is "escape," and in broaching the subject at the bull ring Yvonne has insisted they would not be "just escaping." But in his dream the Consul himself has decisively linked "the northern region" with purification—Himavat beheld with "heaven aspiring hearts," etc.—and the rebirth theme in his letter is built around a vision of "some northern country." Thus the line reverberates as a dual refrain, implying flight on one hand, salvation on the other. And implied concurrently must naturally be any number of other "escapes": the disappearance of the Consul's father, Blackstone, Dante's exile, Oedipus' flight from Corinth, etc.

A clock says "twelve to seven" when Yvonne and Hugh start on the final leg toward Parián, Lowry's two occult numbers falling into dark conjunction. Equally ominous is the sight of the "ruined Grecian temple" mentioned above, an illusion caused by light striking telegraph poles—*Es inevitable la muerte de* Jocasta also. And more prophetic is the statement that "Pegasus pounded up the sky unseen"—though when the real horse does presently hang "petrified in midair" above Yvonne, it will thus develop that in *Under the Volcano* even Jungian archetypes have archetypes.

In that latter instance, an interesting pun will unfold also. In his garden, the Consul has thought of a snake in a tree—"A snake that waited to drop rings on you: whore's shoes." Swimming at the Salón Ofélia, Yvonne mentions a "Horseshoe Falls" in Wales. And soon the horse's shoe is literally to fall.

More. Since this last will occur during imagery of the end of the world, it may not be irrelevant that Vishnu's final avatar will appear as a horse—to be seen in the heavens with one foot lifted. When the hoof strikes earth, the ultimate destruction will occur.

And meanwhile, the gunshots—sounding like "a back-firing car." Hugh laughs, speaking of "more target practice," after which the irony becomes consummate when Yvonne thinks of the explosions as "mundane sounds to hold as relief against the sickening thunder that followed, for they meant Parián was near." A sign on a tree confirms their direction—this with their own "straight way" only now about to be lost—and then Lowry writes that "it began to rain softly and a sweet cleanly smell rose from the woods."

Their straight path has, in fact, been called just that earlier, but now Yvonne approaches a bole across the trail which must be climbed by means of a mildewed ladder. She is leading, and at the top realizes she has "lost Hugh's light." "Yvonne balanced herself someway on the top of this dark slippery log." With "a certain note of triumph," she then proclaims: "Mind you don't get off the path there, Hugh, it's sort of tricky."[334]

It has been necessary to anticipate most of the meanings here in other contexts, though they bear repetition if only in light of the remarkable manner whereby Lowry has again transformed so much abstraction into fictional reality. As for the Consul earlier in fleeing the Salón Ofélia, Yvonne's dark wood is now truly a wood, truly dark. But the path is not Dante's alone, since what is "sort of tricky" is that Cabbalistic symbolism in which the Tree of Life is represented by a ladder—likewise now real. And thus Yvonne's "balance" and her "note of triumph" both have to do with occult elements transformed as well—and all of this, too, after partaking of the symbolic mescal.

Yet even here the dialectic. As we have seen, this balance is crucial because of the nearness of the Cabbalistic ladder to an abyss, meaning that the Tree of Life can open into a wood of death—as it does when still another metaphor turns real and Yvonne "slips" from the log. But within moments, as in Christ's own death upon the "tree," with Yvonne's assumption we will have had the crowning paradox of all: in death, life.

Simultaneously, Lowry's scheme here may suggest a considerably more familiar "ladder" than that of the Cabbala. The Consul's letter mentions a "nightly grapple with death." Elsewhere he recalls having once been mistaken for "that wrestler," and again refers to the "angel of night." Moreover, Jacob is *lamed* in that very wrestling. (Even though the Consul is now simultaneously dying *elsewhere*, it *must* be both irrelevant and coincidental that Gogol's dying words were, "Give me the ladder, the ladder.")

As the horse rears over her, Yvonne is aware that "someone was calling her name far away"—a new sort of "correspondence" insofar as we will find the Consul doing so in his last thoughts at Parián. (Nothing is said of Hugh, here.) She also remembers—in this case perhaps for the benefit of the remedial reader—that "they were in a dark wood." Then, as lightning flashes:

> . . . the horse—Great God, the horse—and would this scene repeat itself endlessly and forever?—the horse, rearing, poised over her, petrified in midair, a statue, somebody was sitting on the statue, it was Yvonne Griffaton, no, it was the statue of Huerta, the drunkard, the murderer, it was the Consul, or it was a mechanical horse on a merry-go-round, the carrousel, but the carrousel had stopped and she was in a ravine down which a million horses were thundering towards her, and she must escape . . . [335]

Her own recent speculations have told us that the scene would, indeed, "repeat itself" in just this way. Disconnected as they appear to be here, meanwhile, each of the progressive images has been equally prepared for. Yvonne Griffaton is the female protagonist in the film of Laruelle's she has remembered, in which the horse "leaping" out at her is itself a statue. But she has also remarked an equestrian statue of Huerta during the morning in Quauhnahuac. The labels "drunkard" and "murderer" fit the man, Huerta being perhaps the arch-villain of the Revolution, president in 1913–14—though of course on a wholly negative plane he becomes one further counterpart for the Consul; by virtue of the symbolic function of the horse the Consul is now "murdering" Yvonne even as he has murdered the Indian. The carousel is naturally a throwback to the fiesta, and the final picture is a transposition also, Yvonne having once recalled an incident in her film career "when she actually had been caught in a ravine with two hundred stampeding horses."

Simultaneously it is here that the imagery of fire is enlarged upon. Yvonne has a vision of escape—"through the friendly forest to their house"—"But the house was on fire . . . everything was burning, the dream was burning." The passage runs for some twenty-five lines, and numerous fired objects are listed —"the old kettle, the new kettle," etc.—virtually all of them familiar from Yvonne's earlier moments of *idyllic* reverie about the house. Too, the Consul's imagined manuscript is seen to be on fire and scattering—as will happen to his letter a year later in Chapter I.

Next the notion of purification by fire is itself connected with myth when the waters upon which the house is built are called "the dark waters of Eridanus," the latter being a mysterious river never seen by mortals, sometimes in antiquity identified with the Styx. In *October Ferry to Gabriola,* Lowry recalls a less negative identification, reminding us that it is also "the river in Virgil's *Aeneid,* which watered the Elysian Fields of Earthly Paradise." Ovid mentions Eridanus in connection with Phaëthon, who falls there after attempting to drive the very chariot of the sun, a mythic adventure causing no few conflagrations on its own part.

Meanwhile this same vision is also apocalyptic of an *ultimate* destruction, as Yvonne then finds that "the tree was burning," a moment later that "the garden" is—which is to say that the Tree of Life, Eden, a world ceases with her. (Since it does, we are again concerned with the question of reality as limited to individual perception, a matter yet to be discussed.) But finally:

> And leaving the burning dream Yvonne felt herself suddenly gathered upwards and borne toward the stars, through eddies of

stars scattering aloft with ever wider circlings . . . among which now appeared, like a flock of diamond birds flying softly and steadily towards Orion, the Pleiades . . . [336]

As might be surmised, it is more than astronomical exactness that gives Orion his prominence in Yvonne's last vision. Orion —who gets drunk, becomes blind as a result, must face east if his sight is to be restored, is aided by the lame god Hephaestus who lives in a volcano, is followed to the heavens by a dog, and whose constellation is nearest that called Eridanus. Whither Yvonne, likewise the Consul.

Here too, however, the "burning dream" must recall the Consul's own earlier description, in that murky passage at Señora Gregorio's, of death as "an awakening from a dream in a dark place." This again is the reality question, but it would also appear to echo a writer Lowry curiously seems nowhere to indicate using, the friar Bernardino de Sahagún, earliest chronicler of post-conquest Mexican culture; according to Sahagún, it was explained to the Spaniards by Aztec priests that "they did not die, but awoke from a dream they had lived." (Sahagún records further that "they said . . . some were transformed into various planets." This would follow the lead of Quetzalcoatl, who, as noted *supra*, became Venus—though Hesiod would have us understand that the same identity was assumed by Phaëthon, and after his very plunge into Eridanus. Or is the Consul himself perhaps en route also—Venus already having been noted as a "horned" star?)

But an unsettling matter must be taken up here also. In the morning, when Yvonne first discusses this same "dream" of rebirth in Canada with Hugh, the latter makes a suggestive remark: "I might have a dream like that in a week or two." What Hugh means literally, of course, is that should his mission to Spain turn out a botch, he too will damned well wish himself elsewhere. But can we possibly infer from this that a botch will indeed occur—i.e., that the "dream" which comprises Hugh's life will definitely soon cease too? Early in the present chapter Yvonne misquotes W. J. Turner's "Romance"—"Chimborazo, Popocatepetl . . . had stolen his heart away"—calling it a poem "the Consul liked," but if we look to the original, two lines leap from the page which may well apply to either of the alter egos: "My father died, my brother too,/ They passed like fleeting dreams . . . " Hugh himself has meanwhile also echoed the Eridanus notion on his own part by having thought longingly of "Sokotra . . . my mysterious island in the Arabian Sea, where . . . no one has ever been."[124] His death is undeniably "true" symbolically, less because of that Byronic strain among his mythic forebears who die on foreign soil than simply because he *must* be read as one of those dead whose resurrection "for one day" forms the novel's basic symbolic *modus operandi.* That "curious fiction" which it is Hugh himself who views earlier, Laruelle's "spiritual property" which seems to disqualify him from Lowry's underworld, doubly strengthens the probability—though all that Laruelle himself can tell us a year later, seeming unaware even then of Hugh's mission, is that he has made his ship.*

Actually, such is the impact of Lowry's final chapter that one tends to forget Hugh entirely after he is abandoned here, and in afterthought it is what Lowry does not tell us about the next *few hours* in his life that creates a far greater extra-fictional reality than the question of his death. One wonders how many readers have visualized him stumbling from the wood with Yvonne's broken form in his arms, into the chaos following the Consul's murder—and there to be confronted in dumb bafflement by his semiliterate fascist acquaintance Weber, the only one present who would make an immediate connection between the two Firmins. It may be an ultimate tribute to Lowry that while his structure precludes any possibility of the scene, it remains as vivid as much that he did write.

But meanwhile the question of Yvonne's assumption—and Lowry's most unequivocal statement of palingenesis. In happening bodily, the event must certainly call to mind the assumption of the Virgin, though Lowry offers no allusions in that regard—

---

*Ideal *textual* proof of Hugh's death, of course, would be the existence of an actual freighter with the same name as his own, one S. S. *Noemijolea,* destroyed by Franco's forces in late 1938. Mrs. Lowry is certain that a connection of just this sort was someway intended, but the present writer must admit to striking a dead end in research here.

perhaps because there has never been anything on the subject in the New Testament to allude *to*. In any case it is again Dante who predominates, the chapter coming full circle with a repetition of the "ever wider circlings" with which it began. Closing Yvonne's life with a reference to the stars, Lowry is adhering to the Dantean pattern which ends each canticle of the *Comedy* with the word "stelle," and just before this, when he has her recall the "myriads of beautiful butterflies" mentioned earlier, again the phrase must suggest Dante's figure for man "who flies to judgment without defense." But in following upon imagery of fire and forest both, the picture would perhaps be closest to the end of the *Purgatorio*, where Dante himself is "born again, even as new trees renewed with new foliage, pure and ready to mount to the stars."

And which is then Lowry's eschatology, as well. "I think I see you with your esposa again soon . . . laughing together in some kernice place where you laugh . . . Far away"—Faust joins Margaret, Dante achieves Beatrice. During the morning, when the Consul thinks of Lucretius, it is to "dispute" with him in regard to the body's ability to "renew itself." But Lucretius denies the immortality of body *and* soul, and by now there can be little doubt that Lowry himself would take issue over the latter as well. If it has been suggested that we would be hard put to unearth anyone's *dogma* in his novel, the same would be true for the later Yeats, for Dylan Thomas, yet we have had few recent writers more "religious," in a most moving sense of the word, than either. And like their own, Lowry's insistence upon catholicity makes no point if not that *all* of man's agony, all of his wonderment, comes to the same end. "What force drives this sublime celestial machinery?" The Consul is made to speak without qualification of a prayer being "answered," Yvonne is carried without metaphor to the heavens—beyond question Lowry holds that *some* force does control those infinite turnings. Like so many of its sempiternal models—from Dante to *Pilgrim's Progress*—as a declaration of the human condition *Under the Volcano* is informed by faith.

CHAPTER TWELVE

In a traditional narrative sense, the final chapter of *Under the Volcano* is the most dramatic in the novel. But things are not as they seem. When the chapter opens the Consul's face is glaring at him from a mirror, and there is a distinct way in which the entire episode occurs on the *other side* of that glass.

In view of what he himself is to call his "mescal-drugged" condition, for example, the Consul's defiance of the fascists in their own stronghold is fantastic on the face of it. But in the midst of that defiance, after enduring an hallucination in which an enormous rooster crows before his face, the man snatches up a machete: "Where was that bloody cock? He would chop off its head." Whereas in *Alice in Wonderland:* "The Queen was in a furious passion, and went stamping about, and shouting, 'Off with his head!' or 'Off with her head!' about once in a minute."

Nor is the analogy isolated:

—In *Alice* the appearance of a remarkable white rabbit is the first "unreal" event. On the first page of Chapter XII the Consul discovers "a white rabbit eating an ear of Indian corn . . . with an air of detachment, as though playing a musical instrument."

—Following the rabbit into its hole, Alice tumbles unconcernedly "down a very deep well." Later the Consul will endure a sustained illusion of "sinking," likening it once to sinking into a "dark well." But even as the chapter opens he contemplates the barranca in patently childlike terms—"a tremendous, an awful way down to the bottom"—while at the same time deciding "he was not afraid to fall either."

—In her queer world, Alice repeatedly questions her own identity and is frequently asked about it by others. A minor thematic motif throughout the novel, the question of the Consul's "identity" now becomes urgent on a strictly literal plane: "What for you lie? It say here too: your name is Firmin," etc.

—Alice desires at one point to enter "the loveliest garden you ever saw." Symbolically, the Consul has been trying to do the same thing all day—but as it happens he here finds himself being led "irresistibly" into a real garden.

—The Hatter and the March Hare, continually taking tea, tell Alice: "It's always six o'clock now." Here the Consul notices a clock "pointing to six"—and when he looks again some time later he finds that it "still said six."

—Alice is shocked by the Queen's perverse notion of due process: " 'No, no!' said the Queen. 'Sentence first—verdict afterwards.' " Compare Weber's "They shoot first and ask questions later"—which will now happen in actual fact, and in Weber's presence.

—The Queen's demand is voiced during the trial of the "Knave of Hearts." In more ways than one the Consul is "on trial" in the chapter himself—and at the hands of such personages as a "Chief of Rostrums," a "Chief of Gardens," etc. (An illiterate sailor takes pains to inform the Consul that "Mozart was the man that writ the Bible. Mozart wrote the old testimony." The puns on legal terminology more seriously enhance the parallel between fascist "justice" and the Queen's.)

—Having occasion to pass through them, the Consul remarks that the rooms in the Farolito grow "smaller and smaller," also that they resemble "the boxes in a Chinese puzzle"—both surely *Alice*like concepts.

—The first thing Alice discovers in Wonderland is a bottle—labeled "DRINK ME."

Actually, Lewis Carroll is cued for us as early as in the Consul's letter, where he suggests that he "should have been producing obscure volumes of verse entitled the Triumph of Humpty Dumpty." That last happy coincidence above to the contrary, meanwhile, an initial point in the *Alice* parallel is doubtless one of innocence. The Consul's death is symbolically inevitable, even symbolically justified, yet like Alice he exists in a self-indulgent dream world—and for all his crimes of *omission* he is plainly a stray lamb among these fascists. In fact it is in contrast with this *operative* evil that he is to be most conclusively identified with Christ.

But as will have suggested itself, another reason for Lowry's use of such materials lies in their correlation with his ever-enlarging scheme of illusion and/or reality. In the Consul's letter, the basic proposition of his work on "Secret Knowledge" is summarized as follows: "Is there any ultimate reality, external, conscious and ever-present etc. etc. that can be realised by any such means that may be acceptable to all creeds and religions and suitable to all climes and countries?"[39] With the appearance of Alice it must finally become evident that the question motivating that book-within-a-book—which, indeed, may itself be unreal—must surely underlie a good deal of Lowry's own interest in *Under the Volcano*.

Much of the subject has been recorded in passing: the Consul's innumerable hallucinations or general "nightmare" existence, Yvonne's illusions, confusions between day and night, references to life as a "dream" or to reality as "loathsome," the occasion upon which the Consul actually holds Yvonne in his arms and is able only to "feel, feel the unreality," and so forth. Equally typical is an incident at the end of Chapter X. In the midst of the final "suspension" of his argument with Hugh and Yvonne, the Consul is newly reminded of the railway station "where he had gone . . . to meet Lee Maitland." But now, despite the detailed re-experiencing of the event which has occurred, abruptly the Consul wonders: "—*had* he gone?"

What is perhaps most immediately provocative about such episodes is that even when Lowry specifically labels them as illusions, they remain indivisible from ordinary reality *as perceived* by his characters. The Canadian house, for example, the waters—Eridanus—are all figments of Yvonne's imagination—yet they have become so real in her mind that it is less the sensible, external world which dies with her than the dream itself. Or again the Lee Maitland passage. It has already been seen as particularly disjunctive, though if the Consul did not go, that disjunctiveness would thus be explained—since he has evidently been reliving an event which had occurred only in fantasy to begin with. Here then he is even *twice removed* from reality—

and still the experience leaves him "oozing alcohol from every pore."

With the possible exception of the dream narrative of *Finnegans Wake*, where of course traditional fictional form itself is distorted, this is almost certainly unique in fiction—philosophic idealism as a *functioning* creative concept. Nor is its operation limited to the perceptions of Lowry's characters alone, witness the Consul's long "anthropological" digression at the Salón Ofélia. Not until it is over does the reader come to understand, any more than the Consul himself, that the man has "not uttered a single word." Lowry has contrived to make it appear as "real" as anything else in the novel *while it is being read*—i.e., while the reader himself perceives it.

This is Bishop Berkeley, of course, whom the Consul says he has been "slap through," although as noted Lowry has taken the concept back to Plato's metaphor of the visible world as a shadowy projection of the ideal, and at one juncture his characters themselves have been transformed into those very shadows. But as a matter of fact he has even paused to satirize the classic schoolroom exercise by which such topics are traditionally introduced. Weighing the "drink situation" after his return from the bathroom at the Salón Ofélia, the Consul makes a neat distinction between the amount he "had drunk in fact, had not drunk so far as the others were concerned." Among the less compulsive, the illustration normally involves trees—or, as E. M. Forster's student has it at the beginning of *The Longest Journey*, "The cow is there." And *has* the Consul consumed drinks if Yvonne and Hugh have not seen him do so? According to the idealist, he has not even *existed* for them in his absence. "The Consul suddenly called from his stone retreat, though it was strange, nobody seemed to have heard him."[296]

Here, perhaps, that "stone" so evident at Señor Cervantes' might be taken as the one kicked by Samuel Johnson in refutation of such matters. But yet again: "To drink or not to drink." If nothing does exist except insofar as the Consul perceives it, and since so much of what he perceives *is* colored by alcohol, to drink is, in his case, a question of "being" or "not being."

But the proposition becomes more complicated. First of all, and as we have seen, the Consul's more extreme "visions" are related to those of the adept, and through the symbolic medium of his hallucinations he becomes a "seer" very like a Paracelsus or a Boehme. In a word, he has mystical experiences. Nor, for that matter, are they always necessarily symbolic. That moment of acute consciousness in his garden, in which the Consul becomes aware of "whistling, gnawing, rattling, even trumpeting," some of it even "from under the earth," is a mystical experience in spades. And the entire phenomenon of the mystical experience itself is nothing if not a transcendence of the normal apprehension of reality—what William James calls the attainment of "potential forms of consciousness."

Thus we are again involved with Lowry's borrowings from such areas as Oriental philosophy, and in a new light, since any such transcendence must certainly bring to mind Nirvana, or again "release"; in fact there is a distinct sense in those philosophies whereby the material world is not only less important, but finally less real, than the spiritual. "Come, amigo," says Dr. Vigil in Chapter I, "throw away your mind." Boehme describes his own mystical experiences as the achievement, simply, of "nothing," which he declares synonymous with "eternity"—meaning that we are back also with the timeless eternity of the Consul's "tomb," likewise with Señora Gregorio's "I have no house only a shadow." Here too then a line not elsewhere quoted becomes vital, in which the Consul likens the entire world to "a bus, making its erratic journey to Tomalín and nothing"—not only echoing Boehme but virtually paraphrasing common metaphors for the so-called "vehicles" of Buddhism. And interestingly, while the Consul has left his copy of Boehme "in Paris," it is at the Cafe Paris that use is first made of the word "release" in this context, as well as where the Consul brings up his "battle for the survival of the human consciousness."

The Consul's madness, read as an ultimate sort of unreality, but additionally as symbolically equal to certain states of religious "rapture," would also implement such themes, as would his "voices." But in sum, then, a theory such as Berkeley's becomes less an end in itself than a point of departure for speculations about the *potential* of perception: if consciousness is all, where might consciousness go? And in this regard Lowry might well be leaning on a writer like Ouspensky, who insists that a higher vision does lie within the realm of human capability.* The first step toward it, Ouspensky says, would be a change in our sense of time, which, again, Lowry himself has adumbrated, and in a way already seen to imply a view of life *sub specie eternitatis.* Spinoza's "eternal mode of thinking," the Jungian creative unconscious, Berkeley—finally *everything* conjoins. We can call this synthesis by any of a dozen names, and in his *Tertium Organum* Ouspensky evokes the fourth dimension, spatial perception, clairvoyance, at last a "cosmic consciousness." Buddha himself, "enlightened" at the age of Dante in the *Comedy*—and incidentally on a night of the full moon—may have been the only mortal ever to take the step absolutely. Yet others so diverse as St. Teresa, Joan of Arc, even the wretched poet Clare "weaving fearful vision," have moved in the same direction. Lowry's subject has not ceased to remain the capacity of man.

A further *Alice* parallel might be noted. At the Salón Ofélia the Consul upbraids Hugh and Yvonne for "interfering" in his personal life, a motif seen to have political implications as well. Here, the theme recurs when he accuses the fascists of interfering with the Indian. While as for Lowry's point:

> " . . . oh, 'tis love, 'tis love, that makes the world go round!"
> "Somebody said," whispered Alice, "that it's done by everybody minding their own business!"
> "Ah, well! It means the same thing," said the duchess.

Most of which is perhaps remote from Parián itself, where, as the chapter begins, we are on more familiar ground. In fact we have heard its opening words before: " 'Mescal,' said the Consul." Missing this time, however, is any qualification of "absent-mindedness"—now truly the "end" he has said the drink would bring. The Consul is in the Farolito—"sanctuary," or so he thinks, and "the paradise of his despair."

The continuity follows close on the heels of his separation from the others, and the tavern is filled with "that ticking,"

---

*Lowry named Ouspensky in conversation as "a best way in" to such areas. Too, *The Varieties of Religious Experience* was once "a bedside book."

meaning that of the "orderly little clock" in the Salón Ofélia. But here it becomes "the ticking of his watch, his heart, his conscience." (In Chapter XI Yvonne recalls the Consul once having heard in El Popo "a soulless draughty death that ticked and groaned." The same ticking is a theme in Lowry's poem "Thirty-five Mescals in Cuautla": "You hear it everywhere, for it is doom;/ The tick of real death, not the tick of time." Since the poem is dated 1937, and also makes reference to an officer with a "bloody hand," more than simply verifying a connection between Cuautla and Parián it would seem all in all a fragmentary anticipation of *Under the Volcano* itself.) Simultaneously the Consul is alert to "a remote sound too, from far below, of rushing water, of subterranean collapse," a characteristic metaphor for the abyss, but in a moment to be understood as descriptive of the actual barranca nearby.

Equally familiar, since Laruelle drinks from one like it in Chapter I, is a bottle of anís "on the label of which a devil brandished a pitchfork." Behind the bar a boy is reading a comic strip called "El Hijo del Diablo," "The Son of the Devil," and then the sight of a dead insect leads to the repetition of a notion seen earlier to fit the Consul himself: "But maybe the scorpion, not wanting to be saved, had stung itself to death."

On the other hand, scorpion imagery has mounted to a degree that, by now, something more may be implied. The date of the novel falls under Scorpio in the Zodiac, and in Chapter XI Yvonne once names the signs consecutively. She has also recited that when "Scorpio sets . . . the Pleiades are rising"—as is happening, in effect, to the Consul and Yvonne respectively. Too, we have had such items as "archers shooting at the sun," rambunctious goats, dying fish, an entire episode concerning Taurus—if not to add Lowry's version of the Scales, otherwise known as *Balance*. An elusive relationship may well exist between all twelve of the signs and Lowry's twelve chapters—or an all too obvious one. In any case it also demands note that Orion, i.e., the Consul, is once hunted by a giant scorpion, in punishment for seducing one of the Pleiades—whom he *eternally pursues* in the heavens. Moreover in certain primitive cultures the setting of the Pleiades meant a death summons for the priest-king, whereas Orion's own rising was said to bring rain and the renewal of the wasted land. The rich get richer.

When the Consul does peer into the barranca, mentally tracing its "circuitous abysmal path back through the country,
through shattered mines, to his own garden," here again Cole-
idge also: "In Parián did Kubla Khan . . ." The actuality of this
particular abyss at a 1938 fascist headquarters might now lead
us to recall more of the original, however:

> And 'mid this tumult Kubla heard from far
> Ancestral voices prophesying war!

It is next that the Consul finds himself truly "under the volcano," after which he considers a crag in the ravine that cannot
"make up its mind to crumble absolutely," yet another inani-
mate symbol for himself. Then from the Farolito's entrance he
studies the Union Militar building, a structure which glowers at
him "with one eye . . . set in the forehead of its low facade," this
the clock saying six. Through an archway he also spies "dun-
geons with wooden bars like pigpens." The pigpens may or may
not be a new allusion to Circe, though undoubtedly implied is
that victims of the fascists are reduced to swine; similarly, if the
building itself is not another cyclops, the Union Militar will
nonetheless prove the literal "monster" in Lowry's fable. Here
too, however, Lowry's insistence upon the hour, even if not
eleven, must again take us to Marlowe:

> Ah, Faustus.
> Now hast thou but one bare hour to live,
> And then thou must be damn'd perpetually!

Hallucination follows, as the Consul watches "some unusual
animals resembling geese, but large as camels, and skinless men,
without heads, upon stilts, whose animated entrails jerked along
the ground"[341]—all now rather beyond the pale for Alice, or
even for Don Quixote. In actuality, "someone who looked like
a policeman was leading a horse up the path, that was all," but
in his recognition of the fact the Consul is dismissing the matter
too hastily; returning to this same vantage point later he will find
the horse, "tied to a small tree he hadn't noticed," and itself

guarded by someone "resembling" a police officer. But in the interim the multiple horrors of the delirium have then been attached to no "casual" object.

Still in mescal focus, the Consul then discovers the face of a beggar "slowly changing to Señora Gregorio's, and now in turn to his mother's face, upon which appeared an expression of infinite pity and supplication."[342] The Consul has had this illusion before; but in occurring this far along, the "appearance" of the mother must now be taken to correspond with the recognition of Jocasta as such by Oedipus. Thus the "pity and supplication," since in Sophocles it is Jocasta who more quickly realizes the nature of their crime and pleads with Oedipus not to pursue the matter on his own part. Too, however, as the Christ parallel materializes, this "presence" will suggest Mary's at Calvary.

Next the Consul pauses to contemplate "the dreadful night inevitably awaiting him," anticipating "his room shaking with daemonic orchestras . . . his own name being continually repeated by imaginary parties arriving . . . the dark's spinets"— i.e., in phrases identical to those used in the letter composed in this same tavern months before, reposing at the moment in the volume of Elizabethan plays. It is during that writing, as has been noted, that the Consul indicates he has some of Yvonne's letters with him, a fact he has forgotten since. Now, as he so to speak "unconsciously" recalls those other phrases of his own, but again not the latter detail, the proprietor of the Farolito suddenly hands him the missing letters.

In his moment of surprise—which is greater than should be the attentive reader's—another line from Racine runs through the Consul's mind: "La rame inutile fatigua vainement une mer immobile . . . " This is the Iphegenia tale again, again the calm before the sacrifice, again perhaps reminding us of "The Ancient Mariner" also. (In lieu of an albatross hung round his neck, the Consul is shortly to feel "as if a black dog had settled on his back, pressing him to his seat.") But in a context of the foregoing discussion of reality, a radically new interpretation may also be demanded by all such images: literally translated, Nirvana means "without wind."

Talking with the proprietor, Diosdado, whose name Lowry renders as "the Godgiven," the Consul draws a map in spilled liquor on the bar. Diosdado is Spanish, and with this in mind the Consul is merely making conversation about his meeting with Yvonne in Granada. But Diosdado is also a fascist, and whatever Granada's significance at this juncture of the Spanish war, the man repeats the name "sharply, in a different, harder pronunciation," then leaves immediately to speak with others whose faces turn "in the Consul's direction."

Distracted, the Consul simply moves into a back room—"not really surprised" to be there confronted by the old woman of the dominoes seen at the start of the day. This is to say that with the Consul's occult orientation, and after the reappearance of the letters, more of this other sort of "correspondence" is but to be expected. But for that matter it might be noted here that the initial incident actually caps an even more intricate syndrome involving letters not only lost but misaddressed, undelivered, even unwritten—as it were a modern postal symbology to reassert the theme of the failure to communicate.

Meanwhile the woman herself almost immediately tries to get the Consul's attention, "opening her mouth and pointing into it." At this, reacting on the basis of another personal "orientation" altogether, the Consul naturally buys her a drink—whereas it will later become evident she has meant to indicate that he is still being talked about.

During this period the Consul endures an illusion that for an instant he is "back in the early morning again," this in opposition to his earlier sensation at the Paris: now even *unreality* becomes Heraclitan. Then there follows a "queer passing feeling" of springing from bed to mutter such remarks as "Coriolanus is dead!"—and of relapsing to "hear, from the street, the soft padding of the eternal ghostly policeman outside."[344] This is possibly an instance in which Lowry can be charged with reading "The Waste Land" instead of Weston, since Eliot speaks of "each in his prison" where, at nightfall, "aethereal rumors/ Revive for a moment a broken Coriolanus." On the other hand it is quite independently of Eliot that Coriolanus himself, like Caligula's steed Incitatus, almost becomes a consul at Rome; Lowry sends the Consul to a death very like Shakespeare gives the man, also.

"Do you remember to-morrow?" Yvonne's words then ask, referring to their wedding anniversary of months past, while the letters more generally speak for the Consul an "abject confirmation of his own lostness." Indeed, they do so too poignantly, so that he wonders "had Yvonne been reading the letters of Heloise and Abelard?" The case appears otherwise, though the reference supplies a new set of prototypal tragic lovers for the pair—cum very genuine prototypal pre-Freudian "castration" as well—while perhaps additionally nodding again in the direction of Conrad Aiken, in whose novel *Blue Voyage* a character does make use of those letters in such a way. The sense of identity between them is reiterated when he reads that "turning I see us in a hundred places"—as is simultaneously *happening* in Yvonne's hallucinations in the preceding chapter—and, with grim irony after the Consul's recent accusations, it further develops that Yvonne has written: "I want your children, soon, at once, I want them." Ultimately, the Consul concludes that "Yvonne had certainly been reading *something*," which is to say that Lowry himself presumably means to tell us she has; precisely what escapes the present reader.

The Consul takes a cigarette, an "Alas," thinking of the "tragic word," thereby again evoking that other impossible love of Echo and Narcissus. (Sooner or later, such parallels must call to mind Dante's tale of the adultery of Paolo and Francesca, if only because there too the husband is cuckolded by a younger brother—or because the husband is named Giovanni the Lame.) Ignoring another ambiguous warning of the old woman's, the Consul then posts himself once more in the entrance, "as sometimes before in the deceptive violet dawn." Pointedly, however, this is not dawn, not for the moment do any hints of Indic "peace" recur. In fact death does, or seems to. Previously, the Consul has seen a soldier "asleep under a tree" at the edge of the barranca; now he questions "or wasn't it a soldier, but something else?" Since a "dead dog" will be near enough at hand to be thrown into the barranca immediately after the Consul himself, and since Lowry does not usually let sleeping "somethings" lie without further identification, he is presumably being even less obtrusive here than with the arrival of the horse—yet, infallibly, getting it all *in.*

It is worth note, if incidentally, that the dawn image has actually seen its polar opposite too, in that after identifying himself
with Judas earlier, Hugh has then thought of "that Madrugada
of Madrugadas"—i.e., the dawn after the betrayal of Christ.
Meanwhile when the dog here *is* flung after the Consul, the
gesture may be less negative than it appears. As noted above, a
dog follows Orion to heaven. A climactic passage in the *Mahabharata* concerns the same sort of event. And in one version of
his death Quetzalcoatl is *reborn* as a dog. All of which, too, might
explain an earlier joking notion of the Consul's, when he has
thought of advertising that he "will accompany corpse to any-
place in east," again a hint of Lowry's own anthropomorphic
awarenesses.

In contrast to the foregoing, the Consul then watches a family
pass, including two children, one of whom abruptly turns "a
succession of cartwheels on the lush grass plot"—in effect the
wheel symbolism now turns human to remark that most elemen-
tary "continuity" missing in his life. Here too, considering the
approaching storm, he decides that two "drunken gods" are
engaged in a "wildly swinging game of bumblepuppy with a
Burmese gong." The game is played in Huxley's *Brave New
World,* another novel about Eden—if of a sort that would reduce
the "nuevo mundo" of Hugh's song to an absurdity.

Led by the "constricted power of aching flesh alone," the
Consul next finds himself acknowledging the overtures of a
prostitute named María, following her first through the "darker
and darker" rooms—once again away from the light, yet simultaneously into the heart of what were once scenes of monastic
worship—and then into the garden already mentioned. This
reminds him "queerly" of his own garden in Quauhnahuac,
"and also of El Popo, where he had earlier thought of going"
—a point being that were he currently in either place, he would
not only be kept from what he calls this "final stupid unprophylactic rejection," but from death itself.

The Consul deliberately listens for his voices, hoping for
"some good advice," but none is forthcoming. Meanwhile he
remarks a curious juxtaposition of purity and corruption in the
girl's room. On one hand he is reminded of "his old room at
college," yet finds the bed "disorderly and covered with foot-

marks, even what appeared bloodstains, though the bed too seemed akin to a student's cot."[348] The girl herself—save for asking in Spanish, "Quiere María?" "Do you want María?"— speaks otherwise "in some strange language, possibly Zapote- can." Since Lowry's Indians generally represent a simple, unso- phisticated good, this primitivism can probably be read in the same regard: in spite of her profession there remains an essen- tial innocence in the girl. The recollection of the Consul's col- lege days would imply something of the same, while on another plane "María" must naturally suggest Mary Magdalene in the later Christ equation. Furthermore the Zapotecan dialect is spoken mainly in the vicinity of Oaxaca, itself long since a nostal- gic symbol. Cf. Yvonne: " . . . at night their cries of love. . . . In Oaxaca they had found each other once," etc.

In fact the girl then "becomes" Yvonne, when it seems to the Consul that "her body" is his ex-wife's. The brief identity is ironic in much the same way as was Yvonne's in drinking the liquor she had failed to drink with the Consul earlier, since the latter is here fulfilling a marital "failure" of his own. Then again, Yvonne has perhaps been the virtuous prostitute all along her- self, if we wish to read an early line in the Consul's garden as evocative of the Dumas heroine: "Oh Geoffrey! Where're my camellias?"

But this "sentimental illusion" dissolves rapidly, the same flesh then transformed into a new kind of "nothing"—"an ab- straction merely, a calamity, a fiendish apparatus for calamitous sinking sensation."[349] The sensation is additionally one of "hor- ror," which Lowry sustains through a sentence some two and one-half pages in length, and in which images of alcoholic mis- ery predominate. Specifically, the Consul does now recall Oax- aca, though an Oaxaca the polar opposite from that which Yvonne has remembered. In this case the vision is of his visit *after* Yvonne's departure from Mexico, mention of which, actu- ally, is what leads to Yvonne's own recollection in the morning, and which is also described in the Consul's letter. But at the same time it develops that the night now being recalled also happens to have been the night before "their wedding anniver- sary"—called to the Consul's mind, doubtless, by Yvonne's let- ter written on that date, but once again then adding a new dimension to a picture essentially self-contained in its earlier presentation.

Said differently, the Consul is now remembering a night of prototypal agony, prompted by Yvonne's reference to the very same evening, during which she herself was enduring the pain of writing one of the unanswered letters just now received—a night of which the reader has been aware for the length of the book *without* knowing of these added correspondences. Moreover the hotel which the Consul now recalls so wretchedly is named in his letter as "the hotel where we once were happy," meaning the same one Yvonne had had in mind in remembering their "cries of love," and *while* it is being recalled the Consul will be cognizant of certain more immediate "cries of love" themselves ironically anything but "happy." This incredibly subtle ordering *within* order, surely, must leave such ostensibly "crafted" fictions as *Les Faux-Monnayeurs* or *The Good Soldier* rather less than exemplary by comparison.

Briefly, the Consul's recollection is of leaving his room at an hour of morning too early to permit entry into a Dantean cantina named "El Infierno"—described as opening at four A.M. and categorized as "that other Farolito"—and in consequence having to wait in the hotel dining room where he steals a drink before making his "escape." The word, in fact, becomes a leitmotif, echoing the "escape" in his poem. The bottle of wine from which he drinks, in his debility of the hour, is almost too heavy for him to lift—"like his burden of sorrow"—and, having recalled this, here now with the prostitute he is reminded of an inadvertent pun of Señora Gregorio's connected with the same topic: "You cannot drink of it." The sentence shifts fluidly from Oaxaca to the present and back, both episodes remaining currently "active" in his consciousness, and it is of this same wine that he decides "it must have been Jesus who sent me this." Whereas again in present time: "God is it possible to suffer more than this, out of this suffering something must be born, and what would be born was his own death . . . for ah, how alike are the groans of love to those of the dying."[349] The protracted sentence ends as he achieves the cantina in recollection and his physical "crisis" in actuality:

. . . standing inside the place with his back to the wall, and his
blanket still over his head, talking to the beggars, the early workers, the dirty prostitutes, the pimps, the debris and detritus of the
streets and the bottom of the earth, but who were yet so much
higher than he, drinking just as he had drunk here in the Farolito,
and telling lies, lying—the escape, still the escape!—under the
lilac-shaded dawn that should have brought death, and he should
have died now too; what have I done?[351]

The passage loses much of its force here, divorced from what
goes before. Nonetheless Laruelle's phrase about "piety" in a
certain scene must again apply—if indeed, the visual picture
itself does not suggest Christ.

Rebirth ensues, with another major symbol now approximat-
ing reality as the Consul discovers "a picture of Canada" on a
calendar beyond the bed. Verbalizing the meaning of the symbol, indeed, he shortly decides that Canada "might have been
a solution," and an opportunity for "a new life with Yvonne,"
if again ironically being made to forget his letter with its vision
of "some northern country": "Why hadn't he thought of it before?" Conversely he also discerns the same calendar to be set
a month into the future: "Where would he be then?"

The picture is of a stag under a "brilliant full moon," which
of itself demands attention. As noted in regard to the Heracles
parallel, the stag is sacred to Artemis (Diana in Roman myth).
Artemis is a goddess of the moon. It is she who causes the
becalming of Agamemnon's fleet, to which Lowry has *twice* now
alluded via Racine, and she does so, furthermore, from anger at
the killing of a stag. Thus the lady would seem to be prowling
somewhere about, all the more so because she is a huntress by
profession and—"incongruously"—there happens to be a
"giant sabre" in María's room. But on top of this Artemis is
eternally chaste: she slays *Orion* for an attempt on that chastity,
and Actaeon is turned *into* a stag for no more than watching her
bathe—whereupon he is torn apart by his own dogs. Ergo,
María's symbolic purity is further corroborated, the Consul will
be turned into a totem animal, the Consul will die at the hands
of "dogs"—and there is still nothing new under the sun (or the
full moon).

Or perhaps there is. In that all-important poem "Thirty-five Mescals in Cuautla," already seen to deal with several other current matters, Lowry similarly makes use of a calendar "set to the future." The picture described in that case is of a man who "thrusts his canoe into the moon," and it is in regard to this image that Lowry adds the aforementioned footnote associating soma with the moon, "who controls vegetation." Here, meanwhile, short moments after leaving María the Consul is aware of "a strange release, almost a sense of attainment," and decides it is as if "out of an ultimate contamination he had derived strength." Now the first of these reactions is obviously again Buddhist or occult, and the latter represents a definite fulfillment of the Consul's wish to "sink lower still." Yet in following so closely after the "unprophylactic" union, this "attainment" must beg new speculation. "Out of this suffering something must be born." There is a bottle of mescal in María's room—i.e., soma, i.e., a fertility potion. Canada, perhaps *the* rebirth symbol of the novel, is as close to transformation into reality as is possible, and the whole point in "sinking lower still" is to be reborn. After the *inordinate* weight of dead-children symbolism, conspicuously out of balance for lack of a polar contrast, is an altogether different "new life" intimated from that involving the Consul and Yvonne? Among all the rest, Artemis is a goddess of childbirth.

Leaving María the Consul does hear his voices at last, like Oresteian furies here "hissing and shrieking and yammering at him." In the mingitorio he sees advertisements offering the services of Dr. Vigil, if for purposes scarcely now those for which Dante looks to Virgil. Here he also finds himself accosted by "an incredibly filthy man sitting hunched in the corner on a lavatory seat," a procurer who announces it was he who "send" María, and whom the Consul thinks of as a "stool pigeon, in the strictest sense of that term." The Consul asks him the time. " 'Sick,' answered the man. 'No, it er ah half past sick by the cock.' " (The sexual pun is apt to obscure the secondary meaning, that the "time" itself is out of order.) More subtly, a poster for the insecticide "666" is altered in the Consul's concern to "606"— i.e., Ehrlich's successful experiment.

The Consul's fourth bathroom scene ends as he wonders "who was it had said earlier, half past tree by the cock?"[352] In point of fact, the phrase has occurred during the afternoon in Tomalín, but since it has also been recalled by the Consul at the Salón Ofélia, Lowry's unusual emphasis may well occur because someone has said the same thing yet "earlier" than this. "And when Immanuel Kant, in his grey coat, cane in hand, appeared at the door of his house, and strolled towards the small avenue of linden trees which is still called 'The Philosopher's Walk,' the neighbors knew it was exactly half past three by the clock." The famous portrait is Heine's; if intimated, the Kantian thesis of "pure reason," i.e., knowledge independent of sense experience and arising from the inherent nature of the mind itself, would obviously add new weight to Lowry's philosophic subjectivity. (Thus somewhere along in here our equally famous "stone" may have become the philosopher's stone, also.)

When the Consul returns to the front of the tavern, for a moment sensations are again exaggerated, and the roll of a drum in the distance seems "a revolution." (Earlier, he has thought of a rolling of drums "heard by some great dying monarch.") He recalls a Canadian Indian belief that "a cock will crow over a drowned body"—as the hallucinatory cock will crow as if in signification of his own demise—and it is at this point that he feels his sense of "release," i.e., while perceptions remain uncommon.

It is next that the Consul discovers the horse, after which he reaches the conclusion that "those Union Militar fellows were at the bottom, in an insanely complicated manner but still at the bottom, of the whole business." Presumably what he means is that in opposition to agrarian collectivism the fascists have robbed the Indian, and then in their role as "police" appear to be investigating their own crime, again contemporary justice epitomized. At a sound of thunder the animal whinnies "uneasily, shaking all over"—Hugh's prophetic notion at the roadside concerning "restive horses" now begins to be fulfilled.

When the man "resembling" an officer—actually resembling a sergeant—asks what he wants, the Consul responds with a "good Mexican joke": "I learn that the world goes round so I am waiting for my house to pass by." (Contrast Laruelle: "At

this rate he could go on traveling in an eccentric orbit round his
house forever.") The policeman is unamused, giving the Consul
"quick suspicious glances" in which the latter perceives "something serious indeed . . . something that bade him escape at his
peril."[355] Yet while also recalling "the look Diosdado had given
him," he nonetheless feels "neither serious nor like escaping,"
a compound irony after the profusion of metaphorical "escapes" in recent pages. Hearing himself called an "Americano,"
the Consul is shoved into the cantina.

He is accused, first, of paying neither for his mescal nor for
the girl—the police being right about the former, whereas nothing at all has been said about the prostitute—and further of
attempting to steal the horse. Reference is also made to his map
of Spain, and the suggestion follows that he is a "Bolsheviki."
"What are you for? Inglés? Español? Americano? Aleman?
Russish? You come a from the you-are-essy-essy?" The Consul
himself then proceeds to expand this new universality by unwittingly replying to a question in French, "Comment non," when
obviously intended is the Mexican idiom "cómo no," after which
he himself is aware of using Portuguese. An ironic if perhaps
again unintentional "Jawohl" caps the meaningful confusion.

Other officials appear in the interim, one "a tall slim man in
well-cut American tweeds with a hard sombre face" whom the
Consul believes he has seen before, another in police uniform.
The first of these is the aforementioned "Chief of Gardens,"
while the second is identified as the "Chief of Municipality."
(Lowry deliberately makes it "Gardens" throughout, whereas
the Spanish, "Jefe de Jardineros," would be "Chief of Garden-
ers"—in other words the "gardener" Hugh has said the Consul
has been without "for so long.") Their actual names pass without recognition, Sanabria and Zuzugoitea, both having been
seen in Laruelle's phone directory. Unnamed, on the other
hand, save insofar as he is the one called "Chief of Rostrums,"
is the "sergeant" who has apprehended the Consul and who will
take his life—doubtless "this fell sergeant, Death," as Hamlet
has it. Harking back to Lowry's epigraph from Bunyan, meanwhile, among all these "chiefs" the Consul himself must again
be seen as the "Chief of Sinners."

Again suggesting Alice—"Who cares for you? . . . You're nothing but a pack of cards!"—the Consul is forced to wonder: "And who were these people, really? . . . Chief of what Gardens? Surely this silent man in tweeds . . . wasn't the one responsible for all those little public gardens?"[358] But Lowry has brought other victims to the bar besides the Knave of Hearts alone. "Who could these men be? What were they talking about? What authority could they represent?" The lines might easily be substituted for the Consul's own; in actuality they come from the arrest in the opening pages of *The Trial*.

The theme of identity is further stressed when the Consul is asked (italics added): "What's your *names?*" Because of his beard someone calls him Trotsky—i.e., the protagonist of Laruelle's proposed Faust film—though not to be overlooked is that Trotsky himself is another exile murdered by "spiders" in Mexico. His residence in Coyoacán at the time of the novel would be why his name comes up to begin with, a reminder that Lowry's whole use of the motif is something less than exaggeration. But then the Consul himself makes the most significant contribution of all to the scheme, changing still another symbol to "reality" as he does: " 'Blackstone,' he answered gravely, and indeed . . . had he not and with a vengeance come to live among the Indians? . . . 'William Blackstone.' "[358]

In addition to the artistic nicety in the contrivance, two meanings seem primary here. First of all the Consul is again identifying with his father, for whom Blackstone has substituted before. But in the same Freudian manipulation Lowry has also brought off a decisive symbolic act on the level of the Oedipus *myth,* since this open proclamation of that identification must obviously correspond with Oedipus' recognition of the displacement of his own father. Thus with Jocasta already "recognized," the moment would signal the end of the Oedipus parallelism in the novel; only Yvonne's death and the Consul's "blinding" remain.

A moment after Blackstone is named, one of the police asks: "You are Juden?" Politically, we can take this as straight realism —meaning straight fascism. Simultaneously, however, this is the first of the detailed Christ equations, since the question is henceforward repeated with the insistence of its counterpart in the New Testament: "Art thou the King of the Jews?" But therein a rather formidable new syllogism: the Consul is his own father,

the Consul is Christ,—etc. Theological complications in abey-
ance, assumably "the Kingdom of God is within you" will ap-
proximate Lowry's meaning in this ultimate of prototypal exten-
sions.

But the Christ parallel must also point up a deliberate ambiguity in this latest reference to "living among the Indians." In
María's room, glancing at a book which, "of all things, was a
Spanish history of British India," the Consul thinks he has seen
mention of Kashmir; then at the point of death he will believe
for a moment that he is "in Kashmir." On one plane this is but
another illustration of the novel's ubiquitousness, "place"
becoming almost as "placeless" as Lowry's time becomes "timeless." But here too the Consul thus becomes not only the traditional Christ but also that Yus Asaf "who had, after being taken
down from the cross, wandered to Kashmir." In other words the
"Indians" at hand are not only William Blackstone's New England red men, but also the very ones with whom the Consul's
real father went to live.

Wherewith, also, a new Indic parallel. According to Oriental
belief a Universal King, or secular counterpart of the Buddha,
appears at certain intervals to guide the troubled world. Called
the *Cakravartin,* his appointment is signified by seven classic
symbols frequently reproduced on Buddhist altars. The seven:

—A Luminous Wheel. The word *Cakravartin* itself translates
roughly as "he who turns the wheel." Buddha's own wheel has
been specifically mentioned *supra.* In the present chapter the
Consul perceives that the Union Militar clock is both "luminous" and "annular."

—A Divine White Elephant. The proprietor of the Farolito, a
site already long associated with Indic themes, has been given
the unusual name "Diosdado," "the Godgiven." The same man,
it develops, is more commonly referred to as "the Elephant."

—A Milky White Horse. Lowry's horse serves too many symbolic functions ever to be restricted in meaning; most telling in
the present regard, however, is that its color is *nowhere* recorded
(the decision has to be deliberate on Lowry's part).

—A Magic Jewel, capable of turning night into day. The Consul has just now endured the latter illusion; and since it will be
death at the hands of a pistol that ends his larger "dark night

of the soul," also to be noted is a pistol once described here as "a bright jewel."

—A Perfect Wife, equally beautiful and virtuous. In a manner of speaking the "virtuous" María is the Consul's only "wife."

—A Perfect Minister of Finance. What money the Consul possesses becomes a subject of special interest from here on; additionally, when it is suggested that the Consul is a "wrider," he will admit for no seeming purpose that he is such—"only on economic matters."

—A Perfect Commander-in-Chief. "Chiefs" already run rampant; but the Consul once speculates that Sanabria, obviously superior to the others, may be "even 'higher' than the Inspector General himself."

Some of this, which is taken from Heinrich Zimmer's *Philosophies of India,* may be tenuous, but certainly the Godgiven Elephant alone would make it clear that Lowry has some Buddhist scheme or other in mind. Near death, in fact, the Consul will see "emerald snow" on Popocatepetl, and the Buddhist "World Mountain"—one more counterpart for the Mountain of Purgatory—is said to have jewelled slopes. But too, the mission of the *Cakravartin* is one of peace, and apropos of nothing save his own musings a drunk is shortly to declare: "Tranquillity means peace. Peace on earth, of all men." (While the line is obviously Christian in its associations, again the East-West, Buddha-Christ parallelism would be one of Lowry's points.) Moreover, in proclamation of that mission the Luminous Wheel appears not only to the *Cakravartin* himself but is placed in the firmament, and the Ferris wheel revolving "over the town" at the end of Chapter I —so to speak proclaiming the "advent" of the Consul in the flashback to follow—is itself a "luminous wheel." (Cf. also a luminous wheel in Yvonne's view of the actual heavens in Chapter XI.)

As a result, then, the notion of living among the Indians might take on still another dimension, suggesting Buddha's seven years of renunciation and meditation in the forest. Or in new paradox, the dark wood becomes a refuge in which to *seek* the light—as it has been for Blackstone all along. (Not to add that Trotsky, one more Jew, even one more writer on "economic matters," was born Bronstein—"brown stone"—or that Bishop

Berkeley, not many years after Blackstone himself, quite literally went to live among the Indians of Rhode Island.)

Further extension of the Consul's Everyman status occurs when he realizes where he has "seen" Sanabria before: "The Chief of Gardens might have been the image of himself when, lean, bronzed, serious, beardless, and at the crossroads of his career, he had assumed the Vice Consulship in Granada."[359] In addition to this identity with one of his own accusers, however, the new manipulation of Granada must be observed; now in retrospect a symbol of the entirely different "path" his life might have taken, its very mention is what has brought him to this present "crossroads." In the same context, meanwhile, "beardless" would imply a pre-Trotsky—i.e., pre-Faustian—persona.

To the same end the Consul also notices Sanabria's "beautiful" hands, an adjective Yvonne has once applied to his own, though here again the deliberate repetition leads to still another Eastern meaning. References by the Consul to both Vedic priests *and* the sacrifice of animals have been quoted *supra.* In the most sacred of all such Vedic ceremonies, the *Ashvamedha* sacrifice, the priest in charge of the offerings was characterized as "the beautiful-handed." The victim of the sacrifice: a horse. (The libation: soma.)

During all of this the Farolito itself is becoming crowded, even "chaotic," with a *Walpurgisnacht* complexion added by celebrants of the Day of the Dead "dressed in long black cloaks streaked with luminous paint to represent skeletons." And when the Consul finally here begins to understand "the tangibility of his danger," it develops that we have not seen the last of Oedipus after all: "Ah, if Yvonne, if only as a daughter, who would understand and comfort him, could only be at his side now! Even if but to lead him by the hand, drunkenly homeward through the stone fields, the forests—"[360] Typically, Lowry has long since prepared for the image by having Hugh think of his guitar as being "like Oedipus' daughter . . . my guide and prop"; and while he is anticipating himself slightly, this is indisputably the right Oedipus after what has gone before, the picture being of Antigone guiding the "drunken" king—read the colloquialism "blind"—*after* the tragic revelations.

The Consul next has a moment in which he sees again "in his mind's eye that extraordinary picture on Laruelle's wall, Los Borrachones," finding in it now "another meaning . . . beyond the symbolically obvious":

> When he had striven upwards, as at the beginning with Yvonne, had not the "features" of life seemed to grow more clear, more animated . . . more *separate* from himself? And had it not turned out that the further down he sank, the more those features had tended to dissemble, to cloy and clutter, to become finally little better than ghastly caricatures of his dissimulating inner and outer self, or of his struggle, if struggle there were still? Yes, but had he desired it, willed it, the very material world, illusory though that was, might have been a confederate, pointing the wise way. Here would have been no devolving through failing unreal voices and forms of dissolution that became more and more like one voice to a death more dead than death itself, but an infinite widening, an infinite evolving and extension of boundaries, in which the spirit was an entity, perfect and whole: ah, who knows why man, however beset his chance by lies, has been offered love?[361]

It would have been difficult for Lowry to put most of this more explicitly, though the question of moral choice demands pause. Obviously, the Consul is here acknowledging the extent of his denial of life, a retreat into the self which has led to the unreality of which he speaks. But here too then the whole scheme of idealism, equated previously with expanding spiritual consciousness, must simultaneously be seen as resulting from a fundamental failure of will. Even now, the Consul could readily extricate himself by facing up to the reality of his predicament and doing something *sensible* about it, in the strict sense of the word, yet when two opportunities for escape are offered he will ignore both.

Where this contradiction leads is difficult to judge, though a line from the Consul's letter appears pertinent: "Sometimes I am possessed by a most powerful feeling, a despairing bewildered jealousy which, when deepened by drink, turns into a desire to destroy myself by my own imagination."[40] Since the Consul is now in essence doing exactly that, rather than any failure of will a perverse triumph may be implied. In "The Forest Path to the Spring" Lowry speaks of a concept of Ortega y Gasset's wherein "a man's life is like a fiction that he makes up as he goes along," and nothing is said to preclude the choice of a tragic ending. The idea is perhaps Miltonic, that man was created "sufficient to have stood, but free to fall." On this more abstract plane, however, it would suggest, again like Señora Gregorio, that our already elusive reality is not merely what *is* perceived, but what one *wishes* to perceive. (Or, alas, perhaps only that Voltaire was right about Dante: "He has commentators . . . another reason for his not being understood.")

In the interim the Consul has been joined at the bar by the "stool pigeon" seen earlier, while at his other side he discovers "a man of uncertain nationality, crosseyed with drink, who resembled a sailor," this the aforementioned creature of Biblical orientation who announces that "Mozart wrote the old testimony." If "Moses" would bring him closer to the mark, a secondary point might nonetheless be that some "artist" was responsible. (Then again it may have been Hugh—who has once remembered being "prepared to lead the whole Jewish race out of Babylon itself," and has also compared himself to Mozart.) But since Lowry goes on to describe the man as "an even obscurer fellow than the stool pigeon," and then for some pages leaves the three inextricably caught up in this relationship, we are of course *in* the "new testimony" too: "And with him they crucify two thieves; the one on his right hand, and the other on his left."

Since it is this same sailor who speaks of "peace on earth," but in terms which at last become a mockery, while the procurer in turn makes certain anti-American remarks the Consul decides are "insults," the analogy goes deeper: "And they that were crucified with him reviled him." Meanwhile the Consul is aware of being discussed on the telephone, and Weber also now appears, repeating lines heard in the morning. Whereupon from a radio: "Quiere usted la salvación de Méjico? . . . Quiere usted que Cristo sea nuestro Rey?"[365] "Do you want the salvation of Mexico? . . . Do you want Christ to be our King?"

Within three pages the question is repeated three times. On

each occasion, and with no indication who is speaking, or in answer to what amid the general confusion, Lowry interpolates as a separate paragraph the single word: "No." These then, as anticipated, the three "denials" before the crowing of the cock.

But then again rebirth, and familiarly, if this time as phrased by Yvonne's letters instead of by Señora Gregorio: "Where did we go, I wonder? In what far place do we still walk, hand in hand?" (Finally, this notion of "some kernice place" must begin to recall something of that equally mystical "shared" identity in *Wuthering Heights;* cf. also Cathy's "I *am* Heathcliff.") And after which Yvonne contrives to reiterate the novel's central premise in a word: "What release can be compared to the release of love?"[367]

Other themes echo concurrently. The Consul is again wearing his dark glasses, making the letters "for some reason clearer," while the noise in the cantina is at last specifically named "the Babel . . . the confusion of tongues." Someone sets a "clockwork skeleton" on the bar—a new "tick of death"—and behind it the boy is munching candy coffins. This is the same boy who has earlier been reading "The Son of the Devil," whereas he himself is in fact the son of the Godgiven, as it were in confirmation of a line the Consul attributes to Baudelaire elsewhere: "The gods exist, they are the devil."

The driver of the afternoon's bus appears, and it is now that his pigeons are referred to as "palomas"; but since he is no longer carrying them, it may be surmised that unlike Aeneas the Consul is to receive no divine guidance from here on—or that unlike Noah, he will be brought no olive leaf from Ararat. Here too, again thinking about "escape," the Consul concludes that there is "nowhere to fly to," a painfully prophetic echo of Laruelle's misreading in Chapter I: "Then will I headlong fly into the earth . . ."

Conversely, he does now receive his offers of mortal aid. First an old fiddler, encouraged by one of the police to play "The Star Spangled Banner," manages to whisper: "Americano? This bad place for you. . . . Bad people here. Brutos. . . . I am a potter. . . . I take you to my home." Here again the Spanish epithet serves the same dual function as in its earlier usage: the fascists are literally "brutes," but like Brutus they are conspirators against the state as well. Simultaneously—while perhaps being a distant cousin of Joe Venuti's—the potter himself represents still another abstraction turned real, the Farolito as indicated being one of those "unimaginable cantinas where sad-faced potters and legless beggars drink at dawn." Thus it is probably unnecessary to confirm that the Consul has already found said beggars in the doorway also.

The second offer comes from a woman who now literally labels the fascists as "diablos," while muttering "Vámonos," "Let us go," but to whom the Consul merely raises his glass in thanks. Only later does he recognize her as the woman of the dominoes. And thus where the woman has seemed an "evil omen" to Yvonne in the morning, what with her two previous warnings to the Consul that original misconstruction would appear more than ironic. Indeed, at the arena Yvonne imagines the woman to be peering over her shoulder, and the possibility suggests itself that she might have been there in fact, a sort of beneficent Consular "demon" hovering throughout the day. Or *was* she? By now such questions have either no answers or too many.

Meanwhile there is actually a third way out for the Consul here —undeniably ironic in this case—since Weber will be seen to glance toward him with "a remote speculation" at hearing the name Firmin, only to turn away again. Which is to say that under certain circumstances the fascist, too, will embrace a policy of "nonintervention."

The Consul's real name is learned when the Chief of Rostrums abruptly empties his pockets under pretext of finding money for the drinks, disclosing Hugh's signed cable, Yvonne's letters in their addressed envelopes, and a card of Hugh's from the *"Federación Anarquista Ibérica."* Since the subject of the cable is anti-Semitism, the Consul is charged with having doubly lied: "It say there: Firmin. It say you are Juden." As abridged by the Consul's own hasty reading, on the other hand, the cable also puns on a concept of a different nature about the fascists themselves: *"German behind . . . interiorwards.* What was this?"[369]

By now, discussion is heated. Still insisting his name to be Blackstone, the Consul protests further at being called an anarchist, whereupon the word undergoes an unobtrusive transfor-

mation from "anarquista" to "antichrista" as mouthed by the
Chief of Rostrums. The Consul is also without his passport;
since it has first turned up missing at the "Máquina Infernal,"
the machine's gears are obviously still meshing. Assorted Spanish obscenities follow, after which, "winking at Diosdado," the
officer confiscates the Consul's belongings. Both this and a recurrent sensation of the latter's that his pockets are being picked
would again imply the presence of "thieves," but probably too
the "casting of lots" at Golgotha.

For some period the Chief of Gardens has been remote, but
now, with an impersonality suggesting Pilate, he tells the Consul
"simply": "I am afraid you must come to prison." It is here that
"writer" becomes "wrider," leading to yet another transformation as the Chief of Rostrums puts in: "You are no a de wrider,
you are de espider, and we shoota de espiders in Méjico."[371] In
addition to the reversal here on the Consul's own paranoia
concerning "spiders," however, he might be viewed as becoming a sort of metaphorical "insect" likewise, much in the meaning of Kafka's *Metamorphosis*. Indeed, in the same breath he is
also labeled "Al Capón," a homely gringo contribution to his
prototypal genealogy, but one into which we can presumably
read a pun on "capon" also—since the Chief of Rostrums suddenly now takes the Consul "by the throat."

At all events only another moment passes—the third "denial"
has likewise been heard—before the hallucinatory cock appears
as well. Hitting out at it, the Consul strikes the Chief of Gardens
"straight between the eyes," and then finds himself shouting
accusations about the death of the Indian. Seeing in the Chief
of Rostrums' expression "a hint of M. Laruelle," and in the
Chief of Gardens' again a hint of "himself," he punches at both
—the sum of such absurdities being comparable to Hugh's intended larger "gesture" in Spain. The clock outside chimes
seven times, and it is on the instant of this symbolic midnight
that the Consul is briefly "blinded"—like Oedipus in self-retri-
bution (the striking at "himself") but equally like Goethe's Faust
before redemption. Dragged toward the door, he falls into his
scapegoat role when a number of bystanders commence to attack him also—communal participation in the ritual-murder of
the priest-king, more particularly to be viewed as the "smiting"

of Christ—and it is here that he snatches up the machete. At
which point:

> The Consul didn't know what he was saying: "Only the poor, only
> through God, only the people you wipe your feet on, the poor in
> spirit, old men carrying their fathers and philosophers weeping
> in the dust, America perhaps, Don Quixote—" he was still bran-
> dishing the sword, it was that sabre really, he thought, in María's
> room—"if you'd only stop interfering, stop walking in your sleep,
> stop sleeping with my wife, only the beggars and the accursed."
> The machete fell with a rattle. . . . "You stole that horse," he
> repeated.[372]

The borrowing from the Sermon on the Mount rings most
obviously—"Blessed are the poor in spirit"—but with his own
pathetic weapon in hand the Consul does not really have to
remind us of Don Quixote either. Considering the fine lines of
distinction in his argument with Hugh, there is equal pathos in
this confused new juxtaposition of political and personal moral-
ity, though the point again emerges that they are one and the
same. The transitional reference to sleepwalking, if literally bespeaking that same confusion, would again appear to raise the
reality question, meaning that the Consul is naturally not the
only one who exists in a "dream." (The same concept might also
newly evoke *Macbeth,* another drama of political "interference,"
in context perhaps seeming to promise a certain aftertaste of
guilt for the fascists themselves.) Since we have actually seen an
old man carrying his father some time before this, that image for
a change represents an instance in which Lowry has transformed
his own reality into metaphor. And in a world where the Consul
has roundly condemned all major political isms, while living in
self-imposed exile from an England he no longer serves, the
invocation of "America perhaps" would appear to sum up
Lowry's personal vision of any immediate hope for the age—at
least at the date of the novel.

But a subtlety occurs here also. This late along, and in such
a recapitulative passage, the reference to "the people you wipe
your feet on" seems strangely "new" by Lowry's standards—
unless it is meant to recall the "footmarks, what even appeared

bloodstains," on María's cot, again then perhaps a suggestive corroboration, if brutally so, of her "innocence." Any "Mary" is obviously relevant at a symbolic death of Christ; but the fact that the Consul thinks of her by name also, when on one level they have had no "communication" at all, would seem equally *pregnant.*

The Consul stumbles at the end of this, and now it is he who is called a "pelado." Before he gets to his feet, the Chief of Rostrums pronounces sarcastically: "You want to be a policeman? I make you a policeman in Mexico." Literally, the notion relates to the Consul's accusations concerning the stolen horse and the murdered Indian—*if indeed, such they are?* To the end, both the theft and even the death remain unverified, Lowry's deliberate ambiguity refusing to pinpoint guilt, or perhaps even any "crime," as an absolute. But there is something else in the line besides the surface implication that here "pelado" and "policeman" are kin. With Yvonne's father having been named "Constable," on a mythic level the Consul is again being identified with the man in Lowry's Electra scheme; more meaningfully, the *Cakravartin* on his own part is traditionally thought of as a "policeman" of *dharma* or moral law.

When the Consul rises he again spies the horse, seeing it "more vividly" than at any time before. The number seven stands out on its rump, and the sore on its hipbone is visible. And then the animal becomes a symbol of sorts for him, himself, as he tears "frantically" at its bridle—as if to set it free in the only act of redemption remaining, or by indirection to "free" himself—and thus of course adding a final irony to the death of Yvonne.

Before firing, the Chief of Rostrums significantly pushes the Consul "back out of the light." In contrast, lightning flashes with the shots, and Popocatepetl is "drenched with brilliance" —the upward way illuminated. Thunderclaps crash—as heard by Yvonne—and the "reborn" horse plunges into the dark wood.

In Marlowe, thunder is indicated for Faust's irrevocable midnight. Here, however, it must presumably also be interpreted as in the final section of "The Waste Land," where Eliot connects it with transcendent human attainment as expressed in the

Upanishads, still another volume on the Consul's shelves. Too, there might be an allusion in the storm generally to the "quaking" and "darkness" at Golgotha, a motif adumbrated by Laruelle's recitation that "the earth had opened all through this country" during the crucifixion—and Laruelle also once uses the figure "tonnerre de dieu."

Rain then falls, also as before Yvonne's death—to be understood as bringing surcease to stricken Thebes, renewal after the death of the Fisher King, etc.—but not until Lowry newly stresses the theme of unbroken continuity by having a bell voice the Dantean notes heard a year hence: *"Dolente . . . dolore!"* And a more subtle repetition occurs when, falling to his face, the Consul thinks: "Christ . . . this is a dingy way to die."[373] Whereas in his letter: "Oh, Yvonne, we cannot allow what we created to sink down to oblivion in this dingy fashion."

Once more then, the Consul has the sensation that his pockets are being picked, but here the concept is intended to recall the theft at the roadside. Almost immediately, the word "pelado" begins to fill his "whole consciousness." "And it was as if, for a moment, he had become the pelado, the thief—yes, the pilferer of meaningless muddled ideas out of which his rejection of life had grown."[374] But in the same period the old fiddler calls him "compañero," a word the dying Indian himself had muttered, if to deaf ears, and this makes the Consul "happy." He hears faint music, in his own turn now confusing Mozart with Moses—this perhaps because we have now reached a different kind of "end of the road," a Pisgah from where, indeed, he simultaneously has a last fleeting vision of England. The music he hears is Gluck's "Alcestis," another tale of devoted lovers who descend into hell but are resurrected. Then the music blends into "the chords of a guitar . . . and what sounded like the cries of love," evoking Hugh and Yvonne respectively perhaps, though a recent line will remind us of what the second sound must be in more immediate actuality: "For ah, how alike are the groans of love to those of the dying."

As in his dream, the Consul then finds himself beneath the Himalayas—making it "all the more remarkable he should suddenly be setting out with Hugh and Yvonne to climb Popocatepetl." Yvonne's warning about bougainvillea is remembered, the "spikes" in context suggesting Christ's thorns, after which the Consul *half* clairvoyantly suspects that she and Hugh have "not only climbed Popocatepetl but were now far beyond it." He imagines himself trudging the foothills "toward Amecameca"— surely now Mecca—alone, then sinking to the ground in exhaustion. "Now he was the one dying by the wayside where no good Samaritan would halt"—in effect the point of the novel in a sentence.

Next the Consul has an illusion of being "rescued at last," in an ambulance carrying him toward the peak—a new way for Mohammed to get to the mountain, or for Dante—and with the "friendly voices" of Laruelle and Dr. Vigil nearby. The pair, he decides, "would make allowances, would set Hugh and Yvonne's minds at rest about him. 'No se puede vivir sin amar,' they would say, which would explain everything"[375]—which indeed they *will* say in Chapter I, and which does "explain everything," for Lowry's purposes if not, as it happens, for their own. The Consul then repeats the phrase "aloud," in fact, making these the last spoken words of the novel as they have been virtually the first.

Convinced that he has "reached the summit," the Consul also thinks to himself: "Ah, Yvonne, sweetheart, forgive me!"—this, most likely, the mystical calling of her name "far away" which Yvonne is *literally* hearing at this time in Chapter XI. He feels "strong hands" lifting him—as is happening, although not for purposes of "succour" as he believes—and then opens his eyes, "expecting to see, below him, the magnificent jungle, the heights . . . like those peaks of his life conquered one after another before this greatest ascent of all had been successfully, if unconventionally, completed." Instead:

But there was nothing there: no peaks, no life, no climb. Nor was this summit a summit exactly: it had no substance, no firm base. It was crumbling too, whatever it was, collapsing, while he was falling, falling into the volcano, he must have climbed it after all, though now there was this noise of foisting lava in his ears, horribly, it was in eruption, yet no, it wasn't the volcano, the world itself was bursting, bursting into black spouts of villages catapulted into space, with himself falling through it all, through the inconceivable pandemonium of a million tanks, through the blazing of ten million burning bodies, falling, into a forest, falling—[375]

Trees close over him, "pitying . . . " And then the last line of the novel reverberates with that impact which can pertain only when purest tragedy transcends even its own inevitability: "Somebody threw a dead dog after him down the ravine."

Meanwhile the illusion of climb will have been seen as one final assertion of hope, of the "dream"—wholly unreal or otherwise—of the striving back toward Eden. And while the overall Christ analogy would make redemption implicit, Lowry deliberately leaves the shock of his ending unmitigated by any such promise. Similarly, the destruction of "the world itself" may suggest philosophic idealism again also, but the last "abyss"— like the "ten million burning bodies" of history's next few years —is real.

The final point is then equally clear. The Consul has been Everyman, true, but the world, Eden, exists for every *man:*

¿LE GUSTA ESTE JARDÍN
QUE ES SUYO?
¡EVITE QUE SUS HIJOS LO DESTRUYAN!

Like the departing commentary by a chorus in Greek tragedy, the familiar words occur after the fact, on a page separate from the body of the novel; separate, it might be said, from the body of the Consul. For this is Malcolm Lowry himself speaking now, intruding at last, the artist who has created and destroyed his own world that through the paradox of tragedy's genius we may perhaps be saved from destroying ours. The lines stand as his reasoned exhortation to mankind—a mankind which, as embodied so triumphantly in the Consul, he has also shown to be *worth* the saving.

AFTERWORD

As indicated in my preface, the manuscript of this book was finished in its present form several years ago, to be specific in 1972. Had I entertained any illusions, even then, that my efforts were exhaustive, they would have been painfully dispelled only a year later with the publication of Tony Kilgallin's *Lowry*. Unarguably, I explore *Under the Volcano* in more detail than he; still, Kilgallin knows things about the novel that eluded me entirely.

Some relevant examples:

—I have recorded a reference of the Consul's to man as "a little soul holding up a corpse." Kilgallin points out that the line is a quotation from Marcus Aurelius, who in turn attributes it to Epictetus—though meaning, among other things, that when Marcus Aurelius *is* mentioned, Lowry has typically (if obliquely) prepared us for his appearance. Indeed, in a line I do not mention, Hugh has asked himself: "What was life but a warfare and a stranger's sojourn?"—yet another borrowing from the same source.

—Chatting with Dr. Vigil, the Consul suggests that the world is sinking, "like Atlantis," and then speaks of "Meropis of Theopompus" and the *"ignivome* mountains," ignored in my own text for reasons of common ignorance. Kilgallin finds them in Jules Verne's *Twenty Thousand Leagues Under the Sea*—incidentally adding a typically Consular universality to that "subaqueous" view of life he endures in his garden.

—Atlantis is mentioned more than once in the novel. Kilgallin notes that the Consul's statement (which I have had to recall frequently) about "intercourse between opposite sides of the Atlantic" is a direct lifting from Ignatius Donnelly in his *Atlantis,*

The Antediluvian World—and in fact Donnelly himself is named by the Consul in his bedroom conversation with Yvonne.

—At the Farolito, the Consul envisions "the uncontrollable face on the barroom floor" (actually he is looking at a rabbit). Kilgallin points to "the uncontrollable mystery on the bestial floor" in a Yeats poem entitled "The Magi"—which would add still another Christ image to the many in Lowry's concluding pages.

—Peering into the barranca from his garden, the Consul proclaims: "Thou mighty gulf, insatiate cormorant, deride me not, though I seem petulant to fall into thy chops." Deliciously Firminish indeed—though the words are taken *verbatim* from a Marston verse called "To Everlasting Oblivion."

Initially, my impulse might have been to incorporate such material into my own pages, but I believe a more urgent point is made by appending it here: no individual commentator is ever going to produce a "definitive" explication of *Under the Volcano* because the depths and echoes in the book would appear almost *infinite.* For that matter it is often possible to *suspect* Lowry of a subtlety and, reading privately, fail completely to pin it down. A few cases in point there also:

—In Chapter I, Laruelle notices a poster of a German actress named Maria Landrock, and again thinks of her as "enigmatic." In his Cape letter, Lowry terms this usage "political." In what exact sense? (Nor do I find a listing of Maria Landrock in any volume on film.)

—The Consul once refers to the Farolito as the "Cafe Chagrin," surely a literary (or perhaps theatrical) borrowing. From where?

—From the doorway of the Salón Ofélia, the Consul finds the sunlight "turning the scarlet flowers along the path into flaming swords." "Even almost bad poetry is better than life," he then speculates. In what actual "bad poem" does the former occur?

—In the same vein, Hugh decides that "death and truth could rhyme at a pinch!" Where do they?

—Hugh also somewhere hears a leaf fall "with a crash," certainly an archetypal concept; but is a more specific allusion intended?

—Lowry allows both Hugh *and* the Consul to speak of killing

"two birds with one stone." His coyness with seeming clichés
has long since been documented. What reference here, then?

—As noted *supra,* Hugh romantically describes Sokotra as an
island where "no one has ever been." Why, when there *is* such
a place (if generally spelled "Socotra")?

—At Señora Gregorio's, the Consul recalls "a phrase read or
heard in youth or childhood: 'For God sees how timid and
beautiful you really are, and the thoughts of hope that go with
you like little white birds—' " Source?

—Only moments before the Consul's death, a relatively long
declamation on "the benefits of civilization" and "the thirsty lips
of the people" in their "bestial tasks" blares from the Farolito's
radio, far too crucially situated to be incidental. Trotsky himself
in deliberately faulty translation, perhaps? *Someone,* almost
unquestionably.

One could go on. Kilgallin himself, in a separate essay on
Lowry's use of the Faust theme (reprinted in Woodcock's *Malcolm Lowry: The Man and His Work*) pursues that subject far more
extensively than I; another scholar is apparently well into a
similarly protracted Dante investigation. Playing Lowry's own
"sortes" game, I have only at this moment—I swear—opened
the book at random and come upon mention of "Tres Marías,"
an actual town near Cuernavaca but surely another deliberate
inclusion to intensify Biblical symbolism (the "three" being
Mary Magdalen, Mary the wife of Cleophas, and Mary the
mother of James, traditionally conjoined because of their alleged prosyletizing in Provence). And yet, and yet, and yet
. . . as recently as in a review of the Douglas Day biography, no
less an admirer of *Under the Volcano* than William Gass felt quite
seriously able to dismiss the very essence of Lowry's *modus* as
literary "namedropping," and to propose—I swear this also—
that Lowry was "not profoundly acquainted with literature."
(One recalls that Samuel Johnson himself could find the metaphysical poets often obtuse; but only after the central perception that "to write on their plan it was at least necessary to
read.")

Probably there are greater novels in the language—whatever
precisely that notion means—and undeniably there are any
number of novelists whose *oeuvre* displaces more weight. But is

any *single* fictional achievement—and I include *Ulysses* in the question—quite so fecund in evocation, so *diverse* in amplification? Indeed, my ultimate suspicion is that *Under the Volcano* should not be read as we read other fictions at all. It is a poem, rather, and a poem in kind with several of its grandest models. I mean with the *Aeneid,* the *Divine Comedy,* with Goethe's *Faust*— each of which, for all the *apparatus criticus* of centuries, remains ever newly open to this same sort of enriching interpretation and delight.

I should perhaps carry that comparison no further for the moment.

APPENDIX
Malcolm Lowry: A Reminiscence

(The following appears essentially as written in 1965. A version published by The Nation *in 1966, and which has been reprinted elsewhere, was severely abridged because of space requirements.)*

For seven or eight days, in the summer of 1952, I visited with Malcolm Lowry in the squatter's shack on the beach beyond Vancouver where he had written most of *Under the Volcano.* In September, 1954, while awaiting the departure of a freighter to Italy, he and his wife Margerie lived for two weeks in my New York apartment. The duration of both visits seems greater in retrospect, since time spent with Lowry was somehow concentrated, or *distilled.* Speaking of Dylan Thomas, Lowry told me once, "You know, I never saw him when he wasn't drunk." I have to begin with the same qualification about Lowry.

The man could not shave himself. In lieu of a belt, he knotted a rope or a discarded necktie about his waist. Mornings, he needed two or three ounces of gin in his orange juice if he was to steady his hand to eat the breakfast that would very likely prove his only meal of the day. Thereafter a diminishing yellow tint in the glass might belie for a time the fact that now he was drinking the gin neat, which he did for as many hours as it took him to collapse—sometimes sensible enough of his condition to lurch toward a bed, though more often he would crash down into a chair, and once it was across my phonograph. Then he would hack and sputter through the night like some great defective machine breaking apart.

Yet what one remembers is somehow less the excess than Lowry's own attitude toward it, a remarkable impression he conveyed that he could never take any of it quite seriously. He had an acute sense of his own dissolution, eternally chagrined at being a nuisance, apologizing hourly after small disasters, but what he sensed equally was the underlying absurdity in it all: the very idea, a grown man and that is the third burning cigarette I have misplaced tonight. So he laughed; and most often, one felt, with the delight of a naughty child who has "gotten away" with something.

One afternoon in New York Margerie and I had to leave him alone for a time, though at his promise that he would remain "safely" within the apartment. Because a party was being given for him that night, Margerie had done her best to establish what Lowry termed her "tyranny of five o'clock," a prohibition against hard liquor before then. Such gin as I had was hidden, and we left him with six or eight cans of beer. I was the first to return, about three hours later. Within moments, Lowry had commenced to giggle. Sheepish, but no less transparently gleeful, he glanced about furtively before he confessed: "I have a funny story to tell you, about something that happened when you were out." Something had "happened," as opposed to being done. A day or two before, I had bought fresh shaving lotion. I did not ask what it had used to dilute itself.

One jokes because Lowry joked: this was mischief only. Though the mischief was somehow cosmic too, as if ordained. In his autobiographical narrative *Ushant,* Conrad Aiken remembers a younger Lowry as "visibly and happily alight with genius," and the phrase means exactly what it says. Lowry *looked* like a genius, there was a gleam not within but *behind* his eyes that seemed to transcend any ordinary alertness or mirth. The notion will prove more provocative if one recalls the Consul's "demons" in *Under the Volcano,* and how often those demons are "in possession"—though I am still aware that I risk exaggeration.

A typical instance comes to mind. Lowry is in the midst of a conversation. Making some point or other, he prefaces it thus: "As old Stendhal might say, if he were here . . . " Abruptly he pauses. That "look" is there, far more than speculative, as he considers a vacant chair, perhaps even a window ledge. "And probably he *is* . . . " When he glances back he is full of merriment again. There is even a hint of self-mockery in it—or would be, if the observer did not endure the unsettling feeling that it was he himself for whom the allowances were being made.

Lowry had "Norse" eyes, with a certain whiteness in the pigmentation of the lids that complemented that demonic glitter. But his upper teeth protruded slightly, suggesting a grin whether one was intended or not—though one generally was—in the end making of him a roguishly improbable Faustus at best.

He was really too "bookish" for the role too, even if there was a distinct manner in which he cared less about the written word than about the shade of the man who had put it down. A novel became a kind of introduction, for Lowry, to the author personally, and it would follow that an insight likened to one of Stendhal's, say—or Kafka's, or Melville's—would often be one that the latter had never anywhere expressed, but that only he among writers might have. Lowry could be uncanny in this regard.

Then again his "familiars" were not necessarily always his peers. During another New York conversation, and after another un-predicated pause, the talk had been taken up again for some ten or fifteen minutes before Lowry announced, "Incidentally, there was an owl perched outside there just now. You saw it, of course?"

An owl. On West 113th Street. Well, it was not impossible. Anyway it more than suited the general run of Lowry's conversation, which, again like the Consul's, was wholly unpredictable, wholly implausible, if not to say so full of involution and subordination that even the most simple statement was rarely completed: every owl reminded Lowry of twelve other owls. One afternoon, drinking with friends, he began an anecdote about a French hospital where, apparently, several kindly but ill-advised nuns had supplied him with litre after litre of red wine. The story also seemed to have something to do with his Cambridge friend John Davenport, the English critic. It was started at least eight times. But after digressions about the China sea, and Mexican jails, and the reading habits of James Joyce, and certain Manx fishing customs, it spiraled finally into absolute incoherence:

"Malc, will you for heaven's sake tell us what you are talking about?"

"Well, it's difficult. But you have to listen. It's . . . *contrapuntal!*" (Expresses delight as he fixes upon the word.)

"And there *was* an owl!"—this also a typical Lowryism, declaimed not on the night of the bird's alleged visitation, but a week later perhaps, and apropos of nothing in the new conversation save that same unreadable, *reflexive* consciousness.

The story of the Davenport visit was told, insofar as it was, in a midtown hotel, under circumstances that were themselves characteris-tic. Lowry was to meet his agent there about noon. After various confusions he arrived at approximately four, wearing baggy denim trousers, a boyish sports shirt without a necktie, and a zippered denim jacket of the sort one might golf in, but hardly designed to gain admit-tance into an exclusive British enclave on Manhattan's East Side. In fact he was in the process of being turned away, until another member of the party was recognized by the doorman—though Lord Peter Churchill's status at the hotel has presumably been in question since.

A point should be made that such situations did not arise because of the drink alone, though they had nothing to do with anything like Bohemian protest either; rather there was a kind of naivete in the man, and a considerable innocence. Lowry simply did not *think* about such things as neckties. But too, he had lived in removal from normal society for so long, in Cuernavaca and in British Columbia, that it was rarely necessary for him to be anything other than himself. In the Dollarton woods, where the Lowrys had neither electricity nor plumbing, an "appointment" meant a casual invitation to drop in for seafood at the shack of some fellow squatter a hundred yards down a stony beach.

As it happens, Lowry and I did take a more "formal" excursion up there one day, or what began as such. The Dollarton house was situated on one of the deep-water inlets east of Vancouver Island, which is to say off the Strait of Georgia, which is really to say off the Pacific. Somewhere to the south, though out of sight beyond a thrust of headland, lay a town called Port Moody that Lowry decided we might inspect. It was "just around the bend," and we could be there in thirty minutes. In bathing trunks, carrying our clothes, we set out via dinghy: "Around the Horn to Valparaiso!"

The latter was more like it. We were an hour making the bend itself, in that case because there were flora and fauna to be investigated along the wooded shoreline. But even then, no Port Moody; instead we were next evidently in the great Strait itself, banging about amid currents, inspecting the looming, rusted underbellies of freighters at anchor a mile or more from any docks, absurd though maybe intrepid too in our tiny craft. Only after four hours did we make fast, our tour of Port Moody now to be taken in twilight—save that we were able to venture no farther than to the first dockside tavern. Somehow, en route, Lowry had lost his pants over the side.

Undaunted, we had the required drinks. Yet even after some hours Lowry was reluctant to depart, and again for other than the ordinary Lowry reasons. Now what held him was a special flavor of the tavern itself, of the sea at its door and of men who followed the sea. More often than literature, or Mexico, the sea colored Lowry's talk, recollections of his one long boyhood voyage to the East, of other passages thereafter, and for all his remoteness from it now, it lured him still. This stocky, clumsy, shy little man, just turned forty-three, unkempt hair spilling into his eyes, without a cent in his pockets—for that matter without pockets—appearing on the threshold and grinning ingenuously, yet timidly too, which was characteristic of him among strangers . . . and yet within a moment being grinned at in turn, his obvious pleasure infectious and winning. Men lifted their glasses, they called hello. There is a line in one of the stories: "The very sight of that old bastard makes me happy for five days. No bloody fooling." Long after recording it, Lowry remained too pleased to admit that he had overheard it being said about himself.

But at last departure: water, mountains on every hand, a starless night sky. Once Port Moody was behind us, and the random night lamps of the freighters drifting at mooring had faded to port, the darkness was absolute. "Now listen, Malc, do you recognize this inlet?" "Oh, it's near, it's near." He, himself, all but invisible in the stern, sprawling, dragging one arm or another in our wake. "There are whales here now and then, have I told you?" Shadows loom and disappear, we have lost all landmarks now, and were I not pulling at the oars I would be shivering from the cold. Then from somewhere in the hills the eerie "Zinnnnng! Zinnnnng!" of a sawmill running through the night. "Ha! There is old Kafka, leading his orchestra. He must have been a splendid fellow, Kafka. I prayed to him once, and he answered my prayer. Incidentally, that could very well be a whale just off to starboard, the shadow that glistens that way—"

It is well past midnight when we locate the solitary dim gleam in the distance. Still, we may be rowing an additional half-mile out of the way. But no, it is the shack, Margerie has left a kerosene lamp in the window. She has been asleep for hours. "Oh, I knew you chaps would have some adventure or other." To which, Odysseus: "I say, you do have the decency to offer us a drink?"

In Dollarton, and evidently in Sicily too, before the last trip to England, Lowry swam for half an hour or more each morning, whatever the weather. It may have saved him, certainly it postponed the inevitable. He was all chest, though in that aging athlete's way of going to fat so that chest and stomach become one, stumplike. He had short arms that often seemed to flop about ineptly, like the appendages of some beached sea thing.

Yet he had been handsome, and, as the photos show, with his beard the face expressed a kind of gravity and wisdom in the last days. But at this time he was weathered, and turning fleshy. Interestingly, the older Errol Flynn, cast as the boozy Mike in *The Sun Also Rises,* took on a look almost precisely like Lowry's.

I have said there was something naive or ingenuous about him. On another level it was simply honesty—one was convinced he had never in his life been motivated by pettiness. But he was also able to talk about love, in an essentially masculine, Platonic sense, without being accused of mawkishness, or something more extreme. A case in point involves Aiken, who had filled an *in loco parentis* role for him in his youth, and whom he had not seen for nineteen years before the New York visit.

Aiken was on Cape Cod when the Lowrys arrived, and Margerie sent a telegram. After two decades, and though he was sixty-five then himself, Aiken still knew his man. It was he who took a train.

Unfortunately, his arrival coincided with the aforementioned party. For some years Aiken had maintained a cold-water flat in the East 30's, and a meeting was planned there first. It was five or six. Lowry was still in fair shape outwardly, the after-shave "bracer" to the contrary. (He had this faculty: musing, perplexed by unmentioned private visions, he could be teetering at the edge of the abyss and for a time not seem drunk at all, merely abstracted. Eventually, of course, he would come back to reality like a bridge collapsing.) At Aiken's, the fare was martinis. Lowry had been elated for days over the prospect of seeing the man again, but here too he was initially shy, and there were false starts. Finally Aiken asked Lowry what he had been writing. In rough form at the moment was the novel, *October Ferry to Gabriola.* For some minutes Lowry endeavored to summarize its nonexistent plot, after which: "Well, nothing happens. Nothing should, in a novel." Whereupon Aiken, whose *Blue Voyage* Lowry readily acknowledged as the critical influence on his own concept of fictional subjectivity: "No. No *incidents.*"

Lowry talked a good deal about his condition of the moment also, laying it in part to his distress at having to leave Dollarton, where the squatters faced eviction. "I have to slide through this time of crisis on my unconscious," was a statement repeated more than once. During the conversation he was beset by the shakes, and discussed this "professionally" also. (Shortly after his arrival in New York, having to sign a paper before a notary, he had been unable to write his name. Three martinis had remedied the difficulty, though he had spilled the first and the second had had to be held for him.)

Margerie had gotten him into a tie and jacket for the evening, and I had shaved him—one relived portions of *Under the Volcano* with his presence—so at the party itself his appearance may again have been briefly deceptive. Present were his friends James Stern and James Agee, his former editors Albert Erskine and Frank Taylor, and two or three wives. The night was exceptionally hot; Agee, apparently already ill himself, stood through most of it in a pool of sweat that had literally dripped from his chin to the floor. Almost at once, Lowry drifted into a kind of rapt silence, likewise sweating profusely, gazing at nothing; perhaps an hour passed in which he spoke to no one at all, nor did he move from his chair. Then, suddenly, cupping his hands to his mouth, he commenced to make sounds that can only be described as "beeps" —though one who knew could infer jazz, more specifically tunes associated with Bix Beiderbecke: "Singin' the Blues," "I'm Comin', Virginia," "In a Mist." For half an hour at least, even more absolutely lost to the rest of us now, the man rendered the Dixieland he had loved as a youth. ("I learned to write listening to Beiderbecke," he had remarked in Dollarton, meaning something about a kind of "controlled" freedom. He owned an ancient, hand-cranked phonograph and a collection of scarred recordings to which he could listen for hours. "Oh, what pure art!" he might cry, or, "Ah, the discipline!" When he heard some of the same pieces in New York, from reissued LP pressings, he immediately noticed elisions in several "breaks"— nor did it take seconds for him to perceive that my turntable revolved too slowly.)

The private recital ceased only when Aiken announced his departure: "Good night, disgrace." Then, however, Lowry insisted upon seeing him home—this with no idea where Aiken was headed, and, chances were, with no money in his possession either, since Margerie normally handled all cash. Once again Aiken knew what he was up against. In the street, in jest but in sadness, the two began to wrestle as a taxi drew up. Breaking Lowry's hold, Aiken tumbled to the floor as the vehicle took him off.

Those next moments, gazing into the empty street where only now a small rain, like a mist, had begun to fall, Lowry could not have appeared more sober. "He is an old man," he said. "And now I will never see him again." He was right enough, if for a wrong reason; and for a time he wept.

By morning, the twinkle had returned. Aiken had spoken of a nine o'clock train, and Lowry did not begin to function until well past that hour. "Listen," he insisted nonetheless, "I know Conrad, he won't have made that train. Let's go see him off." And again: "After all, he is my father, and I haven't seen him in fifty-eight years. How can you keep me from him?" And yet again: "Of course, I would have gone to Massachusetts myself if I had to, even on all fours." In the end he settled for a telegram: *Was on deck 7 A.M. to see you off Wednesday but was offset by hurricane am going to encounter Monday afternoon off Cape Hatteras* . . . (There was in fact a hurricane along the coast that week, called "Edna," which Lowry talked about incessantly, and which he insisted he had "invoked.")

At the same time he was able to regret what he determined had been "rudeness" at the party, apologizing too for the mounting havoc in my apartment: glasses broken, books and bottles and half-smoked cigarettes scattered everywhere, if not to mention the sheaf of manuscript poems reposing for days now beneath the kitchen sink, or the blood that had mysteriously appeared on his blanket. Conversely: "You simply do not understand at all"—this should anyone suggest he postpone the next drink.

Meanwhile, a year before my Dollarton visit, I had written a master's essay on *Under the Volcano* which led to frequent repetition of another sort of admonition altogether: "Whatever a writer does, he must make notes." Those that follow I revise as form demands, but they appear in essence as recorded in 1952 and 1954.

DOLLARTON

He and Margerie bicker, insignificant household disagreements. Always, Lowry cuts it short with a word: "I love you, do you know?" Or: "My God, you are beautiful."

Jimmy Craige, an old Manx boatbuilder, stops by one evening, bearing a gift of live sea crabs. The man is rough hewn, essentially unlettered—and a cherished friend in this wilderness. Gossiping, radiating affection, Lowry communicates with him totally. Irish songs are sung, then sea chanties and hymns. The man tells an anecdote about a stranger in the area, "a Greek fellow." To which Lowry: "Like Aristotle."

Lowry talks of having known "a poet" of seventeen or so, in London —"a wild boy who insisted he was already dying, smashing glasses after each drink, that sort of thing." Some years later he had begun to admire the work of "one" Dylan Thomas, whom Margerie then met during a visit to London without Lowry. "And how is ruddy Malc?"— this with Margerie certain Lowry did not know the man. Nor could Lowry himself make the connection until a new Thomas volume appeared with the Augustus John portrait as a frontispiece.

He is overwhelmed, even almost ill, when I extend the good wishes of a reader of *Under the Volcano* whose comment has been, "Tell him I'm glad he's alive." "Oh, my God," Lowry sobs.

The jazz figures he names most often, after Beiderbecke: Django Reinhardt, Stephane Grappelly, Eddie Lang, Joe Venuti, Frankie Trumbauer.

On types of authors: "You cannot trust the ones who are too careful. As writers or drinkers. Old Goethe cannot have been so good a man as Keats or Chatterton. Or Rimbaud. The ones that burn."

A private myth: "I arrived in America with one football boot and a copy of *Moby Dick.*" He claims, too, that seeking out Aiken in Boston for the first time, confused over currency and arguing with a cab driver, he stopped a passerby for assistance—and the passerby was Aiken.

O'Neill and Conrad "sent me to sea," he declares, though both finally "wrote from the bridge," which is to say they did not know the stokehold. With the exception of Melville's, the best sea novel is Nordahl Grieg's *The Ship Sails On.*

Grieg is a second writer with whom Lowry "identified"—his word—as a youth. Several times, he speaks of occult "correspondences" involving the man. To have written a novel (*In Ballast to the White Sea,* a manuscript destroyed by fire) about a boy who loves a book, and who composes imaginary letters to its author, and then to seek out that author in reality and find him living *exactly* as in the book you yourself have conceived. Or to have changed the name of a ship that figures in Grieg's novel, and to discover that one's substitution is identical with the name of the actual vessel used by Grieg as a model. Or, immediately after the fire in which one's manuscript is lost, to move in with a friend who that day has been assigned to write Grieg's obituary.

More of the same. One morning at the shack, he says, a bird twice plummeted from a tree to crash against a window. Horrified, but assuming it drawn by some sort of reflection, Lowry threw open the glass. Yet the bird came on one more time, now to enter the house, circle, and at last depart. The question to be asked at Margerie's return, for Lowry, was self-evident: "Is there mail? Someone is trying to get in touch with me." It is almost redundant that Margerie carried a letter from a complete stranger, the last line of which read: "You have got to write to me." [No one who knew Lowry made light of any of this. In New York, Thomas had once started to scribble a note that he asked I pass along to Dollarton. In it, he mentioned a James Travers, a Cambridge friend of Lowry's who had burned to death in a tank in North Africa. On second thoughts, Thomas tore up the sheet. "Christ, no, the old boy will have nightmares." As evidently Lowry had, *before* learning of Travers's death.]

One evening, Margerie reads aloud the unpublished manuscript of "The Forest Path to the Spring," which, if a beatification, captures their life here in absolute detail. With water slapping at the pilings beneath the house, branches scraping at the roof, gulls wheeling over the inlet in the twilight, I endure the curious sensation that I am

somehow "inside" the story as I listen. Lowry himself remains diligently absorbed through it all, feigning "thoughtfulness"—though
here and there unable to disguise the self-conscious grin of approba-
tion.

Lines from the novels, or from stories in progress, are often repeated in conversation, though in their original context. A favorite,
voiced by a local fisherman in outrage at the sightseeing ferry that had
almost run him down: "What's the matter with you? You look as
though you'd swallowed Pat Murphy's goat and the horns were stick-
ing out of your arse!"

Hart Crane, Lowry comments, "must have been a wretched sort of
man." Also: "I don't think the bridge is a good sort of symbol." When
pressed, he cannot explain, seeming to mean it static. Yet there is a way
to read the full poem as "genuine tragedy."

Proudly, he tells of once having recognized Joyce—"smiling"—in
the Luxembourg Gardens. He insists they spent the day together. But
details are lost to the usual digressions.

"Every French writer I ever met was a homosexual. Most of them
were not good people either, except for Gide."

On the night before my departure, Lowry surreptitiously presses
into my hand a tiny medal, his own from Mexico, from the church of
"the Virgin for those who have nobody with." But I am not to tell
Margerie. "She'll be sure something might happen to me if I no longer
have it." And when I protest: "Believe me, it is all right to *give.*"

NEW YORK

He borrows a copy of *The Confessions of Zeno* from James Stern, a book
he has not read. He contrives to spend two full hours describing its
plot, however. "And I am going to learn from it, a method of treating
the consciousness."

Whenever he leaves the apartment, the generous impulse: "Here,
here, let me pay." Then the hand at the pocket, the sigh of frustration.
"Well, later, Margie has money." Neither will he forget, ultimately
demanding that she contribute "my share, at least," to an accounting
not worth the notice.

Much of his wit plays on alcohol itself. Someone quotes a line about
the ghost in *Hamlet:* "What, has this thing appear'd again tonight?"
"You know what that is, of course?—that is old Will's way of presenting the d.t.s." Or again, in reference to virtually anyone's masterpiece:

"Naturally you understand he was tight as a tick when he wrote it?"
Yet in all seriousness he cannot seem to comprehend the notion of
working for a living; one morning, when a friend is already hours late,
he commences a "note" to the latter's employer explaining the delin-
quency. "Here, we can take care of all that."

Amid the baggage is a ukulele. A string is missing, however.

"I never quite understood that," he says of opera, as recordings are
played. "I mean, I never really got it."

Only one evening does he face up to the complications of a meal at
a respectable restaurant. He allows Margerie to order for him, then
eats only a few peas—one or two at a time.

Like the Consul, he himself is hardly unaware of the extent to which,
finally, he can become a trial. One night when he has been making no
sense whatsoever for hours, but has refused short of physical force to
return to the apartment, in a 4 A.M. explosion of ruptured patience I
deliberately smash a full bottle of gin against a curb. Perhaps four days
pass before a word about this is spoken, and then only: "That was
wasteful, do you know?" After which the gleam: "Ha! Because I had
already crossed the street you thought I was too drunk to see!"

One night we lose him completely, a check of every bar in the
neighborhood proving fruitless. Then at dawn I discover him asleep
in a chair outside my apartment door. "Well, after all, I didn't want to
wake Margerie." (The story unfolds only some days after this. By
chance, he had run into a woman to whom I had introduced him
earlier, who in turn had taken him home to meet her husband, an
admirer of *Under the Volcano,* but who in his own turn had misinter-
preted the entire situation—and had thrown Lowry out before his
name had been mentioned. Evidently Lowry had slept in *that* corridor
first.)

"But I will pull out of all this in Sicily. Under Etna, wait and see."

They are to sail, via an Italian line, from Brooklyn. With great glee,
he proclaims that the ship is certain to carry high explosives.

He thinks *The Hamlet* "a great book," Ike Snopes and the cow
"tragic." Parts of *A Farewell to Arms* are "Homeric," but most of Hemingway is "not much." He shakes his head wistfully over a copy of
Finnegans Wake: "I did not give this as much time as I should have."

Ushant—"You Shall Not, by God!"—is a "further manifestation of
Aiken's genius." But he admits to annoyance at the portrait of himself,
apparently over certain ultimate privacies intruded upon; nor will he
permit Margerie to read the book. [Lowry appears as "Hambo" in the
work; only in an edition republished after Lowry's death did Aiken
append an identification.]

Other recently read fiction that has impressed him: *Demian*, *The Barkeep of Blemont*, *The Wild Palms*, *Oblomov*, and Dostoevski's short novels, particularly *The Gambler*. Also DeAssis and Broch.

His *big* books, however, would at the moment remain these: *Moby Dick*, *Blue Voyage*, the Grieg, *Madame Bovary*, Conrad (particularly *The Secret Agent*), O'Neill, Kafka, much of Poe, Rimbaud, and of course Joyce and Shakespeare. *The Enormous Room* is a favorite, as is *Nightwood*. Kierkegaard and Swedenborg are the philosophers most mentioned, and in another area William James and Ouspensky. Also Strindberg, Gogol, Tolstoy.

Lifting a Maupaussant from a shelf (nothing has been said of the man before this): "He is a better writer than you think."

Of Djuna Barnes: "I was in the same room with her once, and wanted to rush up and scold her for not writing more."

En route to the docks, on the morning of departure, he is much taken with the Brooklyn Bridge, is "almost tempted" to revise his judgment on Crane. He comments, too, on the "drama" of the New York skyline as seen from the cab. Ever loyal, he reminds me that I must read the stories of Jimmy Stern, which are "brilliant," and Agee's *Let Us Now Praise Famous Men*. Likewise Aiken's *Great Circle*—"Though I did not write that. The only one I wrote in another life was *Blue Voyage*." And throughout the drive he repeats a line, cum spurious Mississippi accent, that he attributes to Faulkner: "Ah can stand anything. Ain't nothin' wrong with me that a good bour-bon won't cure."

In fact he stands the first few hours well. At breakfast the shakes are extreme, but he acknowledges without argument that he must be shaved. And he achieves the freighter in relative sobriety, again in jacket and tie, visibly excited, with passport in hand. But the sailing will be seven or eight hours delayed, by which time he will be semi-conscious in his bunk.

"I must see the skipper. If he is not a company man, this will be a happy ship." Meanwhile he impresses upon Margerie the urgency of tipping the steward at once: "Italian ships have holds *full* of chianti."

Then final words which will perhaps be allowed in a reminiscence of this sort: "I'm a pretty bad man, but you should really come to Sicily with us. We love you, you know, but not so that you have to shove a cork up your arse, old man."

In my apartment, a carton full of empty bottles. Abandoned across a chair, a torn shirt. There is blood on the collar.

Three years and intermittent letters later, the cablegram: MALCOLM SUDDENLY DEAD—MARGERIE.

And *vale*—since words do not recapture him anyway. One was convinced, at last, that the demons were real; but what one remembers is the innocence withal, the mirth, the sheer *abundance.*

"*. . . for I loved the man, and do honor his memory on this side idolatry as much as any.*"

INDEX